Methods Of Extractive Speech Summarization for Binary Neural Networks

Afsar

Contents

Chapter 8

Conclusion and Future Direction

8.1 Conclusions

Most existing extractive speech summarization systems rely heavily on clean transcripts and large annotated corpora. However, speech transcriptions in low-resource languages are often noisy or unavailable, and the required datasets for prosody-based summarization remain missing. The lack of robust extractive summarization systems for these languages, especially ones that work directly on speech, marks a significant research gap. This thesis addresses the above gap through the following contributions:

- **Corpus Creation (Chapter 3):** A prosodically annotated speech corpus is developed for Assamese and Bengali, supporting segment-level summarization and feature extraction.
- **Transcript Error Analysis (Chapter 4):** The effect of ASR errors on summary quality is analyzed using real-world audiobook transcripts.
- **Text-Based Benchmarking (Chapter 5):** A comparative evaluation of summarization methods (e.g., TF-IDF, FastText, BERT, etc.) on clean vs. noisy transcripts is conducted.
- **Prosody-Based Summarization (Chapters 6 and 7):** Both heuristic and neural models are developed to perform summarization directly from speech using acoustic-prosodic features.

The following table provides a high-level comparison of the capabilities of existing systems versus the contributions made by this thesis.

This thesis is intended as groundwork for building effective speech summarization systems in low-resource language settings. The goal was not to develop a complete end-to-end system, but to explore what is possible when resources are limited. The work focuses on understanding how ASR errors affect summary quality, how

Table 8.1: Summary of Existing Work and Gaps Addressed in This Thesis

Aspect	High-Resource Languages (Prior Work)	Low-Resource (Assamese/Bengali)	Addressed in This Thesis
Speech Summarization Corpora	AMI, ICSI, MATBN, TED-LIUM	No summarization corpora	Chapter 3
ASR Error Impact Studies	Known issue in English corpora	Underexplored for Indic scripts	Chapter 4
Transcript-Based Summarization	TextRank, LSA, BERTSum, MMR, etc.	Partially explored; lacks robustness under ASR noise	Chapters 4–5
Prosody-Based Summarization	Limited studies (mostly in English or Mandarin)	No prior work for Assamese/Bengali	Chapters 6-7
Neural Summarization Models	BERTSum, Pointer-Generator, LSTM, Transformer	Rare due to data scarcity; models not adapted	Chapter 7

prosodic features can help when transcripts are unreliable, and whether simple neural models can work with limited data. Each part of the thesis tackles a different practical challenge and proposes methods that are realistic and easy to build on. Instead of assuming ideal conditions, this work focuses on what can be done under real-world constraints. The aim is to set a strong foundation that future research can build on, especially for languages that lack annotated data and reliable tools.

The thesis presents five core contributions as highlighted above, each aligned with a specific research objective:

Corpus development: In this thesis, we address many limitations by developing speech summarization systems for Assamese and Bengali—languages with minimal prior work in this domain. In doing so, this work adds to the growing literature on practical, deployable summarization tools in low-resource environments. A prosodically annotated speech corpus was created for Assamese and Bengali broadcast news. This was necessary to support experiments on prosody-based speech summarization, especially since no such resources previously existed for these languages. The corpus includes speaker-normalized features and spans multiple speakers and genders to allow for generalization across speech variability.

Analysis of ASR transcription errors: Using Bengali audiobook data, the impact of ASR-generated transcript errors was studied. Two unsupervised extractive summarization methods—sentence ranking and K-means clustering—were applied to evaluate how error-prone transcripts degrade summary quality. The results showed that disfluencies, deletions, and substitution errors not only reduce but a set of approaches that demonstrate what can be done when working within real-world constraints. This foundation is meant to support future work—not just on Bengali and Assamese—but for the broader problem of speech processing in underrepresented languages.

8.2 Future Directions

This thesis opens several directions for further exploration in speech summarization for low-resource languages.

First, the methodologies developed here can be extended to larger and more diverse speech datasets. Expanding beyond broadcast news and audiobooks to include conversational, spontaneous, or multilingual speech could reveal how well the proposed approaches generalize. Building annotated corpora for such domains remains a crucial step, especially for evaluating summaries based on both textual and prosodic information.

Second, while this work used relatively simple feature-based and shallow neural models to keep the methods practical, there is room to explore more sophisticated architectures. For instance, hybrid models that combine acoustic-prosodic cues with lightweight pretrained embeddings or cross-modal attention mechanisms could offer improved performance while staying within the constraints of low-resource settings.

Third, the use of prosodic features in summarization remains an underexplored area. Future work could investigate unsupervised or self-supervised techniques for prosodic modeling, as well as explore more fine-grained prosodic annotations—such as prominence, intonation contours, or discourse-level structure—to improve summary coherence and informativeness.

Finally, one promising direction is to move towards semi-supervised or weakly supervised summarization methods. These could leverage small sets of annotated data to guide summary generation in larger unlabelled corpora, especially when full manual annotation is infeasible.

The methods developed in this thesis are designed to be modular and interpretable, making them suitable starting points for these future efforts. Each of these directions would further strengthen the feasibility and reach of speech summarization in truly low-resource environments.

readability but also cause misidentification of important content, especially when summarization relies purely on lexical matching.

Text-based summarization experiments: Several sentence embedding methods were evaluated for extractive summarization on clean text transcripts, including TF-IDF, Word2Vec, and BERT-based embeddings. This helped assess the strengths and limitations of standard extractive pipelines when applied to transcribed speech. The findings showed that while contextual embeddings improved performance on clean data, they offered limited gains in noisy conditions, underscoring the need for robust methods beyond lexical similarity.

Text-independent summarization using acoustic-prosodic features: A prosody-aware summarization framework was proposed and evaluated on the developed corpus. This method avoids transcription entirely and selects important content using pitch, pause, and energy patterns. The study demonstrated that even simple heuristics using prosodic cues can identify salient regions effectively, particularly when ASR is unreliable or unavailable.

Neural approach using 1D-CNN: A neural model was designed to identify summary-worthy segments directly from prosodic and acoustic features. Despite limited data, the 1D-CNN showed promising performance, especially in capturing temporal patterns in speech that correlate with informational prominence. This model complements the heuristic method and shows that simple architectures can be effective even in low-resource settings.

Together, these contributions explore different points in the design space of speech summarization under low-resource constraints—ranging from traditional text-based pipelines to prosody-driven and neural approaches. All evaluations were carried out on a custom-built corpus, primarily because publicly available speech summarization datasets do not exist for Bengali and Assamese. Extending these methods to other corpora would require time-consuming annotations and language-specific resources, which lie beyond the scope of this work.

The restricted evaluation setup is a limitation, but it reflects the core challenge of working with low-resource languages. Instead of overextending to artificially clean or unrelated datasets, the thesis focuses on methods that are realistic to implement and grounded in practical conditions. Future research can scale this work by collecting larger corpora, refining prosodic annotations, or adapting models to other speech domains such as conversational data or classroom lectures.

In summary, this thesis offers a feasibility study on speech summarization for languages where clean transcripts, annotated data, and off-the-shelf tools are scarce. It shows how simple, interpretable techniques can be assembled into useful systems, and where the main bottlenecks lie. The contribution is not a final solution,

Chapter 1

Introduction

Summarization is the task of shortening a large amount of information—either spoken or written—into a smaller, more manageable form, while keeping the most important points [32, 79]. It helps users understand key content quickly without having to read or listen to everything in full. This is useful in many situations, such as when people want to scan the news, review long legal documents, go through research papers, or analyze customer opinions [28]. In each of these cases, summarization can save time and help people make decisions more easily.

The need for summarization has become even more important in recent years, as digital content has grown rapidly across websites, social media, video platforms, and other sources [51, 102]. People and organizations now deal with more information than ever before. Summarization helps manage this overload by giving users just the parts that matter most. It also supports technologies like search engines, recommendation systems, and digital assistants by helping them deliver more focused and useful content.

At the same time, summarization is a difficult task. A summary needs to be short, but also clear and complete. It should avoid repeating the same ideas, and it should preserve the original meaning without adding errors or changing the message. Summaries must also sound natural and stay connected to the original topic. These challenges make summarization a complex problem in language technology [74, 88].

In the past, summarization systems were built using hand-crafted rules or simple algorithms. These systems worked in limited ways and often struggled with more complex language. Today, newer systems use machine learning, especially deep learning, to learn patterns from large datasets [59, 113]. In recent years, data-driven methods, especially those based on deep learning, have largely replaced rule-based techniques. These approaches learn to identify important information from large datasets, allowing for more accurate and flexible summarization.

As summarization methods improve, they are expected to play a larger role in how people interact with digital content. They can support better access to information, help organize knowledge, and make communication between humans and machines more efficient. The goal is not just to shorten content, but to help users focus on what matters—especially in settings where time, space, or attention is limited.

1.1 Extractive Summarization

Summarization techniques are generally divided into two types: extractive and abstractive [29]. In extractive summarization, key sentences or segments are selected directly from the original content to form a summary. The summary is made by identifying the most important parts of the input and putting them together without changing their wording. In contrast, abstractive summarization involves generating new sentences that rephrase or rewrite the original content in a shorter form. This requires a deeper understanding of language and meaning, and is more challenging to design and control.

Extractive summarization has been widely used because it is simpler to implement and easier to evaluate. It ensures that the summary remains grammatically correct and factually consistent, since it uses parts of the original input without altering them. Early systems used rule-based methods and hand-crafted features, such as sentence position, term frequency, or the presence of specific keywords. As the field evolved, these approaches were replaced by statistical and machine learning models that can learn to rank sentences based on their importance.

Today, extractive summarization methods often rely on vector-based representations of text and neural networks that can model patterns in language and discourse. These systems are used in many real-world applications—such as summarizing news articles, meeting transcripts, and customer reviews—where it is important to condense information while retaining the original phrasing. As extractive summarization does not rely on generating new sentences, it is more stable and interpretable in many cases. It is also easier to apply to different domains and input types. These features make it a practical choice for tasks where the availability of resources is limited, and where reliability and transparency are important.

In the context of this thesis, extractive summarization is chosen for both practical and resource-driven reasons. Many low-resource languages, including those used in this work, either lack usable ASR systems or produce highly error-prone transcripts. This makes abstractive summarization— which requires clean, reliable text as input—difficult to apply. Unlike extractive methods that simply select existing sentences, abstractive models must understand and generate coherent new text that accurately reflects the meaning of the original. In speech summarization, the input to such models typically comes from automatic speech recognition (ASR). When ASR output is noisy—due to substitutions, deletions, or segmentation errors—the quality of abstractive summaries degrades significantly. Extractive methods, on the other hand, are more robust in these conditions, as they do not rely on sentence generation and can even operate directly on prosodic features when text is unavailable. They also offer greater transparency, which is especially important in spoken content like news, where factual consistency must be preserved. Table 1.1 outlines the key differences between extractive and abstractive summarization, with a focus on their suitability for speech tasks in low-resource settings.

For these reasons, this thesis focuses on extractive summarization not because it is easier, but because it is the only practical option for many low-resource speech settings where clean transcripts are unavailable or unreliable. By designing models that work with either prosodic features or noisy ASR output, this work addresses a real problem that current abstractive systems cannot solve. It contributes useful methods and new understanding for building summarization systems in languages and conditions where transcript-based approaches break down.

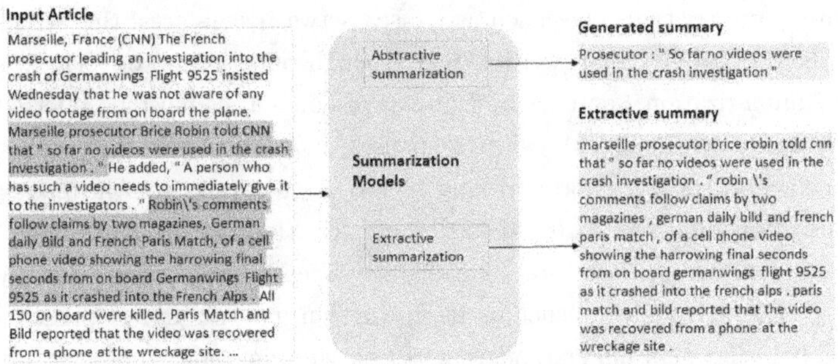

Figure 1-1: Extractive vs Abstractive summarization.
Extractive summarization is where segments are selected from the source document to be included in the summary. In abstractive summarization, new sentences are generated to represent the theme of the source document.

1.2 Spoken Document Summarization

Most research in summarization has focused on written documents. Whether extractive or abstractive, the common assumption is that the input is clean, struc-

Table 1.1: Extractive vs. Abstractive Summarization in Low-Resource Speech Settings

Aspect	**Extractive Summarization**	**Abstractive Summarization**
Input Dependency	Can operate on raw or prosodic speech segments	Requires clean, accurate transcriptions
Factual Reliability	High — reuses exact utterances	May introduce hallucinations or paraphrase errors
Resource Requirements	Low — works with limited annotations	High — needs language models, large corpora
Suitability in this Thesis	Used for both acoustic-only and ASR-based tasks	Not feasible due to transcript noise or absence

tured text. But in many real-world scenarios, the information people want to summarize exists in audio form—spoken news, interviews, meetings, lectures, and so on. This is where speech summarization comes in [38].

Speech summarization, also known as spoken document summarization, deals with spoken content which brings a different set of challenges. Unlike written text, speech is often messy and unstructured. People hesitate, repeat themselves, change direction mid-sentence, or speak in fragments. The lack of punctuation, formatting, or clear sentence boundaries makes it harder to identify what information is important. Although read speech derived from structured text are better structured, and contains cues such as pauses between sentences, this structure is not explicitly encoded as in written text through punctuation or formatting. In speech summarization, sentence and discourse boundaries must be inferred from acoustic and prosodic signals, such as pauses, intonation, and emphasis, which can vary across speakers and speaking styles. As a result, even in read speech, summarization differs from text-based summarization, as the underlying structure is implicit rather than directly available. Speech also carries extra layers of meaning—through prosody, such as pitch, rhythm, pauses, and emphasis. These features help listeners understand tone, focus, and emotion, and they are often key to interpreting what is being said.

Most speech summarization systems try to work around this by converting speech to text first, using an automatic speech recognition (ASR) system. The summary is then generated from the transcript. This pipeline works reasonably well when the ASR is accurate, but the quality drops quickly if the transcript is noisy or incomplete—which is often the case in spontaneous speech or under-resourced languages. Moreover, once speech is converted to plain text, all the prosodic cues are lost. This means that systems built only on transcripts miss out on how the speaker delivered the content—not just what they said.

This makes speech summarization fundamentally different from text summarization, not just in terms of input but also in how information must be processed and interpreted. Text summarization methods assume clear sentence boundaries, grammatical structure, and consistent vocabulary. In contrast, speech summarization must deal with disfluencies, speaker variation, and background noise. It also requires handling timing and prosodic patterns—features that do not exist in written text. These differences affect both the design of summarization algorithms and the evaluation of their output, especially when working with spontaneous or noisy speech.

Table 1.2: Comparison of Text Summarization and Speech Summarization

Feature	**Text Summarization**	**Speech Summarization**
Input Type	Structured text with clear sentence boundaries	Unstructured audio requiring preprocessing
Processing	Direct analysis of lexical and syntactic features	Requires speech-to-text conversion (ASR) and feature extraction
Challenges	Handling ambiguity, redundancy, and context	ASR errors, background noise, accents, disfluencies, lack of punctuation
Features Used	Lexical, syntactic, and semantic features	Acoustic-prosodic features (pitch, tone, pauses) + lexical features
Complexity	Lower; operates on cleaner, structured input	Higher; requires segmentation, error handling, and disfluency removal
Segmentation	Clear sentence boundaries in text	No predefined structure; sentences must be identified from speech
Applications	News summarization, document analysis, legal text processing	Meeting summarization, podcast and broadcast news summarization
Real-time Use	Not typically required	Often required for applications like live meeting summarization

To address this, some recent approaches skip transcription altogether. These text-independent methods analyze the audio directly, using acoustic and prosodic patterns to decide what parts to include in the summary. While harder to build, such methods can work even when ASR fails or when no language-specific tools are available. They also offer a more natural way to handle spoken material by treating speech as its own modality—not just a noisy version of text.

Speech summarization is becoming increasingly important as audio content continues to grow. From podcasts and voice messages to video lectures and broadcast news, spoken information is everywhere. Making this content easier to scan, search, and consume requires summarization systems that can handle the complexity of speech directly.

1.2.1 Types of spoken documents

Speech can be categorized into read and spontaneous speech, each with unique characteristics and challenges. Read speech, like audiobooks and news broadcasts, is recorded in controlled environments with clear, fluent, and structured grammar. It lacks disfluencies, making it ideal for ASR training and summarization tasks focused on coherence, though it misses conversational nuances.
Spontaneous speech, on the other hand, is unplanned and highly variable, including hesitations, false starts, and interruptions. This makes it harder to process and summarize, as it lacks clear sentence boundaries. Examples include meeting summaries, interview highlights, and conversational analytics, where capturing key content amid disfluencies is critical. This is further illustrated in Figure 1-2.

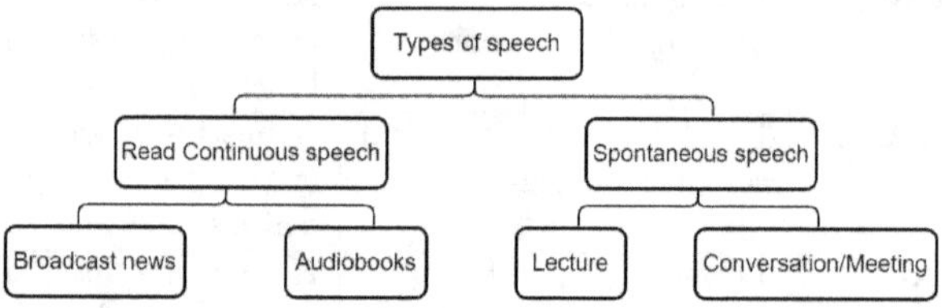

Figure 1-2: Types of speech-data and their real-world examples.

1.2.1.1 Spoken-documents of read-continuous speech

The major types of read-continuous speech in this thesis are as follow:

1. **Broadcast news** programs, such as those on TV and radio, represent a rich and diverse source of spoken content, making them highly valuable for extractive speech summarization. These programs cover a wide array of topics and often feature large volumes of spoken material. Moreover, broadcast news is frequently transcribed, either manually or automatically, to enhance accessibility, providing a convenient text corpus for text-based summarization approaches. While ASR-generated transcripts enhance accessibility, they often contain errors, posing challenges for summarization. Integrating prosodic and acoustic features alongside textual data helps identify key segments more accurately, leading to more effective summaries that capture the essence of broadcast news.

Compared to audiobooks, broadcast news is more structured and information-dense. While audiobooks distribute key details across long narrative sections, broadcast news presents concise, topic-specific segments, making it easier to extract meaningful content. Sentences within content-rich sections of news broadcasts are more likely to be summary-worthy, streamlining the summarization process.

2. **Audiobook** spoken documents provide a valuable yet challenging resource for extractive speech summarization. Unlike broadcast news, which is concise and topic-specific, audiobooks span diverse genres, including fiction, non-fiction, and instructional material, making them structurally and stylistically varied. Their narrative-driven nature presents unique summarization challenges, as key information is often dispersed across long, uninterrupted speech sections rather than concentrated in specific segments. Extracting meaningful insights requires techniques that capture long-range dependencies and contextual relationships across the audiobook.

   Automatic speech recognition (ASR) systems generate transcripts for audiobooks, but their length and contextual richness make ASR errors more problematic, distorting meaning in narrative passages. Integrating prosodic and acoustic features—such as pitch, intonation, and pauses—can help identify critical segments despite ASR imperfections. Compared to broadcast news, audiobooks have lower information density, containing descriptive or embellishing sentences that do not contribute to the core message. Effective summarization must distinguish between key narrative points and auxiliary details, ensuring that only essential content is retained.

This thesis focuses on broadcast news and audiobooks as two distinct yet complementary forms of spoken content, each posing unique challenges for extractive summarization as detailed in Table 1.3. Broadcast news offers structured, topic-driven speech with clear segment boundaries, making it highly suitable for developing and evaluating extractive summarization methods. Audiobooks, on the other hand, provide consistent, well-articulated narrative speech, which is particularly useful for studying the role of prosody in conveying meaning. These domains enable systematic analysis while also covering a wide range of linguistic and acoustic phenomena relevant to speech summarization. Other forms of speech, such as meetings and spontaneous conversations, introduce additional complexities like dialog dynamics, speaker overlap, and informal discourse, which fall outside the current scope. By focusing on these two domains, the thesis targets settings that are both practically important and methodologically aligned with its research goals—particularly for low-resource languages where well-structured spoken data is more readily available than spontaneous conversational corpora.

Table 1.3: Differences between Broadcast news and Audiobooks

Aspect	Broadcast News	Audiobooks
Content Structure	Typically structured into short, concise segments (e.g., headlines, reports, interviews).	Often structured as long, continuous narratives or dialogues.
Information Density	High information density, with frequent key points in short durations.	Lower information density; information is spread across long stretches of narrative.
Speech Style	Formal, clear, and often monotone; aimed at delivering news efficiently.	Expressive and engaging; designed to captivate the listener and convey emotion or character.
Prosodic Features	Minimal variation in pitch and tone, with a professional and neutral delivery.	High variation in pitch, tone, and pace to reflect emotions, characters, and narrative events.
Relevance to Summarization	Easier to identify key points due to high density and structured content.	Harder to identify key segments as important content is spread across longer durations.

1.3 Low-resource Languages

Low-resource languages refer to languages that lack the digital infrastructure, linguistic datasets, and computational tools necessary for developing effective natural language processing (NLP) systems. These limitations typically include a lack of annotated corpora, lexicons, part-of-speech taggers, dependency parsers, and large-scale pretrained models. In contrast, high-resource languages such as English, Mandarin, and Spanish benefit from decades of investment in language technologies, supported by academic, industrial, and governmental initiatives. For many low-resource languages, basic language processing tools are either missing or remain underdeveloped and fragmented, making downstream tasks such as machine translation, automatic speech recognition (ASR), and summarization significantly more difficult to implement.

The notion of "low-resource" is also dynamic and context-dependent. It does not necessarily correlate with the number of native speakers or the cultural significance of a language. Instead, it reflects the availability and quality of computational resources for that language. Many languages with millions of speakers—such as Bengali, Marathi, or Hausa—remain low-resource in the NLP landscape due to the absence of standardized data pipelines, shared benchmarks, or reusable tools.

Others, like several indigenous or tribal languages, are doubly disadvantaged by low speaker populations and a lack of institutional support for digitization or preservation. In such cases, even basic digital literacy tools or speech-enabled interfaces are out of reach, limiting access to digital services and participation in information economies. The resulting technological exclusion compounds existing social and educational disadvantages, reinforcing the digital divide between well-resourced and under-resourced language communities.

In the domain of extractive speech summarization, the challenges associated with low-resource languages are magnified. Most state-of-the-art summarization systems assume access to high-quality transcriptions generated by robust ASR systems, supported by extensive text corpora for training language models or extracting semantic features. These assumptions break down in low-resource contexts. ASR systems for under-resourced languages often produce noisy or unreliable transcriptions, especially when trained on small or mismatched datasets. Errors in word boundaries, misrecognitions of proper nouns, and inconsistent punctuation can significantly degrade the performance of summarization pipelines that rely on textual coherence or syntactic cues. Moreover, due to the scarcity of reference summaries and the absence of large-scale summarization datasets, supervised learning approaches are often infeasible.

In such settings, alternative cues—particularly those derived from acoustic and prosodic features—become essential. These include pitch movements, intensity variations, pause durations, and other suprasegmental signals that may serve as proxies for sentence importance, discourse structure, or speaker emphasis. However, the use of these features is also hindered by the lack of publicly available prosodically annotated corpora for most low-resource languages. Unlike English or Mandarin, where speech corpora with phonetic and prosodic layers are common, languages like Assamese and Bengali have very limited resources for studying speech dynamics beyond raw audio or transcripts. This severely restricts the development of systems that aim to leverage prosody for summarization, particularly in a text-independent manner where reliance on acoustic signals is a necessity rather than a design choice.

Given these constraints, this thesis focuses on two linguistically rich but computationally under-resourced languages from Eastern India: **Bengali** and **Assamese**. Both languages present a unique combination of challenges for speech summarization — including tonal and rhythmic variation, dialectal diversity, and sparse availability of annotated corpora. Bengali, one of the most spoken languages globally, lacks accessible prosodic resources despite a growing digital footprint. Assamese, like Bengali, belongs to the Eastern Indo-Aryan branch and shares some typological and script-level similarities. Although less widely spoken, Assamese is known to exhibit tonal variation and flexible prosodic timing, which makes it a linguistically interesting candidate for studying acoustic-prosodic patterns in speech.

These two languages serve as *representative case studies* throughout this thesis, allowing us to explore the practical feasibility and modeling challenges of text-independent summarization in low-resource environments. The speech corpora created for this work include audiobook and broadcast news data in both languages, with sentence-level annotations and speaker metadata. The following section provides an overview of these corpora and the design choices made to support summarization tasks.

1.3.1 Bengali

Bengali (or Bangla/ বাংলা) is an Indo-Aryan language spoken by more than 230 million people, making it one of the most widely spoken languages in the world. It is the official language of Bangladesh and one of the 22 scheduled languages of India, with a strong presence in the state of West Bengal, as well as in Assam, Tripura, and several diaspora communities abroad. Bengali has a long and vibrant cultural history, with a strong literary tradition and a prominent role in poetry, music, and cinema across South Asia. It remains central to education, media, and public discourse in the regions where it is spoken.

Despite this large speaker base and cultural significance, Bengali remains under-resourced in the field of speech and language technology. Publicly available corpora for Bengali speech, especially those annotated for specific downstream tasks like summarization, are extremely limited. Most existing resources are focused on basic tasks such as speech recognition or keyword spotting, often relying on studio-quality recordings or scripted prompts. Large-scale annotated speech datasets with natural, domain-rich content—such as news or audiobooks—are rare. Tools for prosodic analysis, speaker segmentation, and summary evaluation are also less developed than for high-resource languages like English or Mandarin. These gaps restrict the development and evaluation of robust models for Bengali speech applications, especially in low-resource or real-world conditions.

Including Bengali in this study is therefore both timely and necessary. Bengali offers a compelling case for summarization research in low-resource settings, due to its large speaker base, under-representation in annotated speech corpora, and the real-world relevance of domain-rich spoken content in the language. It allows us to address a well-recognized gap in language technology research while demonstrating the challenges and feasibility of speech summarization in settings where data and tools are scarce.

1.3.2 Assamese

Assamese (or Asomiya / অসমীয়া) is an Indo-Aryan language spoken by approximately 15 million people, primarily in the northeastern Indian state of Assam. It is the easternmost Indo-Aryan language and shares several linguistic features with Bengali, including script origin, syntactic structure, and phonological traits. Assamese holds official status in Assam and is used widely in education, media, and government. Despite its relatively smaller speaker base, it plays a key role in the cultural and political identity of the region, with a rich tradition of poetry, prose, and journalism.

Like Bengali, Assamese is significantly under-resourced in the field of speech and language technology. Publicly available speech corpora for Assamese are rare, and those that exist are often small, narrowly scoped, or limited to controlled environments. Annotated datasets for higher-level tasks—such as summarization, prosody modeling, or discourse analysis—are virtually non-existent. The scarcity of tools for speech processing, particularly in domains like broadcast news or expressive reading, makes it difficult to develop models that operate reliably in practical settings.

Assamese was included in this study not only because of its linguistic and regional importance, but also because it provides a compelling comparative case with Bengali (Table 1.5). The two languages share structural similarities (Table 1.4) but differ in usage patterns, speaker variation, and technological resources. Studying both allows for a more grounded understanding of how summarization methods generalize across related low-resource languages, while also contributing essential annotated data for a language that has received limited attention in computational research.

Table 1.4: Sentence Structure Comparison Between Bengali and Assamese

Aspect	**Bengali**	**Assamese**
Original Script	আমি বাজারে যাবো	মই বজাৰ লৈ যাম
Romanized	*āmi bāzār-e jābo*	*moi bāzār-loi jām*
Gloss (Word-by-word)	I market-LOC go-FUT	I market-TOWARDS go-FUT
English Translation	I will go to the market.	I will go to the market.
Word Order Type	SOV (Postpositional)	SOV (Postpositional; directional emphasis)

Including Assamese in this study, alongside Bengali, allows us to explore two different levels of resource scarcity. Bengali provides a moderately low-resource case, where tools and data exist but remain insufficient for complex tasks. Assamese represents a more severe low-resource condition, where foundational resources are minimal. This contrast helps evaluate the robustness of speech summarization methods across a spectrum of linguistic and infrastructural constraints, and makes the case for practical solutions that work under both.

Table 1.5: Linguistic Overview of Bengali and Assamese [13, 64, 66, 83]

Linguistic Property	Bengali	Assamese
Language Family	Indo-Aryan (Eastern)	Indo-Aryan (Eastern)
Primary Regions	India (West Bengal), Bangladesh	India (Assam)
Number of Speakers	~230 million	~15 million
Script Used	Eastern Nagari	Eastern Nagari (Assamese variant)
Phonology	Non-tonal; aspirated stops, nasal vowels	Non-tonal; velar fricatives, retroflex variation
Word Order	SOV (Subject-Object-Verb)	SOV (with pragmatic flexibility)
Stress	Weak lexical stress	Variable, generally non-contrastive
Intonation	Phrase-final pitch rise common	Dialectal pitch variation in intonation patterns
Morphology	Moderately agglutinative; rich verb forms	Similar; verb endings differ in person/tense handling

1.4 Motivation of the research

Despite major progress in summarization for high-resource languages, low-resource languages remain largely overlooked—especially when it comes to spoken document summarization. Many of these languages lack the basic tools needed for developing summarization systems, such as annotated datasets and accurate speech-to-text models. In contrast, languages like English and Chinese benefit from well-developed NLP tools and highly accurate ASR systems. This creates a significant gap in how different languages are supported in digital speech technologies.

As digital content becomes more complex and varied, summarization systems need to do more: they must process audio, handle context, and adapt to different language structures. For low-resource languages, these demands are even harder to meet because the necessary infrastructure simply does not exist. Most summarization methods still rely heavily on text-based inputs generated by ASR systems—tools that work well only when large datasets and clean transcripts are available. These problems are especially severe in Indian languages like Bangla and Assamese. Their linguistic diversity, complex writing systems, and regional dialects make it difficult to reuse tools developed for better-resourced languages. Even when ASR systems are available for low-resource languages, they are often unreliable and produce noisy or incomplete transcriptions. These transcriptions capture only the textual content of speech and fail to represent prosodic features such as pitch, pauses, and intonation. In many languages, these prosodic cues are essential for conveying meaning, emphasis, and sentence boundaries. Ignoring them leads to summaries that miss important information and do not reflect how the content was actually spoken. These prosodic features carry meaning in spoken language and help the listener understand emphasis, intent, and structure—especially in languages where grammar alone doesn't always convey the full message. Adding prosodic features into the summarization process offers a way to reduce dependence on clean transcripts. It helps capture how meaning is delivered in speech, which is critical in languages where textual tools are not reliable or mature.

India's multilingual setting highlights why this issue matters. Millions of people speak Bangla and Assamese, yet they remain digitally underserved. Without tailored solutions, these communities risk being excluded from the benefits of automated speech technologies. This thesis directly addresses these challenges by focusing on Assamese and Bengali as case studies of under-resourced Indian languages. Both languages are spoken by tens of millions of people and have rich literary and oral traditions, yet remain marginalized in the landscape of speech technologies. The absence of annotated corpora, domain-specific ASR models, and standardized evaluation benchmarks makes it difficult to build scalable solutions for tasks like summarization. By constructing a manually annotated corpus and exploring both acoustic-prosodic and minimal textual features, the work presented here explores practical and linguistically informed approaches for summarization in the absence of conventional NLP infrastructure. This thesis responds to that need through a multi-pronged approach. It presents a series of methods for extractive speech summarization that are designed to function effectively in low-resource settings. These include the creation of prosodically enriched corpora, the analysis of transcription errors in ASR outputs, and the evaluation of both text-based and text-independent summarization techniques. While Bangla and Assamese are used as case studies, the methods are not specific to these languages and are designed to generalize across other low-resource linguistic contexts. By addressing the limitations of current approaches and developing practical tools tailored to real-world constraints, this work aims to support more inclusive access to speech technologies.

Ultimately, the goal is not to build fully-fledged systems that rival those available for high-resource languages, but to lay the groundwork for principled, modular solutions that operate under real-world constraints. The thesis aims to demonstrate that even with limited data and partial supervision, it is possible to make progress on core speech understanding tasks—provided that modeling strategies are adapted to the realities of low-resource environments. This includes exploiting linguistic cues that are robust to transcription noise, using simpler classifiers that require less data, and designing evaluation protocols that reflect the practical limitations of working in such settings.

1.5 Research Objectives

The main objective of this thesis is *to study the extractive speech summarization methods in the context of low-resource languages, and to design an effective summarization framework that addresses the unique challenges associated with these languages.* In order to achieve this, the following objectives have been carried out.

1. Development of a prosodically annotated speech corpus capable of extractive summarization, covering read continuous speech in both Assamese and Bengali.
2. A detailed analysis of speech-to-text transcription errors in Bengali spoken documents, showcasing the limitations of ASR-based summarization in low-resourced settings.
3. Evaluation of state-of-the-art text-based extractive speech summarization methods using various sentence embeddings, applied to Bengali as a representative case of ASR-dependent low-resource languages.
4. Development of a text-independent summarization framework using handcrafted acoustic-prosodic features, applied to Assamese as a case study for ASR-absent (or extremely poor ASR) lower-resource conditions.
5. Design of a neural summarization framework based solely on acoustic-prosodic features, demonstrating the viability of speech summarization in languages like Assamese where no reliable speech-to-text transcript exists.

1.6 Thesis Contributions

This thesis takes a grounded approach to the problem of extractive speech summarization in low-resource settings. Instead of pursuing a single end-to-end model, it isolates key challenges that arise when working with languages like Assamese and Bengali—lack of annotated data, unreliable ASR output, and underexplored prosodic features—and designs targeted solutions for each.

Each objective is chosen to address a specific weakness in the pipeline. Chapter by chapter, the work explores what is possible under real-world constraints: How far can we go with limited transcribed speech? What role does prosody play when lexical information is noisy or missing? Can simpler models, informed by linguistic cues, perform competitively in low-resource conditions?

The work does not assume scale. It assumes difficulty. And it responds with focused, practical methods that aim to extend the reach of summarization research to languages that are often excluded.This thesis makes several key contributions to the field of extractive speech summarization, particularly in the context of low-resource languages. While the experiments focus on Bangla and Assamese, the proposed methods are not language-specific and are designed to generalize effectively to other low-resource settings. The main contributions are as follows:

1. One of the key contributions of this thesis is the development of a manually annotated speech corpus in two low-resource Indo-Aryan languages—Assamese and Bengali (Bangla)—tailored specifically for speech summarization. Despite their widespread use, with Bengali spoken by over 230 million people and Assamese by approximately 15 million, both languages suffer from a lack of digital resources and annotated data essential for building speech and language technologies. The curated corpus includes broadcast news recordings collected from Akashvani Guwahati and Kolkata between April and August 2020, covering significant regional and national topics, particularly those related to the COVID-19 pandemic. In addition, expressive audiobook recordings were sourced from the public domain to provide variation in prosody and speaking style. All recordings were carefully segmented at the sentence level to enable precise alignment between speech and text. Human-written gold summaries accompany each document, serving as ground truth for evaluating summarization systems. Furthermore, approximately 60% of the corpus includes manual prosodic annotations created using Praat's TextGrid environment, enriching the dataset for speech-based modeling beyond lexical features. This corpus stands as a foundational resource to support research in speech summarization and broader NLP tasks in low-resource Indian languages.
2. Another significant contribution of this thesis is the development of a typology of Automatic Speech Recognition (ASR) errors encountered in transcriptions of Bengali spoken documents. These errors, though varied in nature, consistently impact the readability and informativeness of speech-derived

texts—ultimately affecting the quality of downstream applications such as summarization. The typology is drawn from empirical analysis of ASR-generated transcripts and highlights key error categories including: deletion of initial or final words due to low pitch detection thresholds; substitution errors arising from vowel and consonant misrecognition; boundary misidentification caused by the absence of pause-based segmentation; and critical misinterpretations of dialectal speech, given the mismatch between regional varieties and the standard language model of the ASR system. Through qualitative examples and speech-text alignment visualizations, this analysis reveals how even small transcription errors can lead to severe contextual loss or semantic distortion. The categorization proposed here is among the first such systematic efforts in the context of low-resource languages like Bengali and serves as a foundational reference for improving ASR error handling. Moreover, the thesis conducts comparative summarization experiments on both ASR-generated and manually transcribed documents to quantify the impact of these errors, offering deeper insight into their practical consequences on information retrieval from speech.

3. A key contribution of this thesis lies in its comprehensive evaluation of extractive summarization methods in the presence of automatic speech recognition (ASR) errors, specifically within the context of Bengali—a low-resource language. Building on the prior typological analysis of transcription errors, this investigation offers a first-of-its-kind empirical study that rigorously examines how such errors affect summarization quality. While extractive summarization is traditionally framed as an Information Retrieval (IR) problem, existing literature and tools are overwhelmingly developed and benchmarked on high-resource languages. These systems assume a certain level of transcription fidelity, often maintained by advanced ASR models trained on large-scale annotated corpora—resources that are unavailable or insufficient for languages like Bengali.

   This study challenges that assumption by evaluating the performance of widely adopted unsupervised summarization algorithms—Sentence Ranking, TextRank, Latent Semantic Analysis (LSA), Latent Dirichlet Allocation (LDA), and Maximal Marginal Relevance (MMR)—on both manually transcribed and ASR-generated versions of Bengali speech documents. The use of semantically rich, higher-order embeddings such as FastText, GloVe, and XLM-RoBERTa (XLM-R, full form Cross-lingual Language Model – RoBERTa), which are typically robust to noise in high-resource settings, was found to be significantly less effective in mitigating transcription errors for Bengali. Performance metrics, measured using ROUGE, reveal a pronounced decline in summary quality when operating on noisy ASR transcripts.

The findings underscore a critical gap in the field: that techniques presumed to be state-of-the-art for summarizing spoken content fail to generalize to low-resource linguistic contexts when transcription quality is compromised. By demonstrating this limitation through a controlled, data-driven analysis, the thesis makes a substantial and original contribution to speech and language processing for underrepresented languages. It not only questions the generalizability of current NLP paradigms but also provides the empirical foundation for future work that develops summarization models tailored to the realities of low-resource, error-prone transcription environments.

4. A significant contribution of this thesis is the development of a text-independent framework for extractive speech summarization that effectively addresses the limitations of conventional, text-dependent methods in low-resource language settings. In many such languages, the absence of robust ASR systems or the presence of high word error rates in transcriptions severely affects the quality of text-based summarization. This work introduces a novel approach that bypasses the need for accurate transcripts by leveraging acoustic-prosodic features—such as pitch, intensity, and duration—to identify important content directly from speech. A prosody-based sentence-importance scoring method is proposed to capture emphasis and prominence within spoken utterances, offering a linguistically motivated way to estimate sentence relevance. By framing the task as a binary classification problem, the study demonstrates how combining prosodic and lexical cues can effectively distinguish summary-worthy sentences from the rest. This approach not only provides an alternative path for summarization in resource-constrained scenarios but also establishes the viability of using speech signal properties themselves as meaningful indicators of salience. As such, it represents a foundational step toward building summarization systems that are independent of transcription quality, thereby extending the reach of speech technologies to truly low-resource linguistic contexts.

5. The final contribution of this thesis presents the design, implementation, and evaluation of a lightweight neural architecture for extractive speech summarization in a fully transcript-free setting. The proposed model is a one-dimensional convolutional neural network (1D-CNN) trained solely on handcrafted acoustic-prosodic features, without relying on lexical input, language models, or ASR transcriptions. Evaluated on manually segmented Assamese broadcast news data, the model achieves competitive classifica-

tion and ROUGE-based summarization performance compared to deeper neural variants (e.g., CNN+BiGRU, CNN+Attention), despite its architectural simplicity. This is the first known application of a 1D-CNN model for prosody-only summarization in a low-resource language. The model's robustness under class imbalance, limited training data, and absence of textual supervision demonstrates that effective summarization is achievable in speech-native form. Beyond model accuracy, this contribution establishes a clean, reproducible experimental pipeline that offers a scalable and interpretable solution for summarization in languages with little to no ASR support. It also lays groundwork for future extensions in multilingual speech summarization, self-supervised acoustic modeling, and spoken document processing under extreme resource constraints.

1.7 Outline of the Thesis

The thesis is organized into eight chapters.

Chapter 1 introduces the motivation for speech summarization in low-resource languages, outlines the research problems, objectives, scope, and contributions of the thesis.

Chapter 2 presents a thematic review of existing research in extractive summarization, both for textual and spoken content. It covers foundational techniques in extractive summarization, the impact of ASR errors on summarization quality, prior efforts on summarization in low-resource languages, and the role of prosodic features in spoken language processing. The review identifies key limitations in prior work, particularly the lack of text-independent approaches and under-exploration of prosodic cues in low-resource settings, motivating the research contributions of this thesis.

Chapter 3 describes the creation of a bilingual speech corpus of Assamese and Bengali, including broadcast news and audiobook data. The chapter details the data collection process, annotation pipeline, and design principles used to ensure sentence-level alignment, speaker diversity, and quality control. Gold-standard summaries and partial prosodic annotations are also included, forming a critical resource for subsequent experiments in this thesis.

Chapter 4 presents a typology of transcription errors commonly observed in Bengali speech-to-text outputs. It evaluates their impact on summarization quality and sets the groundwork for justifying text-independent approaches.

Chapter 5 investigates how various sentence embedding techniques (e.g., FastText, GloVe, XLM-R) and unsupervised summarization methods perform when applied to both manual and ASR-generated transcripts. The results highlight the limitations of applying high-resource techniques to low-resource contexts.

Chapter 6 proposes a framework for extractive speech summarization that eliminates dependency on text transcriptions. The approach models sentence-level importance using prosodic cues such as pitch, intensity, and duration. Sentences are classified as summary-worthy using ensemble machine learning methods trained on prosodic and lexical features. A novel prosody-based sentence importance scoring mechanism is introduced, and the results show that prosodic signals can reliably guide summarization in the absence of clean textual input.

Chapter 7 extends the previous approach by developing a 1D-CNN architecture trained solely on handcrafted acoustic-prosodic features. The model eliminates the dependency on textual data and demonstrates promising results for Assamese broadcast news.

Chapter 8 summarizes the key findings of the thesis, discusses the implications of text-independent summarization, outlines limitations, and suggests possible directions for future research.

Chapter 2

Literature Survey

Research on speech summarization has evolved at the intersection of automatic speech recognition (ASR), natural language processing (NLP), and audio processing. While substantial progress has been made in high-resource settings, most existing methodologies, datasets, and benchmarks are designed for languages like English, Mandarin, or French. These resources often assume the availability of high-quality transcriptions, well-annotated corpora, and pretrained models — conditions that do not hold in low-resource scenarios. This chapter presents a comprehensive survey of existing literature and datasets relevant to extractive speech summarization. The goal is to critically examine the building blocks of the field, identify gaps in current research, and position the contributions of this thesis within the broader scholarly context.

2.1 Introduction

Speech summarization has been an active area of research for over two decades, with growing relevance in domains such as broadcast news, meetings, lectures, and spontaneous conversations. Traditional approaches have predominantly relied on automatic speech recognition (ASR) systems to convert speech into text, followed by the application of extractive or abstractive text summarization techniques. This has proven effective in high-resource settings where accurate transcriptions, large annotated datasets, and pretrained models are readily available. However, these assumptions do not hold for many low-resource languages, such as Assamese and Bengali, where ASR systems remain unreliable, large summarization corpora are absent, and pretrained models either do not exist or fail to generalize. The gap between state-of-the-art methods and their applicability in such settings motivates a closer examination of existing summarization approaches and their underlying dependencies. In this context, this chapter provides a background information on

Through this survey, the chapter lays the foundation for the problem formulations, corpus design, and modeling strategies adopted in subsequent chapters.

2.2 Spoken Corpora for Summarization

Research on speech summarization has historically depended on corpora developed for high-resource languages such as English, Mandarin Chinese, and Japanese. These corpora typically consist of spoken content—often meetings, lectures, or broadcast news—paired with manual or semi-automatic summaries. In most cases, the speech recordings are transcribed and aligned at the sentence or segment level, enabling researchers to apply both text-based and speech-based summarization methods. Table 2.1 provides a comparative overview of widely used speech summarization corpora.

These corpora have served as benchmarks for both automatic speech recognition (ASR) and summarization, enabling systematic evaluation across a range of domains. However, they share several limitations:

- They are primarily designed for high-resource languages, such as English, Chinese, and Japanese.
- They assume the availability of accurate ASR transcriptions.
- They focus on structured domains like meetings, lectures, or news broadcasts.

Such corpora have enabled the development of a wide spectrum of summarization models, ranging from statistical extractive techniques to advanced neural abstractive methods. However, they remain unavailable for the vast majority of low-resource languages. This gap—both linguistic and methodological—is the focus of the next section.

While these benchmark datasets have shaped current progress, they are each defined by particular design trade-offs. AMI [46] and ICSI [41]target multi-party meetings, useful for dialogue modeling but limited in linguistic and prosodic diversity. TED-LIUM [92] and How2 [93] offer clean, monologue-style speech, which supports semantic modeling but lacks natural disfluencies and prosodic richness. Corpora like MATBN [107] and JNSC introduce language diversity but are domain-bound and not always publicly accessible. A further constraint is that most of these corpora provide abstractive summaries, while extractive annotations—crucial for sentence-level summarization—remain scarce. Moreover, none address the unique challenges of speech summarization in low-resource languages.

Table 2.1: Overview of Existing Speech Summarization Corpora

Corpus Name	Language(s)	Domain	Summary Type	Speech Source	Duration / Size	Link
AMI [46]	English	Meetings	Abstractive & Extractive	Multi-party meetings	100 hrs	http://groups.inf.ed.ac.uk/ami/corpus/
ICSI Meeting Corpus [41]	English	Meetings	Abstractive	Multi-party meetings	75 hrs	[41]
TED-LIUM [92]	English	Lectures/Talks	Abstractive	TED Talks	452 hrs	https://www.openslr.org/19/
How2	English, Portuguese	Instructional Videos	Abstractive	YouTube videos	300 hrs	[93]
CC-News-En	English	Broadcast News	Extractive	TV/Radio news	19.6 hrs	[61]
MATBN	Mandarin	Broadcast News	Abstractive	TV news reports	198 hrs	[107]
CSJ	Japanese	Simultaneous Interpretation	Extractive	Live simultaneous speech	20 hrs	[62]

2.3 Spoken Corpora for Low-Resource Languages

In contrast to the rich resources available for English and other high-resource languages, low-resource settings rarely offer corpora that support end-to-end speech summarization research. Although various initiatives have focused on ASR and speech recognition for Indian and other underrepresented languages, few, if any, provide paired speech-summary data. This gap severely restricts the development and evaluation of summarization models in such languages.

Table 2.2 lists a range of corpora developed for low-resource languages, categorized by their modality and relevance to summarization.

Despite these expanding resources, no existing corpus provides:

- Spoken documents with aligned extractive summary labels
- Acoustic-prosodic annotations suitable for prosody-aware modeling
- Full support for training and evaluating speech-to-summary pipelines in low-resource languages

This persistent data gap strongly motivates the corpus development efforts undertaken in this thesis. Speech corpora for Bengali, Kannada, and Assamese—such as MUCS and OpenSLR—primarily support ASR development and are devoid of summary annotations. Even well-resourced platforms like Common Voice and MLS offer only transcriptions or read speech, with no alignment to summarization tasks. On the text side, datasets such as FIRE-2021, XL-Sum, and WikiLingua provide multilingual abstractive summaries for written content. While useful for evaluating language models, they contain no speech data and cannot inform models that integrate acoustic or prosodic information.

To the best of our knowledge, no existing corpus—regardless of modality—provides aligned speech-summary pairs for any low-resource language. This lack of data has been a consistent roadblock in expanding speech summarization research beyond high-resource settings. Addressing this shortfall is a core contribution of this thesis, which introduces manually segmented, prosody-annotated speech data in Assamese and Bengali with aligned extractive summaries.

2.4 Transcript-Based Techniques for Extractive speech Summarization

Research in speech summarization has evolved significantly over the past two decades, starting from early rule-based methods to more recent automatic,

Table 2.2: Existing Low-Resource Language Corpora (Speech and/or Summary)

Corpus Name	Language(s)	Data Type	Summary Available	Domain	Size	Link
MUCS	Bengali, Hindi	Speech (ASR)	No	Conversational	200 hrs/lang	[6, 7, 36]
OpenSLR ASR Sets	Assamese, Bengali, Kannada...	Speech (ASR)	No	News, Read speech	20–300 hrs/lang	https://www.openslr.org/
Common Voice [2]	100+ languages incl. Assamese, Bengali	Speech (crowd-sourced)	No	General read speech	Varies per lang	https://commonvoice.mozilla.org/
MLS	Multilingual (some Indic)	Speech (audio-book)	No	Audiobook readings	50–100 hrs/lang	https://www.openslr.org/94/
IndicTTS	13 Indian languages	Speech (TTS recordings)	No	Phoneme-rich sentences	4–10 hrs/lang	[94, 100]
FIRE-2021	Bengali, Hindi	Text + Summary (text only)	Yes (textual)	News articles	300 docs/lang	[65]
XL-Sum	44 languages incl. Assamese, Bengali	Text + Summary (abstractive)	Yes	BBC News	1 million+ pairs	[33]

data-driven systems. In the early 2000s, summarizing spoken documents was often tackled using hand-crafted heuristics or manually curated templates. These systems typically relied on shallow linguistic cues, such as cue phrases, sentence position, or speaker turns, and were often built on domain-specific speech corpora [25, 77, 82, 115].
Murray et al. [77] investigated the role of speaker and discourse-level features in improving speech summarization performance on meeting data. Using the ICSI Meeting Corpus, they incorporated indicators such as speaker activity, turn-taking patterns, and discourse cues into a summarization system, hypothesizing that these elements signal informational relevance beyond what text-based methods can capture. Their approach combined traditional extractive techniques with features like speaker dominance, floor-holding behavior, and dialogue structure, all of which influence how listeners perceive importance in spontaneous conversations. Evaluation using both ROUGE scores and human judgment showed that even relatively simple heuristics—such as emphasizing content from key speakers or detecting topic shifts through discourse markers—led to improved summaries over baseline text-only models. This study was among the first to demonstrate that integrating speech-specific interaction cues can enhance summarization quality, especially in dialogue-rich domains like meetings, where lexical content alone may fail to reflect communicative intent.

As automatic speech recognition (ASR) technology matured, extractive summarization methods adapted to work with transcribed speech. Many of these early systems borrowed techniques from text summarization—such as sentence ranking, graph-based centrality, and clustering—but faced new challenges when applied to speech. Unlike written documents, spoken language contains disfluencies, false starts, filler words, and redundant phrasing [95]. These elements often confuse models that assume grammatical well-formedness [26, 119].
In their work on summarizing spontaneous speech, Furui et al. [26] explored both speech-to-text and speech-to-speech summarization approaches, targeting the unique challenges of handling unstructured spoken content. The study emphasized the need for preprocessing techniques to manage disfluencies, speaker overlaps, and fragmented utterances that are typical in conversational or informal speech. For the text-based summarization pipeline, they employed automatic speech recognition (ASR) followed by sentence extraction using statistical and heuristic methods. In parallel, the speech-to-speech system generated spoken summaries using concatenative speech synthesis, allowing for audible output summaries. Their experiments showed that direct summarization from speech — bypassing full-text transcription — can be beneficial when ASR output quality is low, particularly in

noisy or low-resource settings. The paper's findings highlight that speech-specific processing methods, such as pause detection and prosodic segmentation, can complement lexical cues and help produce more coherent and concise summaries. This work was notable for framing summarization as a multi-modal task, extending the field beyond traditional text-centric paradigms.

Another major challenge comes from ASR errors. Even state-of-the-art systems produce word-level inaccuracies, especially in noisy or low-resource language settings. Substitution, deletion, and insertion errors in ASR output can significantly degrade the performance of transcript-dependent summarization methods, as they interfere with keyword detection, sentence coherence, and embedding quality [76, 106]. This limitation has encouraged research into alternatives that rely more on speech signals—such as prosody, energy, and pauses—rather than the lexical content alone.

Tündik et al. [106] investigated how automatic speech recognition (ASR) errors influence the semantic representation of spoken documents and, consequently, affect the performance of summarization systems. Their study introduced the concept of semantic space bias, where word-level ASR errors—particularly substitutions and deletions—distort sentence embeddings generated by models such as TF-IDF or Word2Vec. By conducting controlled experiments on spoken Hungarian datasets, they demonstrated that even low ASR word error rates (WER) could significantly shift vector representations away from their clean-text counterparts. The authors quantified this distortion and analyzed its downstream impact on extractive summarization quality. Importantly, they highlighted that semantic degradation is not always linearly correlated with WER, meaning that even small transcription inaccuracies can disproportionately impact sentence scoring and ranking. This work underscores the importance of ASR-aware or ASR-robust methods in summarizing spoken content and motivates the use of alternative or auxiliary features—such as prosody or structure—to mitigate the limitations of purely lexical summarization pipelines in noisy conditions.

Several benchmark corpora have supported the development of speech summarization systems. Notable examples include the ICSI Meeting Corpus [41], AMI Corpus [46], TED Talks [92], and Broadcast News datasets [31, 107]. These resources have enabled comparative evaluation of extractive and abstractive methods across different domains, including meetings, lectures, and news reading. However, these corpora are primarily in English, Chinese, and other high-resource languages, limiting their applicability in under-resourced contexts.

Over time, research has expanded from purely text-based extractive approaches to include multimodal strategies that integrate acoustic-prosodic features. This shift is particularly important in low-resource or noisy ASR environments, where transcript quality is unreliable or unavailable altogether. The next sections survey these developments in more detail, contrasting transcript-based methods with prosody-aware approaches.

2.4.1 Extractive Methods Using ASR-converted Transcripts

Text-based extractive speech summarization assumes that the spoken document has first been transcribed—manually or using automatic speech recognition (ASR). Once speech is converted to text, summarization techniques select a subset of sentences deemed most informative. These methods differ in how they model sentence importance: using frequency statistics, similarity graphs, topic distributions, embeddings, or a mix of these.

(a) Statistical and Frequency-Based Methods

Early extractive summarization relied on simple statistical cues like word frequency and sentence position. In these approaches, sentences with high TF-IDF scores or those containing predefined cue words were ranked higher. While these methods are fast and interpretable, they depend heavily on word accuracy and frequency statistics, making them fragile under ASR-induced noise.

Examples include: Luhn's frequency-based scoring [58], Edmundson's cue-word strategy [19], and Zechner's adaptation for speech [114]. Zechner presented one of the early comprehensive efforts toward automatic summarization of open-domain, multiparty spoken dialogues across diverse genres. Unlike monologue-based summarization tasks, this work tackled the complexity of spontaneous human conversations—where overlapping speech, disfluencies, and topic shifts pose major challenges. The proposed method combined speech recognition transcripts with shallow linguistic processing and heuristic features to identify salient segments. Zechner incorporated speaker turns, cue phrases, and term frequency metrics to score utterances for extractive summary generation. The study was notable for its domain diversity, including meeting dialogues, interviews, and panel discussions, which made the system robust to variability in structure and interaction patterns. Evaluation on human-annotated summaries revealed that even basic models—when adapted to conversational structure—could achieve meaningful compression without major loss of content. This work laid foundational groundwork for later efforts in dialogue summarization and emphasized the need for dialogue-aware and genre-specific strategies beyond standard sentence-ranking techniques derived from text summarization.

(b) Graph-Based Methods

Graph-based summarization represents sentences as nodes in a graph, with edge weights reflecting semantic similarity. Methods like TextRank [72] and LexRank [20] compute sentence importance using centrality scores, selecting the most connected sentences for the summary. These models are unsupervised and domain-independent, but their reliance on accurate similarity measures makes them vulnerable to ASR errors, which can distort sentence embeddings or term overlaps.

(c) Latent Semantic and Topic Models

Latent semantic approaches aim to capture deeper topic structure. Latent Semantic Analysis (LSA) [30] uses singular value decomposition on a term-sentence matrix to uncover important sentence-topic alignments. Kong and Lee [45] explored the application of Probabilistic Latent Semantic Analysis (PLSA) to improve the summarization of spoken documents. Recognizing the limitations of surface-level text features in capturing semantic relevance, particularly in noisy ASR outputs, they proposed a topic-based representation framework using PLSA. This approach modeled latent topic distributions over utterances, allowing the system to group semantically related content even when lexical overlap was low. Importantly, their method addressed the data sparsity and noise typical in transcribed speech, which often degrades the performance of frequency-based or lexical matching methods. Experiments demonstrated that integrating topic modeling significantly enhanced the selection of summary-worthy sentences in broadcast news and lecture data. Their results indicated that PLSA could outperform traditional summarizers in identifying thematic coherence within spoken documents, making it a promising direction for speech summarization tasks involving semantic abstraction and redundancy reduction.

Topic models like Latent Dirichlet Allocation (LDA) [9] assign probabilistic topic distributions to sentences. These models can capture redundancy and thematic importance, but performance drops when transcripts are fragmented or noisy, which affects co-occurrence statistics. Hazen [35] proposed a latent topic modeling approach for summarizing large audio corpora without relying entirely on textual transcriptions. The core idea was to represent spoken documents in terms of their latent semantic structures, learned through unsupervised topic models, specifically Latent Dirichlet Allocation (LDA). Unlike transcript-dependent summarization methods that assume clean and reliable ASR output, this work emphasized the need to work effectively even when transcriptions are noisy or unavailable. Hazen demonstrated that topic representations derived from speech features could be used to group semantically related utterances across an entire corpus and select representative segments for summarization. The approach was validated on large-scale spoken document collections, including broadcast news, showing that latent topic structures could capture salient information even in the presence of disfluencies and transcription errors. This work was among the early efforts to decouple summarization performance from transcript quality, paving the way for more robust speech-first summarization models.

(d) Redundancy-Controlled Ranking

Maximum Marginal Relevance (MMR) [12] was designed to avoid redundancy in summaries by selecting sentences that are both relevant and novel. MMR has been used in speech summarization, particularly in meeting and news data, where repetition is common. However, it still depends on reliable similarity scores between sentences, which noisy transcripts may compromise. Xie and Liu [111] extended the Maximum Marginal Relevance (MMR) framework for meeting summarization by incorporating both corpus-based and knowledge-based semantic similarity measures. Recognizing that ASR transcripts often contain sparse and inconsistent lexical information, the authors aimed to improve sentence selection by combining traditional TF-IDF similarity with external knowledge from lexical resources like WordNet. This dual approach allowed the system to better capture semantic overlap between utterances and reduce redundancy in summaries, even when ASR output was noisy. Their experiments on meeting data showed that integrating multiple similarity metrics led to more informative and diverse summaries, outperforming baseline MMR approaches that relied solely on word overlap. This work contributed to improving robustness in extractive summarization by addressing semantic sparsity and distortion in spoken transcripts.

(e) Embedding-Based Enhancements

Modern approaches leverage dense vector embeddings to compute semantic similarity:

- **Static Embeddings:** TF-IDF, GloVe, and FastText have been used to encode sentences as vectors, which are then ranked using cosine similarity or clustering. FastText is slightly more robust to ASR noise due to its subword structure [112].
- **Contextual Embeddings:** Transformer-based models such as BERT [90], XLM-R [60], and SBERT [90] produce context-aware sentence embeddings. These improve salience estimation in clean text but tend to underperform on noisy or low-resource ASR transcripts, unless specifically fine-tuned.

  Weng, Lo, and Chen [108] proposed a contextual language modeling framework designed to enhance extractive speech summarization through the integration of augmented features. Their approach augmented BERT-based contextual embeddings with linguistic and acoustic-prosodic features—such as part-of-speech tags and pitch-based indicators—capturing both the lexical and suprasegmental cues within speech. By encoding these enriched feature sets into the summarization model, they demonstrated improved resilience to ASR errors, particularly in spontaneous speech settings. Experiments conducted on Mandarin broadcast news showed that the model outperformed baselines relying purely on text embeddings. The study highlighted the importance of hybrid feature integration, especially for speech summarization tasks where lexical noise or loss of intonational cues can misguide purely transcript-based methods.

While extractive text-based summarization remains a foundational approach, its performance on ASR-transcribed speech—particularly for low-resource languages—is limited by transcription quality. Our study confirms that simpler or noise-tolerant models often outperform more complex ones under these conditions.

2.4.2 Robustness Under Noisy Transcripts

While extractive summarization methods built on clean transcripts have shown strong performance, applying these techniques to *ASR-generated speech transcripts* poses significant challenges. Automatic speech recognition (ASR) systems often introduce errors — including deletions, insertions, substitutions, and disfluencies — especially in low-resource settings where acoustic and language models are poorly trained. These imperfections directly affect the performance of text-based summarization systems, which rely heavily on lexical and syntactic coherence.

Types of ASR Errors and Their Impact

Common ASR error types include:

- **Deletion errors**, where important content words are skipped, reducing the informativeness of a sentence.
- **Insertion and substitution errors**, which introduce out-of-context or phonetically similar words, lowering lexical cohesion.
- **Disfluencies**, like repetitions or filler words, are often retained in transcripts and increase noise in sentence representations.

These distortions reduce the accuracy of methods such as sentence ranking, topic modeling, and embedding-based similarity. For example, sentence similarity scores used in TextRank or LexRank may become unreliable when key terms are misrecognized. Similarly, semantic embeddings generated from corrupted transcripts fail to capture intended meaning, making sentence ranking and selection unstable [98].

Performance Degradation in Noisy Conditions

Several studies have evaluated the *performance gap* between clean and ASR-transcribed inputs. In most cases, summarization models trained or evaluated on noisy transcripts show significant ROUGE score drops compared to those operating on gold-standard text [55, 56]. Liu, Liu, and Chen [55] introduced a hierarchical neural summarization framework tailored for spoken document summarization, aiming to address the limitations of flat sentence-level models. Their architecture combines a sentence encoder and a document-level summarizer, leveraging hierarchical attention mechanisms to capture both local and global discourse structures within ASR-transcribed speech. The model integrates acoustic-prosodic features alongside word embeddings, allowing it to better model prominence and salience even in the presence of ASR errors. Evaluations on Mandarin broadcast news data showed that this hierarchical design significantly outperformed traditional flat summarization models in both ROUGE scores and summary coherence. The work underscored the value of structured modeling in spoken language summarization, especially when input transcripts are noisy or contain incomplete discourse cues.

This degradation is more severe in languages where ASR word error rates (WER) are high due to code-switching, limited vocabularies, or domain mismatch. Liu et al. [56] proposed a positional language modeling approach for extractive summarization of broadcast news speech, addressing the observation that summary-worthy content tends to appear in specific structural positions within a news segment. Their method integrates sentence-level language models with position priors, effectively biasing the summarizer to favor early and central portions of the document where critical information often resides. The model is further enhanced by incorporating acoustic cues and relevance scores derived from statistical features. Experiments on Mandarin broadcast news data showed improved performance over traditional frequency-based and statistical baselines. This work highlights how structural and positional heuristics can significantly boost summarization accuracy in domain-specific spoken content.

Additionally, *fragmentation* of utterances and improper punctuation in ASR outputs can disrupt the sentence segmentation assumed by many extractive methods. This leads to poorly formed input units for summarization, reducing the quality of extracted summaries.

Approaches to Mitigate ASR Impact

To address these issues, researchers have explored:

- **ASR-aware scoring techniques**: Some methods down-weight low-confidence words based on ASR confidence scores or use alternate hypotheses from ASR lattices.

- **Noise-robust embeddings**: Domain-adapted or fine-tuned contextual embeddings (e.g., BERT variants) have shown some improvement in summarizing ASR transcripts, but results are mixed without domain-specific adaptation [117].
- **Transcript-cleaning or preprocessing**: Removing disfluencies, normalizing punctuation, or applying sentence boundary detection improves summarizer stability.
- **Non-lexical or multi-modal features**: Acoustic-prosodic cues, such as pitch or pause duration, have been proposed as complementary signals that are immune to transcription errors [77].

In summary, transcript noise remains a *major bottleneck* for summarization systems in real-world, low-resource conditions. This motivates the need to explore **text-independent approaches**, which either add-to or entirely bypass ASR output — a direction that will be further explored in Section 2.5.

2.5 Extractive Speech Summarization using Text-Independent approaches

Extractive speech summarization traditionally depends on automatic speech recognition (ASR) to convert spoken content into text, which is then processed using standard summarization techniques. However, in low-resource languages or noisy conditions, ASR systems often produce unreliable transcriptions, severely degrading summary quality. Given the continual issues with ASR-generated transcripts, especially in low-resource languages, researchers have explored summarization methods that use *non-lexical* information—most notably, acoustic-prosodic features such as pitch, pause, intensity, and speaking rate. These features are directly observable from the audio signal and can serve as indicators of emphasis, boundaries, and salience, even in the absence of clean transcripts.

2.5.1 Speech Prosody and Acoustic-prosodic features.

Prosody refers to the rhythm, stress, and intonation patterns present in spoken language [17, 49]. Unlike lexical or grammatical content, prosodic features operate at the suprasegmental level—spanning across phonemes, syllables, and phrases— to convey information about speaker intent, emphasis, emotion, and discourse structure. Key prosodic cues include pitch (fundamental frequency), intensity (loudness), duration, pausing, and contour shapes over time.

In the context of speech summarization, prosody plays a crucial role in signaling salience, often guiding human listeners in identifying important or emphasized segments of speech [68]. For instance, final pitch rises or pauses may signal sentence boundaries, while pitch peaks and increased energy often correspond to focal or informative content. These patterns are especially valuable when working with noisy or incomplete transcripts, as prosody provides a text-independent signal for sentence importance [77]. As such, prosodic features are increasingly being explored as an alternative or complementary source of information in summarization systems, particularly in low-resource or ASR-error-prone settings where lexical features are unreliable [110].

In computational speech processing, prosody is operationalized through acoustic-prosodic features—quantitative measurements extracted directly from the audio signal. These features include pitch-based measures (e.g., minimum, maximum, mean pitch), energy-related features (e.g., root mean square energy, energy range), durational statistics (e.g., speaking rate, utterance length), and contour descriptors (e.g., slope, rise-fall patterns, number of peaks) [111]. Unlike text-based cues, these features can be obtained without transcriptions, making them especially valuable for text-independent summarization and for languages where reliable ASR systems do not exist. Recent work has shown that such features can be used to train lightweight classifiers or integrated into hybrid models, often yielding robust results in low-resource or noisy environments where traditional summarization approaches tend to fail.

Motivation for Text-Independent Approaches

Text-independent summarization is motivated by several factors:

- **ASR-Independence:** In languages with poor or unavailable ASR systems, relying purely on audio features enables summarization without needing transcription [77].
- **Language and Script Independence:** Since prosodic patterns are signal-based, they can generalize across languages, making these methods attractive in multilingual or under-documented settings. One of the earliest and most cited contributions to this line of work was by Maskey and Hirschberg [69], who proposed a hidden Markov model (HMM)-based system for extractive summarization of broadcast news using prosodic cues. Their model extracted features such as pitch range, energy, and pause durations and trained an HMM classifier to assign salience labels at the sentence level. Crucially, they compared their prosody-only system against baseline sys-

tems that relied on text transcriptions and found that the text-independent approach could achieve ROUGE-1 scores within 5 points of transcript-based methods on broadcast news. This was one of the first demonstrations of summarization feasibility in a no-text setting.

- **Complementary Cues:** Even when transcripts are available, prosodic signals can serve as a supplementary modality, improving robustness under noisy conditions [110].

Use of Acoustic-Prosodic Features

Early studies have used features like fundamental frequency (F0), energy, and duration to identify sentence boundaries and segment-level prominence. For example, pitch contours that rise and fall within a segment often signal closure or emphasis, and long pauses may separate discourse units [49]. In read or formal speech, such as broadcast news or audiobooks, these prosodic features tend to be more structured and reliable [37].

Several studies in speech summarization have explored the role of prosodic cues as primary or auxiliary features, especially in scenarios where textual transcripts are noisy, unreliable, or unavailable. These methods generally fall into three categories: heuristic scoring, contour modeling, and transcript-free summarization.

Heuristic Scoring Approaches: Early work in this approach used simple pause-based thresholds or pitch discontinuities to detect sentence boundaries or emphasize important phrases. For example, longer inter-utterance pauses were treated as potential sentence or topic boundaries[98], while abrupt pitch resets were associated with discourse-level prominence [37, 67]. Maskey and Hirschberg [67] conducted a comparative analysis of multiple feature types—lexical, acoustic/prosodic, structural, and discourse-level—for the task of extractive speech summarization. Using broadcast news as the testbed, they systematically evaluated the impact of each feature set on summary selection accuracy. The study found that while lexical features (such as TF-IDF) were strong baselines, prosodic cues like pitch range, pause duration, and energy levels significantly enhanced performance, especially when combined with structural and discourse indicators such as sentence position and speaker change. Their results demonstrated that prosodic and structural features offer complementary strengths and are particularly valuable in noisy ASR scenarios where lexical reliability is reduced. This work is a foundational reference in multi-modal speech summarization, providing early empirical evidence for the role of non-lexical cues in capturing salience.

These rule-based methods are easy to implement and can be interpreted; but they often suffer from low generalizability across speakers or domains.

Contour-Based Modeling: More refined models represent prosodic signals—such as pitch and intensity—as time-series contours. Studies have used contour shapes (e.g., rise-fall, monotonic rise) to infer sentence modality or prominence [50, 91]. Some methods extract slope, curvature, or peak structure of contours and use them as features for sentence classification. These approaches are especially useful in monologue or read-speech scenarios, where prosodic phrasing closely aligns with discourse structure.

Transcript-Free Summarization: Several recent works have explored entirely text-independent summarization. These systems use acoustic-prosodic features—such as pitch mean, energy RMS, pause duration, and MFCCs—to train classifiers or neural models for identifying summary-worthy segments. For example, the authors [77] demonstrated that a combination of pitch range and pause duration could outperform baseline lexical methods in noisy environments.

These prosody-focused approaches are particularly relevant for low-resource languages, where ASR systems are either unavailable or error-prone, and where training data for text-based summarization is scarce. However, a major limitation in the field remains the scarcity of publicly available prosody-annotated speech corpora, especially in non-English languages.

In summary, text-independent summarization represents a *practical and theoretically grounded* solution for scenarios where ASR fails or is unavailable. While still a relatively niche area, especially in low-resource speech processing, this approach opens up summarization to a broader range of languages and use-cases where text-based methods struggle. Its growing feasibility is driven by advances in prosodic modeling, deep neural encoders, and fusion strategies. As research expands to new languages and domains, and as evaluation frameworks improve, these methods are set to become a mainstream alternative to ASR-dependent summarization.

2.6 Neural Networks models for Extractive Speech Summarization

Deep neural networks (DNNs) have become foundational in modern natural language and speech processing tasks, including summarization. Their strength lies in their ability to automatically learn abstract representations from raw or lightly processed inputs, eliminating the need for extensive feature engineering. In the context of extractive speech summarization, neural networks have enabled systems that can model both local and global dependencies across audio and/or text inputs, with promising performance even in low-resource or error-prone environments.

2.6.1 Neural Models for Speech Summarization

Neural models for speech summarization can broadly be grouped into two categories: those that operate on transcribed speech, and those that attempt to summarize directly from audio features without textual transcriptions.

Recurrent Neural Networks: Early neural models adapted from text summarization frameworks typically use Long Short-Term Memory (LSTM) or Gated Recurrent Unit (GRU) networks to capture sequential dependencies across sentences in transcribed speech. These models encode a sequence of sentences and predict which ones are important based on a binary classification or ranking objective. Attention mechanisms are often integrated to better model long-range dependencies and to weight sentences differently based on context. Liu et al. [53] proposed an enhanced language modeling framework for extractive summarization of broadcast news speech, integrating proximity-based relevance and sentence relatedness information. Unlike traditional language models that treat sentences independently, their approach estimates sentence importance based not only on word occurrence but also on the semantic and positional relationship between neighboring sentences. This enables the model to better capture discourse structure and topical coherence within spoken documents. Evaluated on Mandarin broadcast news, the framework achieved notable gains in summary precision and recall compared to standard unigram or positional models. The study demonstrates how incorporating discourse-aware features into statistical language modeling can significantly improve extractive speech summarization, especially in structured domains like news.

These models assume relatively clean ASR outputs, and often underperform when transcription quality is poor.

Recurrent neural networks (RNNs), especially long short-term memory (LSTM) and gated recurrent unit (GRU) architectures, became popular for modeling sequential dependencies in speech. These models could capture temporal context across sentences or utterances and were often employed in multi-layered configurations. Bidirectional LSTMs were particularly effective in modeling both preceding and succeeding context, which is vital in determining the relative importance of content in speech. A notable study proposed a hybrid CNN-LSTM model where CNN layers were used to extract local patterns from pitch-energy contours and the LSTM layers captured long-range utterance relationships. This model outperformed flat MLP and CNN-only models on ROUGE metrics over a Mandarin broadcast news corpus [104].

End-to-End Speech-to-Summary Models: A more recent trend involves building end-to-end models that take raw audio or acoustic-prosodic features as input and directly generate summaries without relying on intermediate text. These systems typically combine convolutional layers for local feature extraction with recurrent or transformer-based layers for temporal modeling. Zhang et al. [117] introduced Summ , a multi-stage summarization framework specifically designed for handling long-form input such as dialogues and multi-speaker documents. The system adopts a hierarchical pipeline that first performs segment-level summarization, then aggregates these summaries using a higher-level encoder-decoder model to produce the final output. This structure is particularly effective for long or loosely structured spoken content, such as meetings or interviews, where end-to-end summarizers struggle with context retention. Summ outperformed baseline models on several long-input datasets, demonstrating improved fluency and factual consistency. While developed for general text and dialogue summarization, its modular design holds potential for adaptation to spoken document summarization, especially in low-resource or noisy conditions where intermediate representations can stabilize performance.
While promising, such models require substantial paired data (speech and summary) and are challenging to train without large corpora and robust annotation. Their use is also constrained by domain specificity—models trained on English TED talks or meeting speech do not generalize well to regional news in low-resource languages.

Transformer-Based Architectures and Pretrained Audio Models: Transformer-based models, especially those pretrained on large audio corpora (e.g., wav2vec 2.0, HuBERT), have been used to derive high-level representations of speech segments [3, 39]. When combined with summarization heads (e.g., sequence classifiers or extractive rankers), these systems can bypass the need for ASR in some settings. However, their computational demands, large parameter counts, and dependence on domain-matched training data make them less practical in low-resource environments. Additionally, pretrained models may not support underrepresented languages due to lack of training data in those languages.
Attention mechanisms, and later, transformer-based models, allowed for more flexible modeling of relationships across utterances. Attention enables the model to dynamically weigh different parts of the input, improving the model's ability to detect globally salient content. In one study, a transformer encoder was trained

on Mel-spectrograms with positional encodings and achieved F1 scores of 0.73 on summary selection from lecture recordings [115]. Other works proposed multi-task transformer models jointly trained on ASR and summarization objectives, demonstrating better generalization to noisy inputs [54].

2.6.2 Neural and Low-Resource Approaches

Neural networks have significantly influenced the development of automatic summarization systems in recent years. These models have the capacity to learn complex patterns in both linguistic and acoustic data, making them well-suited for tasks such as sentence scoring, representation learning, and even direct summary generation. However, such advancements often rely on the availability of large-scale, well-annotated datasets, computational infrastructure, and pre-existing language resources—factors that are frequently absent in low-resource language contexts such as Assamese and Bengali. This section reviews key neural methods for speech summarization and the specific challenges they face in data-scarce environments.

2.6.3 Challenges in Low-Resource Scenarios

While neural approaches continue to evolve, their application in low-resource settings faces several pressing challenges:

(a) Scarcity of Labeled Summarization Data: Supervised neural models rely heavily on paired data—speech utterances aligned with human-generated summaries. For most low-resource languages, such datasets are either extremely limited or non-existent. Manual annotation is expensive and time-consuming, especially for summarization tasks that require understanding both content and prosodic emphasis.

(b) Poor ASR Support: Transcription quality plays a crucial role in the effectiveness of text-based neural summarizers. For languages like Assamese and Bengali, available ASR systems are either non-existent or produce high word error rates, especially in real-world broadcast settings. This limits the effectiveness of all summarization models that depend on reliable lexical representations.

(c) Limitations in Infrastructure and Resources: Training large-scale transformer or sequence-to-sequence models typically requires multiple GPUs, long training cycles, and access to memory-efficient hardware. In many academic or institutional setups in low-resource regions, such resources are unavailable. This makes training and deploying state-of-the-art models infeasible, regardless of their theoretical capabilities.

(d) Practical Need for Compact Architectures: Given the constraints outlined above, simpler models offer a feasible alternative. These models operate directly on acoustic-prosodic features and are less sensitive to data scarcity, overfitting, and transcription noise. They are also easier to understand, can be trained in parts (step by step), and can run on devices with limited computing power. Recent works have also looked at importance prediction using handcrafted features combined with neural classifiers [77]. While not always positioned as summarization systems, such methods are foundational to content selection tasks. Additionally, several have proposed innovative combinations of neural encoders and feature fusion mechanisms that may be relevant for future low-resource summarization pipelines.

Despite these advancements, challenges remain. Neural models often require large datasets, which are scarce for most low-resource languages. Moreover, models trained on textual transcriptions may inherit ASR errors, degrading performance. This has led to growing interest in designing purely acoustic models—trained on prosodic and spectral features—that can work even in the absence of reliable transcripts. However, such models are still in the early stages of exploration, with limited benchmarking and inconsistent evaluation practices. In summary, The key to designing neural models for low-resource speech summarization is to keep the model simple enough to work well with limited training data, support less commonly used languages, and be easy to use in real-world applications.

2.7 Summary Evaluation Strategies in Prior Work

Evaluation remains a central challenge in speech summarization, particularly in low-resource and noisy settings. Most prior studies have relied on automatic overlap-based metrics such as ROUGE (Recall-Oriented Understudy for Gisting Evaluation) to compare system-generated summaries against human-written references [52]. ROUGE computes unigram (ROUGE-1), bigram (ROUGE-2), and longest common subsequence (ROUGE-L) overlaps, providing recall- and precision-oriented variants. Mathematically, for ROUGE-N (where N is the n-gram length), the recall is calculated as:

$$\text{ROUGE-N}_{\text{recall}} = \frac{\sum_{S\in\{\text{Reference Summaries}\}} \sum_{\text{gram}_n \in S} \text{Count}_{\text{match}}(\text{gram}_n)}{\sum_{S\in\{\text{Reference Summaries}\}} \sum_{\text{gram}_n \in S} \text{Count}(\text{gram}_n)} \quad (2.1)$$

where $\text{Count}_{\text{match}}(\text{gram}_n)$ denotes the number of overlapping n-grams between the system summary and reference summaries.

While widely used in text summarization benchmarks, ROUGE assumes well-formed lexical inputs and suffers when summaries are derived from noisy ASR transcripts [47, 118].

In speech summarization, the presence of ASR errors—such as deletions, substitutions, or disfluencies—can significantly reduce lexical overlap with human references, even when the summary content is semantically adequate. Studies have shown that transcription noise disproportionately affects recall-based ROUGE scores, particularly in morphologically rich or under-resourced languages [? ?]. Moreover, sentence segmentation inconsistencies and word-level mismatches further degrade the reliability of these surface-level metrics.

Some works have attempted to address these limitations by incorporating semantic similarity measures such as embedding-based metrics. BERTScore [116], for example, computes similarity based on contextualized token embeddings. Given a candidate summary $C = \{c_1, c_2, \ldots, c_m\}$ and reference summary $R = \{r_1, r_2, \ldots, r_n\}$, the precision score is computed as:

$$\text{Precision} = \frac{1}{|C|} \sum_{c_i \in C} \max_{r_j \in R} \text{cosine}(E(c_i), E(r_j)) \tag{2.2}$$

where $E(\cdot)$ denotes the BERT embedding of a token, and cosine similarity is used for matching. Similar equations apply for recall and F1 variants.

However, these methods are resource-intensive and have limited reproducibility in low-resource scenarios.

In speech-only or text-independent summarization systems, the lack of textual alignment presents additional challenges. Since ROUGE and similar metrics depend on lexical overlap, they are less suited for evaluating summaries derived from acoustic or prosodic cues. Recent studies have advocated for task-specific proxy metrics, such as classification accuracy of predicted important segments, coverage of key time-stamped events, or perceptual relevance via user studies [77, 110].

In summary, while ROUGE remains a standard baseline for comparison, its limitations are especially pronounced in speech-based and low-resource contexts. In this thesis, ROUGE is used with caution—as a proxy for content overlap—while recognizing that such surface-level metrics may not fully reflect the quality of summaries derived from spoken input. This underscores the broader challenge of evaluating summarization in settings where transcripts are noisy or unavailable, which remains an open direction for future work.

2.8 Chapter Summary

In this chapter, we reviewed various strands of work on extractive speech summarization, ranging from transcript-based and prosody-aware approaches to neural models in low-resource scenarios. We examined how classical methods, neural architectures, and multimodal features have been adapted for summarizing spoken content, particularly in challenging low-resource settings. Special attention was given to the role of prosody, emotion, and ASR-related distortions in shaping the design of summarization systems. While the field has seen major progress for high-resource languages like English and Mandarin, this progress has not translated to low-resource (as well as Indic languages) such as Assamese and Bengali. These observations motivate the present thesis which aims to address these challenges, detailed in the following chapters.

Chapter 3

Corpus Creation and Development for Extractive Speech Summarization

The corpus comprises data from two languages—Assamese and Bengali—which were selected to represent distinct types of resource constraints. Bengali offers partial support for automatic speech recognition (ASR) and basic linguistic tools, making it suitable for transcript-based experiments that evaluate how ASR errors affect summary quality. Assamese, by contrast, does not have reliable or publicly available ASR systems suitable for summarization tasks, and is therefore used to explore transcript-free modeling based solely on acoustic-prosodic features. This dual-language design allows the corpus to reflect two realistic low-resource scenarios: one where noisy transcriptions exist, and one where they do not. The corpus thus serves as the empirical foundation for developing and evaluating language-appropriate summarization models under different resource assumptions.

3.1 Introduction

This chapter presents the design and structure of a speech corpus developed for extractive summarization in low-resource language settings, covering both Assamese and Bengali to address different levels of transcription availability. The corpus consists of two distinct but complementary sub-corpora: one made from literary audiobooks and the other from broadcast news recordings, with data available in both Assamese and Bengali. These two domains were carefully selected because they represent contrasting speech styles—narrative and expressive on the one hand, factual and formal on the other. While audiobooks provide flowing, expressive speech with rich variation in prosody, broadcast news offers a more compact, information-focused delivery with clearer prosodic boundaries. Together, they form a balanced resource for investigating how acoustic-prosodic features can help identify summary-worthy content in spoken language.

In this work, speech is treated as the main data source. Each spoken document is segmented into smaller units—either full sentences or utterance-level chunks. These segments are then described using feature vectors that capture acoustic-prosodic properties such as pitch, intensity, rhythm, and duration. Human-created summaries are used to label these segments as either important or not, allowing the dataset to support both supervised learning models and summary-level evaluation.

The goal of this resource is not to serve general-purpose speech applications, but to support summarization research under real-world constraints typical of low-resource settings. The remainder of the chapter discusses the data sources, design decisions, and annotation procedures in detail.

3.1.1 Spoken Documents in Read-Continuous Speech

The speech in this corpus belongs to a specific category called **read-continuous speech**. This refers to audio where a speaker reads aloud from a written script, without interruptions, spontaneous speech, or turn-taking. Both audiobook narration and professional news broadcasts fall into this category. Read speech is generally smoother and more structured than spontaneous or conversational speech. It also tends to have clearer articulation and more deliberate use of prosody—making it a stable and reliable choice for studying how acoustic patterns relate to the importance of spoken content.

- **Broadcast News.** Public radio broadcasts, such as those from Akashvani Guwahati and Kolkata, are a strong example of structured, formal speech. Each session—typically around 15 minutes—covers several news topics and follows a predictable, well-paced delivery style. Because the content is dense, and transitions between topics are clear, the speech naturally divides into meaningful sentence-level segments. This makes it easier to detect which sentences carry the most important information. The prosody used in broadcast news is more standardized than in other speech types, often marked by shifts in pitch or loudness to signal emphasis or transitions[1]. Also, the professional quality of the recordings—with minimal noise and few speech

[1] In this context, "prosody" refers to the rhythm, pitch, and loudness patterns in speech that help structure information and guide listener attention. Throughout this thesis, we refer to prosody as the combination of acoustic features—such as pitch, loudness, and duration—that convey emphasis, boundaries, or speaker intent in spoken language. Detailed in Section 2.5.1

disfluencies—helps ensure accurate extraction of acoustic features. In many low-resource settings, where high-quality ASR (Automatic Speech Recognition) is unreliable or unavailable, these prosodic features offer an alternative way to identify salient information without relying on the text alone.

- **Audiobooks.** Audiobook recordings, in contrast, are longer, more expressive, and driven by narrative flow. The content is often descriptive and spread across multiple sentences, with key information embedded in storytelling rather than stated directly. This makes it harder to detect important content using only surface-level word statistics or lexical features. However, audiobook narrators typically use expressive prosody—like rising or falling pitch contours (changes in vocal pitch that signal questions, emphasis, or boundaries), sudden changes in loudness (used to stress important points), and rhythmic pacing (the deliberate timing or pauses that shape how the speech flows and where listeners should focus)—to guide the listener through the story. These prosodic signals often correspond to moments of emotional emphasis, narrative transitions, or the ends of meaningful segments. For this reason, acoustic-prosodic features can be a powerful tool for summarizing long-form narrative speech. Moreover, since ASR systems often struggle with expressive and stylistically complex speech, relying on the speech signal itself becomes an even more important strategy in low-resource language scenarios. Audiobooks also tend to include filler or decorative content—sentences that are grammatically well-formed but not central to the story. A good summarization system must learn to tell the difference, and prosody offers valuable cues for doing so.

Together, these two types of read speech—broadcast news and audiobooks—cover a wide range of speaking styles and use cases. Despite their differences, they share an important property: both are based on written scripts. This ensures that the speech is coherent and grammatically well-formed, making it easier to segment and analyze. It also provides a consistent framework for examining how prosodic patterns align with sentence-level importance. These qualities make the corpus a strong foundation for developing and evaluating speech summarization systems that rely on acoustic-prosodic features—particularly in low-resource language settings where textual tools like ASR or language models may not be reliable.

Table 3.1: Common Prosodic Signals and Their Communicative Functions

Prosodic Feature	What It Sounds Like	What It May Indicate
Pitch Contours	Rising or falling melody of the voice	Rising pitch may signal a question or continuation; falling pitch often marks the end of a sentence or important point
Loudness (Intensity)	Sudden increase or decrease in volume	Emphasis on key words, speaker emotion, or shift in topic
Rhythm / Pacing	Speeding up, slowing down, or use of pauses	Slow pace or pauses often signal boundaries or important points; fast pace may indicate less important filler content
Pitch Range / Variation	Wide or narrow changes in pitch levels	Greater variation may signal emotional or salient content; flat pitch may indicate monotony or low importance
Pause Duration	Short vs. long silence between words or phrases	Longer pauses often indicate end of a unit or shift in meaning/topic

3.2 Overview and Motivation behind the Development of the Corpus

The speech corpus developed in this work was created with a clear purpose: to support extractive summarization of spoken content using prosodic and acoustic cues, without relying on automatic speech recognition (ASR) or textual features. This need emerged from a practical challenge — for many Indian languages like Assamese and Bengali, reliable ASR systems, named entity recognizers, and deep semantic embeddings are still limited in performance, especially in spontaneous or expressive speech. While recent efforts have expanded tool availability, accuracy and domain generalization remain challenging for downstream tasks like summarization.

3.2.1 Why a New Corpus Was Needed?

Most of the existing summarization datasets are text-centric. Even speech summarization benchmarks often assume high-quality transcripts, which can be processed using standard NLP tools. However, this assumption does not hold in low-resource scenarios. For many regional languages, transcriptions may be noisy, inconsistent, or entirely missing. Moreover, when ASR systems are available, they often suffer from high word error rates[2], especially in spontaneous or expressive speech.

[2]Word Error Rate (WER) is a standard metric in speech recognition that quantifies transcription errors by measuring the percentage of words that are substituted, deleted, or inserted

To address this gap, a speech corpus was developed, centered around **speech as the primary input modality**. Rather than depending on transcripts or lexical analysis, this corpus supports models that work directly with prosodic and acoustic features — such as pitch variation, energy changes, timing, and spectral patterns. This speech-first design enables the development of summarization systems that are more robust to ASR errors or even completely ASR-independent.

3.2.2 Handling Challenges of Low-Resource Settings

In many low-resource languages, it is difficult to use traditional natural language processing (NLP) pipelines. This is mainly because tools like ASR (automatic speech recognition), named entity recognizers, or large annotated datasets are either missing or not accurate enough. To overcome these challenges, this corpus was designed with three practical strategies:

- **Minimal Dependence on Textual Processing:** While sentence-level segmentation was guided by punctuation in the original source text (e.g., full stops or *daari*), the overall modeling framework avoids reliance on ASR transcripts or language-specific NLP tools. No deep linguistic processing (such as parsing or named entity recognition) is used. This reduces dependency on accurate transcriptions, which are often unreliable or unavailable in under-resourced languages.
- **Working with Read Speech:** The speech data in the corpus comes from two sources: professional broadcast news and narrated audiobooks. Both are types of read speech. This kind of speech is usually well-articulated, clearly recorded, and has fewer hesitations or background noise. It also follows consistent prosodic patterns (such as pitch changes and pauses), which makes it easier to analyze even without transcripts.
- **Simple Yet Effective Features:** Instead of using deep embeddings or large pretrained models, this corpus focuses on basic acoustic-prosodic features like pitch, loudness (energy), speaking rate (duration), and spectral information (MFCCs), as detailed in Table 3.2. These features are easy to extract using standard tools, do not depend on the language being spoken, and still provide meaningful information across different speakers and situations.

By focusing on these design choices, the corpus is well-suited for research in low-resource settings—especially when there is little to no support from existing language tools or annotated training data [91].

compared to a reference transcript.

Table 3.2: Rationale for Chosen Acoustic-Prosodic Features

Feature Type	What It Captures	Why It Was Chosen
Pitch (F0)	Fundamental frequency of voice	Indicates emphasis, sentence modality (e.g., questions), and prosodic phrasing. Widely studied in prosody-based speech processing.
Loudness / Short-term Energy	Intensity or amplitude of speech	Useful for detecting stressed or highlighted content. Easy to extract from waveform.
Duration	Speaking rate, pause length	Longer or slower-delivered phrases often mark salient content or segment boundaries. No need for ASR.
MFCCs	Spectral characteristics of speech	Capture broader acoustic context and speaker variation. Serve as a compact representation of the audio signal.

These features were selected to strike a balance between ease of understanding, ease of extraction, and relevance to prosodic salience. They are language-independent, require no ASR, and have been validated in prior studies on speech-based classification and segmentation[68, 75].

3.2.3 Reference Summary Creation and Annotation Guidelines

To enable supervised learning and evaluation, each spoken document in the corpus—whether from broadcast news or audiobook—was paired with a human-annotated extractive summary. These reference summaries serve as the gold standard for training and benchmarking sentence selection models.

Annotation Protocol

The annotation process involved five native speakers for each document. For the broadcast news corpus, annotators were selected based on their educational qualifications, with all holding at least a master's degree in fields related to language, media, or the social sciences. This ensured that the selected sentences reflected a strong grasp of both linguistic nuance and informational relevance.

For the audiobook sub-corpus, the annotators were actively engaged in literary communities. These included published writers, poets, literature educators, and local news columnists in Bengali and Assamese. Their deep familiarity with literary form and narrative structure helped maintain coherence and salience in the summaries.

Summarization Guidelines

A fixed summarization ratio of 20% was followed uniformly across all documents. Annotators were instructed to select complete sentences that best captured the central content and intent of the spoken document while adhering to this length constraint. All annotations were based on the manually segmented transcriptions, ensuring that sentence boundaries were meaningful and aligned with the underlying prosody.

Quality Control and Agreement

To assess the reliability of the annotation process, pairwise Cohen's Kappa was computed across the five annotators per spoken document. Each sentence was labeled with a binary value (1 if selected as part of the summary, 0 otherwise), and the agreement was calculated over all sentence positions. Across the corpus, the average pairwise kappa score was **0.68** for broadcast news and **0.61** for audiobooks. According to standard interpretation guidelines [48], this reflects *moderate to substantial* agreement.

A majority-vote approach was used to finalize the reference summary: a sentence selected by at least three annotators was included in the gold-standard summary. To illustrate the annotation protocol clearly and concisely, we include a small example in Table 3.3. Due to scalability constraints, results are shown for a representative subset of 3 out of the 5 annotators. This subset demonstrates how binary sentence labels were collected from multiple annotators and aggregated into a final reference summary.

Table 3.3: Sample annotator labels and final summary decisions for a broadcast news spoken document (Assamese)

ID	Sentence Text (excerpt)	A1	A2	A3	Majority
1	দেশৰ ১৬খন ৰাজ্য অচিৰেই কৰ'নামুক্ত হোৱাৰ দিশত	1	1	1	1
2	২০ মে'ৰ ভিতৰত ভাৰতত নোহোৱা হ'ব সংক্ৰমণ শিৰোনামৰ এটা বাতৰি দৈনিক জনমভূমি কাকতে প্ৰধান বাতৰি হিচাপে প্ৰথম পৃষ্ঠাত প্ৰকাশ কৰিছে	0	0	0	0
3	৮জন ৰোগীক কালি চিকিৎসালয়ৰ পৰা যাবলৈ দিয়া হয়	1	0	1	1
4	অৱশ্যে চৰকাৰী কৰ্মচাৰীসকলে যিহেতু সম্পূৰ্ণ দৰমহা লাভ কৰিছে	0	0	1	0
5	কেতিয়া খুলিব লকডাউন, উদ্বিগ্ন জনতা	1	0	1	1

3.2.4 Unified Design Across Sub-Corpora

Although the two sub-corpora — audiobooks and broadcast news — differ in their structure and narrative style, they were built using a common pipeline and design philosophy. The core steps and principles are outlined below:

- **Speech-Centric Modeling:** The entire pipeline treats speech — not transcripts — as the primary source of information. This design avoids relying on ASR systems, which are either unavailable or inaccurate for languages like Assamese and Bengali. Instead of focusing on lexical content, summarization decisions are based on how a sentence is spoken — that is, its prosodic profile — including variations in pitch, loudness, and rhythm. This approach makes the model resilient to transcription errors and more suited to low-resource environments.
- **Sentence-Level Summarization Units:** Each spoken document is segmented into utterance-level units, which serve as the basic candidates for extractive summarization. These units correspond to meaningful sentence-like segments, manually determined by reading from the original source text (e.g., news scripts or audiobook text) and aligning them with clear prosodic cues such as final pitch drops or pause boundaries. These sentence units form the granularity at which human annotators assign binary importance labels.
- **Feature-Based Representation:** Each utterance is represented using a 21-dimensional vector comprising acoustic-prosodic and spectral features. These include pitch (min, max, mean, slope, range), short-term energy (min, max, mean, RMS), duration, and 13 MFCCs. Such features are chosen for their interpretability, language-independence, and proven utility in prior prosody-based classification tasks. In addition, manually derived features like pitch contour shape (e.g., rise-fall) and number of pitch/intensity peaks help model rhythmic and emphatic variation, which are often strong indicators of salience.
- **Speaker and Gender Normalization:** To minimize the influence of speaker-specific traits (e.g., voice timbre, pitch range), all continuous-valued features are normalized per speaker and per gender using z-score normalization. This ensures that models learn generalizable prosodic patterns rather than speaker idiosyncrasies. Gender normalization is used to account for typical pitch and loudness differences between male and female speakers, further reducing unwanted variability.
- **Consistent Preprocessing:** All speech recordings are preprocessed uniformly using a set of acoustic criteria. Background noise is removed, loudness

is normalized, and long audio files are segmented based on acoustic cues such as pauses, energy dips, and pitch resets. These preprocessing steps improve signal quality and ensure that extracted features reflect genuine prosodic variation rather than recording artifacts.

- **Gold-Standard Labels:** Each utterance is annotated with a binary relevance label (1 for summary-worthy, 0 otherwise), based on manual summaries created by native speakers. For each spoken document, five annotators selected approximately 20% of the utterances as part of an extractive summary. These labels serve as the ground truth for training and evaluating supervised models. Inter-annotator agreement was measured using Cohen's Kappa, and representative examples are shown to validate consistency in annotation.

3.2.5 Significance

This corpus fills an important gap in speech summarization research. It offers a clean, well-annotated dataset that supports supervised training of models even when ASR is missing or unreliable. Because the design is focused on speech signals, the corpus opens new research avenues — including text-independent summarization, prosody modeling, and cross-lingual adaptation in speech-centric tasks. Its simplicity and consistency also make it a valuable baseline for developing and testing future prosody-aware systems in Indian and other low-resource languages.

3.3 Languages and Corpus Design Goals

3.3.1 Language Background

This thesis investigates extractive summarization in two under-represented Eastern Indo-Aryan languages: Bengali and Assamese. While both languages are widely spoken in South Asia, they remain under-resourced in terms of speech processing tools and annotated corpora. This section introduces their phonological and prosodic characteristics, focusing on aspects that influence sentence-level acoustic modeling and speech summarization.

3.3.1.1 Bengali

Bengali (ISO 639-3: `ben`) is spoken by more than 200 million people, primarily in Bangladesh and the Indian state of West Bengal. It has a rich consonant system that includes aspirated stops, nasals, and retroflex sounds, along with a relatively simple vowel inventory. Bengali typically follows a Subject-Object-Verb (SOV) word order, and uses postpositions.

Prosodically, Bengali is often described as a syllable-timed language. Although it is not tonal, intonation plays an important role in signaling sentence boundaries and sentence types. For example, declarative sentences tend to show a falling pitch contour, while interrogatives often involve a final rise or a rise-fall pattern. Sentence-final pauses and pitch resets are common cues marking prosodic boundaries.

There is noticeable variation across dialects, especially in vowel pronunciation, rhythm, and pitch usage. However, in this work, the focus is on a standard variety close to Kolkata Bengali.

Bengali uses the Eastern Nagari script, where sentence-final periods (দাড়ি / দাঁড়ি) were used as references during manual segmentation. However, inconsistencies in punctuation across literary texts required annotators to rely on prosodic cues and contextual judgment in ambiguous cases. Additionally, pronunciation phenomena like schwa deletion can complicate alignment between text and speech, reinforcing the need for transcript-independent approaches.

3.3.1.2 Assamese

Assamese (ISO 639-3: `asm`) is spoken by approximately 15 million people, mainly in the Indian state of Assam. Though closely related to Bengali, Assamese differs in several phonological and prosodic respects.

Assamese is not a tonal language, but pitch variation is more pronounced than in Bengali, especially in marking sentence boundaries and focus. Rising or rising-falling pitch contours are commonly found at the ends of sentences. These patterns contribute to the perception of emphasis or contrast.

In terms of rhythm, Assamese shows characteristics of both syllable-timed and mora-timed languages. This hybrid rhythm affects how syllables are realized in continuous speech and can influence duration-based prosodic cues. Like Bengali, Assamese also relies on pitch movement and pauses to signal sentence-level prosodic boundaries.

The Assamese script is also derived from Eastern Nagari, and sentence-ending punctuation (দাড়ি / দাঁড়ি) was used as a guide for segmentation in the news domain. However, public broadcast speech in Assamese tends to exhibit clearer prosodic resets and fewer disfluencies, which makes sentence-level segmentation more reliable. These properties made Assamese broadcast sessions particularly suitable for acoustic-prosodic analysis in this work.

3.3.2 Corpus Design Goals

The corpus developed in this work was built with clear goals in mind, especially to support research on prosody-based extractive speech summarization in low-resource settings. Each design choice—from selecting the speech data to annotating summaries and choosing features—was made to support practical and effective experimentation under real-world constraints. This section explains the main goals that guided the entire process.

1. Focus on Extractive Summarization

The primary goal of the corpus is to support extractive summarization of spoken content, where the task is to select relevant spoken sentences (utterances) from an input audio document. Each spoken document is segmented into utterance-level units, and each unit is labeled as either summary-worthy or not, based on human-generated reference summaries. The corpus is therefore explicitly structured to support sentence-level classification and summary-level evaluation, making it suitable for training and evaluating supervised extractive summarization models.

2. Emphasis on Prosodic Cues and Acoustic Segmentation

Unlike many standard summarization datasets that focus on lexical or semantic features, this corpus is built around acoustic-prosodic information. Prosodic features—such as pitch contour, intensity, rhythm, and duration—are treated as central indicators of sentence importance. To make full use of such features, the speech data is manually segmented into meaningful utterance-level units, using prosodic boundaries such as pauses, pitch resets, and energy drops. This design allows models to learn from how content is spoken, rather than just what is spoken.

3. Dual Modality: ASR-Free and ASR-Compatible Use

The corpus supports two complementary use cases. First, it enables fully text-independent modeling using only acoustic-prosodic features, which is critical for languages where ASR systems are inaccurate or unavailable. Second, where ASR transcripts exist or can be generated, the same corpus can be used in hybrid systems that combine prosodic and lexical features. This dual-modality design ensures that the corpus is useful both for ASR-independent research and for studies exploring how prosody complements lexical content in summarization.

4. Multi-Tier Annotation: Utterance-Level, Summary-Level, and Prosodic Labels

To support flexible modeling and evaluation, the corpus includes annotations at three levels:

- **Utterance-Level Segmentation:** Each spoken document is segmented into sentence-like units, which form the candidates for extractive summarization.

- **Summary-Level Labels:** Each utterance is tagged as summary-worthy or not, based on human-created summaries. These binary labels enable training of classification models and allow for ROUGE-based evaluation.
- **Prosodic Annotations:** For a portion of the corpus, detailed annotations of prosodic patterns are included. These include pitch and intensity contour shapes (e.g., rising, falling, rise-fall), and the number of contour peaks, which help capture rhythmic emphasis and boundary marking.

This layered annotation strategy ensures that the corpus is versatile: it can be used for utterance classification, prosodic pattern analysis, or full-system summary evaluation. By explicitly separating different levels of annotation, the design also allows researchers to isolate and analyze the contribution of each signal type—acoustic, structural, or summary-level.

Table 3.4: Metadata: Size of Corpus

Spoken Document	Bengali	Assamese	Total
Broadcast News	2h 35min	3h 9min	5h 44min
Audiobooks	4h 30min	3h 52min	8h 22min
			14h 6 min

3.4 Broadcast News Sub-Corpus

The broadcast news sub-corpus was specifically designed to support extractive speech summarization using prosodic and acoustic cues, particularly in low-resource language settings. Drawing from Assamese and Bengali news broadcasts during a critical social period (April–August 2020), the corpus balances linguistic diversity with thematic consistency. Broadcast news offers structured, well-paced speech with clear sentence boundaries and minimal disfluencies—features that are conducive to isolating prosodic markers of information salience. The subsections below describe in detail the source selection, annotation strategy, preprocessing steps, and feature design adopted in building this corpus.

3.4.1 Data Collection and Motivation

The broadcast news sub-corpus was created using professionally read radio news stories broadcast by All India Radio — specifically Akashvani Guwahati (Assamese) and Akashvani Kolkata (Bengali). The speech comprises continuous narration with minimal pausing between words or sentences, making it ideal for studying prosodic patterns in a controlled setting. This genre was chosen for its structured delivery, clear articulation, and formal tone—qualities that make it well-suited for prosody-focused extractive summarization.

Unlike conversational or spontaneous speech, broadcast news follows a recurrent structure: an introductory segment where the speaker announces themselves, followed by a list of headlines and subsequent elaboration of each topic. Additional information not present in the headlines is also discussed, culminating in a standard closing segment. This predictable discourse structure enhances the feasibility of manual segmentation and summarization tasks.

3.4.2 Preprocessing of Speech Data

The original audio files contained background hums and static noise typical of AM radio transmissions. These artifacts were removed using the built-in noise reduction tools available in Audacity. All audio files were converted to mono-channel WAV format to preserve signal fidelity and ensure consistency across the corpus.

Manual inspection and preprocessing were also applied to identify and remove segments affected by severe distortion or overlapping audio. Only clean, uninterrupted speech segments were retained for further annotation and analysis.

3.4.3 Segmentation and Annotation

Each news story was manually segmented into sentence-level utterances. Given the continuous reading style of news speech, segmentation was guided by audible pauses, syntactic cues, and changes in prosody. This sentence-level segmentation allowed for precise alignment between speech units and their corresponding acoustic or summary labels, forming the basic instances for downstream summarization experiments.

Approximately 60% of the broadcast news corpus includes additional prosodic annotations created using Praat TextGrid [3](please see section 3.6 for the rationale behind choosing Praat). These include pitch and intensity contour shapes (e.g., rising, falling, rise-fall) and the number of contour peaks, offering fine-grained representations of prominence, rhythmic complexity, and prosodic boundaries.

[3] Praat is a widely used tool for speech analysis and annotation, developed by Paul Boersma and David Weenink. It allows researchers to visualize, edit, and annotate speech signals, and supports TextGrid files for time-aligned annotations. http://www.fon.hum.uva.nl/praat/

3.4.4 Feature Extraction for Summarization

The motivation for feature selection stems from the observation that humans often rely on prosodic cues—such as pitch movement, stress, and duration—to infer the salience of spoken content. These cues often correlate with summary-worthiness, especially when lexical content alone is insufficient to indicate importance.

For each segmented utterance, the following features were extracted:

- **Prosodic Features:** Pitch-related statistics (min, max, mean, range,), short-term energy features (mean intensity, RMS), and duration.
- **Timbre Features:** Thirty-nine Mel-Frequency Cepstral Coefficients (MFCCs) to represent the spectral envelope, associated with speaker-specific emphasis and voice quality.

In total, 47 features were extracted for each utterance. These features serve as inputs to machine learning models developed for extractive summarization tasks.

3.4.5 Summary Annotation and Labeling Strategy

To support supervised summarization models, utterances were labeled as either **summary-worthy (1)** or **not-summary-worthy (0)**.

The annotation process involved both native and non-native speakers of Assamese and Bengali. Native speakers annotated based on both the semantic content and prosodic delivery of each utterance. Non-native annotators, lacking full lexical comprehension, relied primarily on intonation and prosodic stress. Final labels were decided by majority vote across annotators to ensure robustness. This mixed-strategy design allowed prosody to play a more central role, aligning well with the goals of acoustic-prosodic summarization in low-resource settings.

3.4.6 Corpus Statistics

The broadcast news corpus comprises approximately 5 hours and 44 minutes of speech (2h 35min in Bengali and 3h 9min in Assamese), drawn from 32 unique news sessions. Each session was around 15 minutes in length. The recordings were manually segmented into utterances, each aligned with its transcript, and enriched with both acoustic-prosodic features and summary labels. Roughly 60% of the utterances include detailed prosodic annotations via Praat TextGrid.

3.4.7 Limitations

The broadcast news sub-corpus complements the audiobook sub-corpus by offering high-quality, professionally read speech with formal structure and information density. Its clear prosodic patterns and segmentable content make it a strong candidate for prosody-based summarization research.

However, some limitations remain. The dataset includes only monologue speech from public radio, and though it covers both Assamese and Bengali, the overall duration (under 6 hours) may still be limited for training deep learning models from scratch. Additionally, while 60% of the corpus includes detailed prosodic contour annotations, the remaining utterances may require automatic estimation or exclusion in certain modeling tasks.

Nonetheless, the corpus provides a valuable benchmark for prosody-driven summarization in low-resource settings, with sufficient structure and annotation depth to support a wide range of speech-based summarization experiments.

Table 3.5: Summary of acoustic-prosodic features extracted per utterance/sentence, for both Broadcast news and Audiobooks sub-corpus

Feature Type	**Features Included**	**Count**
Pitch	Min, Max, Mean, Range	4
Energy	Min, Max, Mean	3
Temporal	Audio segment (sentence/utterance) duration	1
Spectral (MFCCs)	M1–M39 (39 coefficients)	13
Total	—	**47**

3.5 Audiobook Sub-Corpus

The audiobook sub-corpus offers a complementary speech domain to broadcast news, allowing the thesis to explore summarization performance under more expressive, narrative-rich conditions. Audiobooks provide high-quality read speech with deliberate prosodic modulation—characteristics that are particularly well-suited to studying the relationship between acoustic features and perceived sentence importance. The following subsections describe the design rationale, speaker and genre diversity, segmentation approach, annotation techniques, and normalization strategies applied to this sub-corpus.

3.5.1 Speech Source and Metadata

The audiobook sub-corpus is composed of Assamese and Bengali audiobook recordings collected from publicly available online platforms and curated repositories, recorded in digital audio format. These recordings feature narrations of literary texts read aloud by professional and semi-professional speakers. Further details of this sub-corpus is given in Table 3.6The genre of read speech is marked by its structured delivery, clear articulation, and expressive intonation—all of which support detailed analysis of acoustic-prosodic features. For tasks like extractive speech summarization, such characteristics are advantageous because they minimize the occurrence of disfluencies, speaker overlaps, or unpredictable intonation changes common in spontaneous speech.

The decision to include audiobooks in this summarization-focused corpus is intentional. Unlike spontaneous speech, i.e. conversational or interview-based speech, audiobook narration tends to have predictable sentence structures, follows a linear narrative structure, with prosodic cues often used intentionally to highlight segmental or thematic boundaries. Prosodic cues in audiobooks — like changes in pitch, loudness, and rhythm — often match the importance of what is being said. For example, sentences that carry a key message are usually spoken with more variation in tone or with greater emphasis. This makes audiobooks especially useful for summarization, where the goal is to find and select the most important parts of the speech. Since how something is said often signals how important it is, these prosodic patterns become helpful indicators when building automatic summarization systems.

Another advantage of audiobooks is that the narration is steady and consistent. Most books are read by the same speaker from start to finish, using a clear and expressive speaking style. This reduces unnecessary variation and makes it easier to recognize which prosodic features (like rising or falling pitch) often signal important content. Compared to everyday speech, which can be messy or unpredictable, audiobooks offer a cleaner and more reliable setting to study how speech features relate to meaning.

In other words, the linear, narrative structure of audiobooks introduces natural segmentation points and topic shifts, which are often marked prosodically. This makes audiobooks an ideal testbed for text-independent summarization models, where the goal is to detect summary-worthy utterances based solely on how they are spoken.

- **Speech Genre:** Read speech (audiobook narration)
- **Languages:** Assamese and Bengali
- **Total Duration:** ~8 hours 22 minutes (Bengali: 4h 30min; Assamese: 3h 52min)
- **Speakers:** 14 total (9 Female, 5 Male), covering a diverse range of pitch and speaking styles; diverse prosodic styles and vocal characteristics
- **Recording Conditions:** Clean, single-speaker audio with no background music or environmental noise
- **Selection Criteria:** Recordings were selected based on narration quality,

prosodic clarity, balanced gender representation, and minimal ambient interference

Table 3.6: Audiobook Metadata

Audiobook ID	Speaker Gender	Title	Author
AA01	Female	Asimat Jar Heral Seema	Bhubanmohan Baruah
AA02	Male	Sahebpurar Boroxun	Anuradha Sarma Pujari
AA03	Male	Sahebpurar Boroxun	Anuradha Sarma Pujari
AA04	Female	Mayabritto	Reeta Chowdhury
AA05	Female	Makam (Chapter 1)	Reeta Chowdhury
AA06	Female	Makam (Chapter 12)	Reeta Chowdhury
AA07	Female	Adhalekha Dastavej (Part 1)	Mamoni Raisom Goswami
AA08	Female	Adhalekha Dastavej (Part 2)	Mamoni Raisom Goswami
AA09	Male	Sahebpurar Boroxun (Part 1)	Anuradha Sarma Pujari
AA10	Male	Sahebpurar Boroxun (Part 6)	Anuradha Sarma Pujari
AB01	Male	Manush	Bimal Mitra
AB02	Female	Satashey Shrabon	Bimal Mitra
AB03	Female	Ghoronti	Bimal Mitra
AB04	Male	Aamrityu	Bimal Mitra
AB05	Male	Porishishto	Ashapoorna Debi
AB06	Male	Obhagir Swargo	Sarat Chandra Chattopadhyay
AB07	Female	Tetultolar Ghat	Bibhutibhushan Bandyopadhyay
AB08	Female	Kankan	Ashapoorna Debi
AB09	Female	Belmotiya	Bimal Mitra

3.5.2 Segmentation and Annotation

To prepare the data for utterance-level modeling, each audiobook was divided into smaller, meaningful segments. An utterance, in this thesis, refers to a speaker's sentence-length segment of continuous speech, typically bounded by pauses or prosodic cues like pitch/intensity resets. This segmentation process was done partly by hand and partly with the help of acoustic cues in the audio signal.

Specifically, long pauses, sudden changes in pitch, and noticeable drops in loudness were used as indicators of natural breaks in speech. These breaks often align with sentence boundaries or major clauses. Each segment created in this way was treated as a separate data point in the dataset, making it suitable for further analysis and classification in the summarization framework.

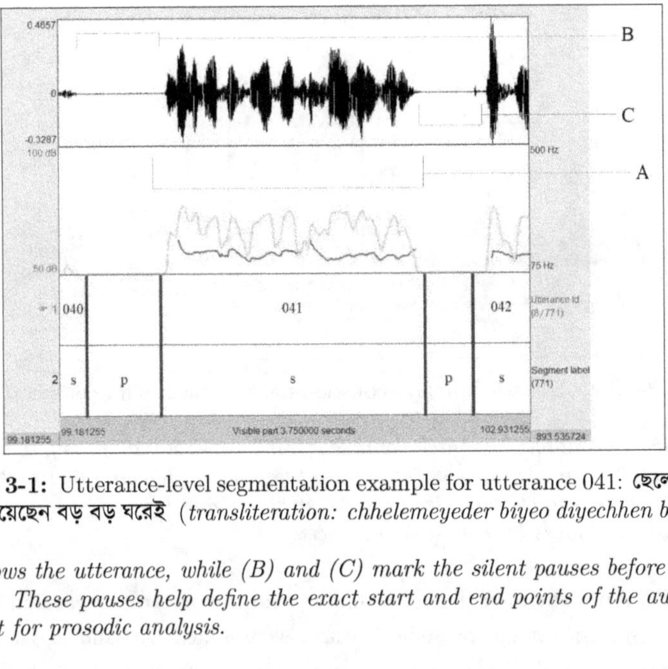

Figure 3-1: Utterance-level segmentation example for utterance 041: ছেলেমেয়েদের বিয়েও দিয়েছেন বড় বড় ঘরেই (*transliteration: chhelemeyeder biyeo diyechhen boro boro ghorei*)
(A) shows the utterance, while (B) and (C) mark the silent pauses before and after it. These pauses help define the exact start and end points of the audio segment for prosodic analysis.

- **Segmentation Rule:** A pause was identified wherever the pitch dropped below 65 Hz and the intensity fell below 40 dB.[4] Voiced regions between these pauses were treated as 'utterances', as shown in Figure 3-1.
- **Utterance Labels:** Each segment was initially labeled as either:
  - s: Sentence-ending utterance
  - ph: Mid-sentence utterance

  These labels were kept in the dataset as extra background information, but they were not used directly in the summarization experiments. While they may be useful for other analysis tasks in the future, they played no role in training or evaluating the summarization models in this study.
- **Annotation Format:** All utterances were aligned using Praat's TextGrid

[4]These values were selected based on typical acoustic ranges for human voiced speech. Pitch below 65 Hz falls outside the common voiced range for most speakers, while intensity below 40 dB is generally inaudible in clean recordings. Empirical inspection confirmed these thresholds aligned with perceptual pauses in the corpus. [87]

files, maintaining time-aligned sentence-level annotations synchronized with WAV files[5].

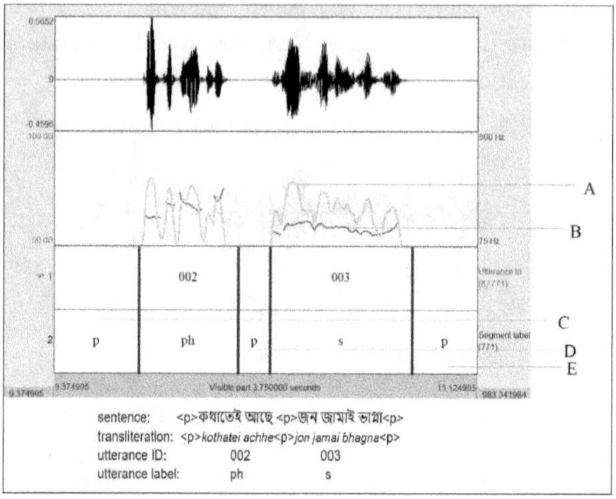

Figure 3-2: Visualization of key acoustic-prosodic features for consecutive utterances.
(A) intensity contour, (B) pitch contour, (C–D) pause durations before and after utterance 002, and (D–E) pause durations before and after utterance 003. These features are used to characterize prosodic structure and inform summary-worthiness in downstream models.

Prosodic Annotations: To better understand the patterns of rhythm and emphasis in speech, certain prosodic features were added by hand at the level of individual phrases. These manual annotations aimed to capture subtle details in how speakers vary their pitch and loudness to highlight important parts of the sentence, also shown in Figure 3-3.

- Manual segmentation and annotation of pitch and intensity contours.
- Shape encoding for both pitch and intensity contours per utterance:
  - R = Rising
  - F = Falling
  - RF = Rise-Fall
  - FR = Fall-Rise

[5]The lower pitch limit in Praat is set to 75 Hz, which corresponds to the default pitch floor commonly used for adult speech analysis. The pitch extraction algorithm does not search below this threshold; therefore, in regions with weak or irregular voicing, the estimated pitch may appear as a flat contour near this lower boundary. Setting the pitch floor excessively low would increase the analysis window and may reduce sensitivity to rapid pitch variations. Since Praat requires predefined minimum and maximum pitch ranges to detect periodicity, weak or aperiodic segments can sometimes be assigned the lowest permitted value.

- Number of peaks in intensity contours were also recorded for each utterance. This peak-count reflects rhythmic variation, pitch prominence, and local prosodic emphasis.

These manual annotations make it possible to measure and analyze how speakers use pitch and loudness to express meaning. By adding this layer of information, we can study more closely how changes in prosody relate to which sentences sound more important or meaningful. For instance, the number of peaks in intensity contours serves as an indicator of rhythmic stress and dynamic emphasis within an utterance. In expressive speech—such as audiobook narration or broadcast delivery—multiple intensity peaks often align with syllabic or phrasal stress patterns that mark content as emotionally charged, structurally important, or syntactically complete. Tracking this variation helps distinguish flat or transitional sentences from those that carry information salience, supporting more accurate extraction of summary-worthy units in a prosody-driven framework.

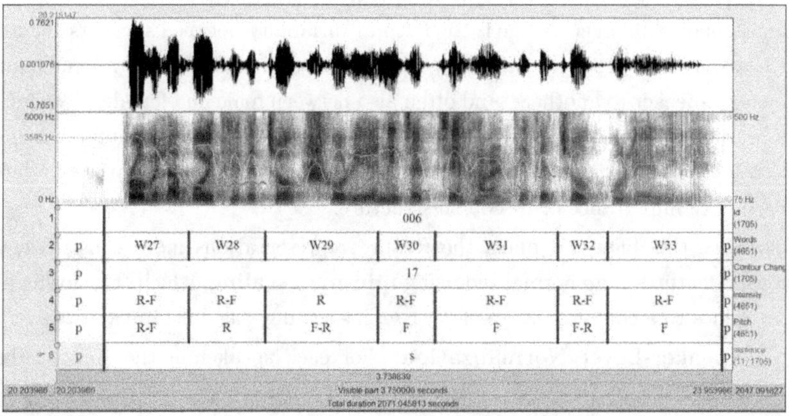

Figure 3-3: Manual segmentation and prosodic annotation of a speech segment using Praat.
Each utterance is annotated with contour shape categories—Rising (R), Falling (F), Rise-Fall (RF), or Fall-Rise(FR) for both pitch and intensity. Also, the number of peaks in intensity contours was also annotated per utterance to capture rhythmic prominence.

3.5.3 Preprocessing and Normalization

Before feature extraction, each recording was subjected to a multi-step preprocessing pipeline to ensure consistency and eliminate distortions that could interfere with acoustic-prosodic analysis.

- **Noise Removal:** Low-level background noise was removed using spectral subtraction [6] in Audacity. A static noise profile was selected for each recording and subtracted from the entire waveform.

- **Loudness Normalization:** Recordings were normalized using RMS-based amplitude adjustment[7] to reduce inter-file loudness variations.
- **Background Music Exclusion:** Any segment containing music, jingles, or transitional sound effects was excluded altogether, ensuring clean prosodic contours in the final dataset.
- **Storage Format:** All preprocessed audio files were stored as 16-bit PCM WAV files (44.1 kHz) to maintain signal integrity and compatibility with standard feature extraction tools.

3.5.4 Normalization of Acoustic Features

In any speech-based analysis, especially when working with prosodic and acoustic signals, one common challenge is the natural variability between speakers. Factors such as pitch range, voice intensity, and articulation style can vary significantly from one speaker to another—and often also between male and female speakers. If this variability is not addressed, machine learning models may focus too much on these speaker-specific traits, rather than on the more meaningful patterns related to sentence importance or discourse structure.

To reduce this bias and make the feature representations more consistent, all acoustic features were normalized using **min-max scaling**, which transforms feature values to a common range of [0, 1]. This scaling was done in two ways:

- **Speaker-Level Normalization:** For each speaker in the corpus, their

[6]Spectral subtraction is a noise reduction technique used in speech signal processing that estimates and removes background noise from the frequency spectrum of an audio signal. It works by first estimating the average noise spectrum during silent or non-speech portions of the signal (called a noise profile). Then, this noise profile is subtracted from the spectrum of the entire audio signal, frame by frame. The goal is to preserve the clean speech components while minimizing the impact of noise, especially in low-energy frequency bands.This preprocessing step is particularly important before tasks such as pitch extraction, since background noise can distort the frequency information and lead to inaccurate pitch estimates.

[7]Loudness normalization using RMS (Root Mean Square) amplitude is a technique used to ensure consistent volume across different audio recordings. RMS amplitude provides a statistical measure of the average signal power over time, and is more closely related to perceived loudness than simple peak amplitude. In this method, the RMS value of an audio signal is computed and compared to a desired target level. The entire signal is then scaled up or down so that its RMS amplitude matches this target. Unlike peak normalization, which adjusts audio based on the loudest point in the waveform, RMS-based normalization considers the energy throughout the duration of the audio, resulting in more perceptually balanced loudness between segments. This step is particularly important in speech processing tasks like summarization, where loudness variations between speakers or utterances can interfere with consistent feature extraction and downstream analysis.

features—such as pitch, intensity, and MFCC values—were scaled independently using min-max normalization. This helped account for individual differences in vocal range and delivery style. By doing this normalization separately for each speaker, we ensured that the unique speaking characteristics of one person did not dominate the overall data distribution.

- **Gender-Based Normalization:** Male and female voices naturally differ in pitch and energy levels. For example, male speakers typically have a lower average pitch than female speakers. To avoid any bias that could arise due to these physiological differences, we grouped all male speakers together and all female speakers together, and applied min-max normalization separately within each group. This ensured that the acoustic range typical to each gender was treated fairly and on an equal footing.
- **Formula Used:**

$$x_{scaled} = \frac{x - \min(x)}{\max(x) - \min(x)} \tag{3.1}$$

Together, this two-level normalization approach allowed the summarization models to focus on meaningful patterns in the data—such as changes in prosody or intensity that signal sentence importance—rather than being misled by speaker-specific or gender-related characteristics.

3.5.5 Feature Design and Use Case

Each segmented utterance in the audiobook corpus is treated as a separate data instance. The task is to decide whether this utterance should be part of a summary or not. Importantly, this decision is made without using the textual transcript of the utterance. Instead, the system relies entirely on **acoustic-prosodic features**, which makes this a **text-independent summarization** approach.

Feature Vector Composition

For each utterance, we extract a fixed set of acoustic and temporal features, which are then combined into a **47-dimensional feature vector**. This feature set captures various aspects of how the sentence was spoken, rather than what was said.

The features include:

- **Pitch-Based Features:**
  - Minimum pitch (F0)
  - Maximum pitch
  - Average pitch

  - Pitch range (difference between max and min)
- **Energy-Based Features:**
  - Minimum intensity
  - Maximum intensity
  - Mean intensity
- **Temporal Feature:**
  - Duration of the utterance in seconds
- **Spectral Features:**
  - 39-dimensional Mel-Frequency Cepstral Coefficients (MFCCs), labeled M1 to M39

Learning Setup

These 39-dimensional feature vectors are used as input to a **binary classifier**. The model learns to predict whether a given utterance is likely to be included in a human-generated summary, based only on its acoustic profile.

Since the audiobook narrators tend to use deliberate prosody—like emphasizing key sentences with longer duration or higher pitch variation—these acoustic cues become powerful indicators of sentence importance. The classifier is trained on this hypothesis: *that expressive vocal patterns can be learned and used to estimate which utterances carry more informational weight.*

Rationale for Feature Choices

Each type of feature was selected based on its ability to reflect sentence-level importance:

- **Pitch variation** often indicates emphasis or a change in discourse structure.
- **Intensity (loudness)** can correlate with the speaker's effort to highlight a segment.
- **Utterance duration** reflects pacing—longer utterances often carry more content.
- **MFCCs** capture the spectral shape and are widely used in speech recognition to characterize phonetic structure.

These features together create a holistic representation of how a sentence was delivered, enabling the classifier to make informed decisions without relying on the words themselves.

Limitations

While this approach opens up promising directions for summarization in low-resource languages and speech-first settings, there are a few limitations to consider:

- **Limited Prosodic Annotations:** Detailed annotations of pitch and intensity contour shapes (such as rising, falling, or rise-fall) are only available for a portion of the data. These patterns can be important for modeling emphasis, but due to annotation constraints, they are not consistently used in training.
- **Manual Annotation Bias:** Some of the contour shape annotations were done manually. Although we followed structured guidelines and observed acceptable agreement among annotators in a pilot study, subjectivity cannot be fully ruled out.
- **Domain Generalization:** Audiobooks provide a clean and expressive environment with minimal noise and disfluency, making them ideal for model development. However, the same features may behave differently in spontaneous or conversational speech. As such, further evaluation on other domains is needed to test the generalizability of this summarization strategy.

Nonetheless, the audiobook setting serves as a valuable starting point. It allows us to build and validate summarization models in a controlled environment where expressive prosody is naturally present and easy to analyze.

3.6 Discussion: Choice of Tool for Prosodic Feature Extraction

In this work, Praat was used as the primary tool for extracting prosodic features such as pitch, intensity, and related statistics. Praat was chosen because it provides a well-established and widely accepted implementation of autocorrelation-based pitch estimation, which has been extensively used in speech and phonetics research across languages and speaking styles. Its robustness and reproducibility make it suitable for corpus-level feature extraction.

The acoustic feature-set in this work consists of pitch, intensity, and duration. While intensity and duration estimation follow largely standardized computation procedures across commonly used speech analysis tools(such as WaveSurfer, Audacity, etc.), pitch extraction involves multiple algorithmic approaches that can produce varying estimates. Therefore, the comparative evaluation focused specifically on alternative pitch extraction algorithms to justify the selection of the Praat-based method.

While several alternative algorithms for prosodic analysis exist, including YIN [18], pYIN [70], and cepstrum [1, 80] pitch detection methods, the choice of Praat was not made arbitrarily. To assess the quality of prosodic feature estimation, comparative experiments were conducted using these alternative methods. Rather than evaluating pitch accuracy in isolation, the comparison was carried out in terms of downstream task performance, specifically sentence-level classification. Prosodic features extracted using different methods were evaluated across five classification algorithms to ensure consistency of observations.

Table 3.7: Sentence classification mean-accuracy (%) obtained using prosodic features extracted with different feature estimation methods across five classifiers.

Model	YIN	pYIN	CEP	Autocorrelation
Extra Tree	62.14% ± 4.67%	64.76% ± 3.95%	61.18% ± 4.27%	66.78% ± 4.07%
Random Forest	64.66% ± 4.50%	65.46% ± 3.37%	60.81% ± 3.80%	67.82% ± 4.78%
Gradient Boosting	62.86% ± 2.52%	65.04% ± 3.87%	61.54% ± 4.21%	66.43% ± 5.14%
K Nearest Neighbour	54.21% ± 4.86%	63.51% ± 4.58%	57.33% ± 3.02%	57.95% ± 2.67%
ADA Boost	63.35% ± 2.68%	64.33% ± 5.22%	61.78% ± 3.17%	60.97% ± 4.08%

Table 3.8: F-score performance of sentence classification using prosodic features extracted with different pitch estimation methods across five classifiers.

Model	YIN	pYIN	CEP	Autocorrelation
Extra Tree	0.5944 ± 0.0488	0.6273 ± 0.0463	0.5849 ± 0.0562	0.6520 ± 0.0442
Random Forest	0.6229 ± 0.0474	0.6394 ± 0.0346	0.5831 ± 0.0483	0.6646 ± 0.0492
Gradient Boosting	0.6079 ± 0.0301	0.6343 ± 0.0398	0.5971 ± 0.0450	0.6529 ± 0.0507
K Nearest Neighbour	0.5238 ± 0.0471	0.6255 ± 0.0500	0.5596 ± 0.0272	0.5683 ± 0.0261
ADA Boost	0.6079 ± 0.0301	0.6343 ± 0.0398	0.5971 ± 0.0450	0.6529 ± 0.0507

The empirical results in Table 3.7 and Table 3.8 showed that features extracted using Praat's autocorrelation-based approach consistently led to better or more stable classification performance compared to features obtained from YIN, pYIN, and cepstral methods. In particular, Praat-based features exhibited fewer pitch tracking inconsistencies and were more reliable in the presence of variability typical of spontaneous and broadcast speech. Based on these observations, Praat was selected for the final corpus development and subsequent experiments.

It is important to note that the use of Praat does not imply that other prosodic estimation methods are unsuitable. Rather, the choice reflects a balance between methodological reliability, empirical performance on the target task, and practical considerations for large-scale corpus processing.

3.7 Chapter Summary

This chapter introduces the speech corpus[8] developed to support prosody-based extractive summarization in low-resource language settings. The corpus includes Assamese and Bengali broadcast speech, selected to represent two common types of resource constraints in speech processing.

Bengali has limited ASR and basic text processing tools, allowing transcript-based experiments that assess how ASR errors affect summary quality. Assamese, by contrast, lacks publicly available ASR systems with sufficient accuracy for summarization, making it a case for fully speech-based modeling. This corpus enables text-independent speech summarization by providing manually annotated sentence-level summaries and acoustic-prosodic features, without relying on ASR transcripts. It supports low-resource languages like Assamese and Bengali, offering a practical testbed for prosody-based modeling, lightweight classifiers, and evaluation under real-world constraints.

This enables the corpus to support both transcript-reliant and transcript-free summarization approaches, forming the empirical foundation for the modeling frameworks presented in later chapters.

[8]The corpus developed in this research is not publicly hosted at this time. As it is a newly created resource, distribution will be managed directly by the author(s)/institution to ensure appropriate academic use. Interested researchers may request access.

Chapter 4

The Effect of ASR Errors in a Low-Resource Language for Extractive Speech Summarization

Automatic speech recognition (ASR) was often viewed as a necessary first step in spoken document summarization. However, in low-resource language settings, this dependency introduces a bottleneck. Most ASR systems trained on limited data suffer from high word error rates (WER), and their errors propagate into downstream tasks — particularly extractive summarization, which relies heavily on lexical fidelity.

This chapter investigates a critical but underexplored question: *How do transcription errors from low-resource ASR systems distort the outcome of extractive summarization?* We address this through a targeted empirical analysis using Bengali speech data, serving both as a diagnostic study and a motivation for later ASR-independent approaches.

4.1 Introduction

In summarization systems of spoken documents, the first step was to convert speech to text using automatic speech recognition (ASR). This transcription was then used as input to a text-based summarization model. However, in practice, ASR systems for low-resource languages like Bengali still exhibit high word error rates (WER), especially when used out-of-the-box without task-specific tuning. These errors can significantly affect downstream tasks, including extractive summarization, which relies heavily on accurate sentence representations. Yet, in most summarization research, the quality of ASR output was either assumed to be acceptable or not analyzed in depth.

This chapter addresses that gap by investigating how ASR transcription errors influence the quality of extractive summaries. Rather than focusing only on WER as a surface metric, we go further to identify the types of errors that degrade summary content — such as the loss or distortion of key words, sentence boundary confusion, and phonological substitutions that alter sentence meaning. Using a subset of our corpus with both human-verified and ASR-generated transcripts, we compare summary quality across these two conditions using simple, unsupervised extractive summarization techniques. By holding the summarization method constant and varying only the input transcript (manual vs. ASR), we were able to isolate and measure the impact of transcription quality itself. Both text summaries and corresponding speech summaries were evaluated by human raters, allowing us to quantify the effect of ASR errors on informativeness and relevance.

This chapter plays a crucial role in the thesis. It builds directly on the corpus described in Chapter 3, and sets the stage for Chapter 5, where we evaluate multiple summarization strategies and sentence embeddings under ASR-induced noise. Before exploring alternative or more resilient models, we must first understand the nature and consequences of the errors introduced by transcription systems in real-world conditions.

In short, this chapter answers a foundational question for low-resource speech summarization: *Can extractive summaries be trusted when their input transcripts were error-prone?* The findings here show that transcription errors do not merely reduce readability — they fundamentally distort sentence importance estimation, often leading to poor summary content. This motivates the exploration of both more robust summarization models (Chapter 5) and non-transcript-based approaches using acoustic-prosodic features (Chapters 6 and 7).

4.2 Methodology

This section outlines the data selection and processing pipeline used for analyzing the impact of ASR transcription errors on summarization quality. We begin by describing the subset of the speech corpus used in this chapter and the preprocessing steps applied to prepare the audio for transcription. This was followed by a description of the ASR system employed and the rationale for its selection.

4.2.1 Speech Corpus and Preprocessing

The experiments in this chapter use a subset of the Bengali audiobook corpus introduced in Chapter 3. Specifically, three annotated audiobook segments—referred to as Audiobook A, B, and C—were selected for their diversity in narration style and clarity of utterance boundaries. These segments were chosen to represent a controlled but realistic testing environment for assessing transcription and summarization quality.

Each selected audiobook segment contains sentence-aligned utterances manually segmented based on prosodic and syntactic cues. This segmentation was performed using a semi-automated procedure in Praat, followed by manual correction. Table 4.1 summarizes the key properties of the three selected segments, including duration, number of utterances, and speaker characteristics.

Table 4.1: Metadata for Audiobook Documents Used in ASR Analysis

Document ID	**Speaker Gender**	**Name of Audiobook**	**Author**	**Duration (sec)**
A	Male	*Porishishto*	Ashapoorna Debi	996
B	Female	*Tetultolar Ghat*	Bibhutibhushan Bandyopadhyay	1159
C	Male	*Obhagir Swargo*	Sarat Chandra Chattopadhyay	1422

Before ASR transcription, all audio files underwent the following preprocessing pipeline:

- **Loudness normalization**: Standardized peak amplitude across utterances using RMS normalization to ensure consistent transcription performance across varying recording conditions.
- **Noise removal**: Low-frequency background noise and static artifacts were removed using spectral subtraction and energy-based filtering.
- **Segmentation**: Each document was segmented into sentence-level utterances using manually aligned TextGrid boundaries to minimize long-span errors in ASR and improve alignment with reference transcripts.

This preprocessing ensured that the quality of ASR output was not confounded by recording artifacts or inconsistent segmentation. Notably, earlier experiments showed that segmentation granularity plays a critical role in ASR accuracy—longer chunks yielded high deletion rates, while sentence-level segments reduced WER considerably.

4.2.2 Transcript Generation and ASR Tool Used

Transcriptions for each segmented utterance were generated using the publicly available Google Cloud Speech-to-Text API [1]. This API was selected for three key

[1]This API was used through Google API client library for Python language, which was a part of the package SpeechRecognition 3.8.1 to be installed in platforms supporting Python. For more details of this package, check https://pypi.org/project/SpeechRecognition/

reasons:

1. **Accessibility**: It was available for Bengali and does not require additional training or customization.
2. **Relevance to low-resource conditions**: The system was used in its default configuration, reflecting realistic usage in low-resource scenarios where fine-tuning was not feasible.
3. **Baseline performance**: While not optimized for domain-specific speech, its transcription output was sufficiently representative of real-world usage in low-resource pipelines.

No custom language models or acoustic model fine-tuning was applied. This allowed the analysis to reflect the kind of performance a typical researcher or application developer might encounter when deploying speech summarization systems for Bengali using off-the-shelf tools

Reference transcripts for each utterance were obtained from human-verified transcriptions created as part of the corpus annotation effort. These were aligned with ASR outputs to allow word-level comparison and facilitate error type analysis in the next section.

4.2.3 Manual vs. ASR Transcript Comparison

To evaluate the impact of ASR errors, we compared the transcriptions generated by the ASR system with corresponding human-verified reference transcripts for each utterance. These manual transcripts were produced as part of the corpus annotation described in Chapter 3, and serve as the gold standard for assessing transcription fidelity.

The ASR outputs were aligned with the reference transcripts at the word level. Word Error Rate (WER) was used as the primary metric to quantify transcription quality. WERwas defined as:

$$\text{WER} = \frac{S + D + I}{N} \times 100 \tag{4.1}$$

where S, D, and I represent the number of substitutions, deletions, and insertions respectively, and $N$was the total number of words in the reference transcript.

Initial experiments revealed that WER varied substantially based on the duration of the audio input. Table 4.2 shows the transcription errors for three randomly selected samples of different lengths. As seen, longer segments had disproportionately higher deletion errors and overall WER.

To mitigate this, we segmented the audio into smaller, sentence-level utterances

Table 4.2: ASR Transcription Errors for Unsegmented Audio

Duration (sec)	Words	Deletions	Subst./Insert.	WER (%)
11	32	4	4	25.0
14	33	17	4	63.6
43	96	77	1	81.25

[2] prior to transcription. As shown in Table 4.3, this significantly improved ASR performance, particularly by reducing deletion errors.

Table 4.3: ASR Transcription Errors after Sentence-Level Segmentation

Duration (sec)	Words	Deletions	Subst./Insert.	WER (%)
11	32	1	4	15.6
14	33	1	7	24.2
43	96	3	5	0.08

These results highlight two key patterns:

- **Deletion errors dominate in longer audio inputs**, where the ASR system fails to decode a large portion of the input due to speech overlaps, disfluencies, or silence thresholds. This leads to total absence of the words in the converted transcript.
- **Utterance-level segmentation was essential** for improving recognition quality in low-resource languages, especially when using generic ASR systems without fine-tuning. However, the number of substitutions and insertions increase because there was an increase of words being converted from the speech signal to text. This increase was not as substantial compared to the previous case, thus the word error rate was significantly reduced.

Thus, all transcripts used in this chapter were generated using sentence-level segmentation. The aligned reference and ASR transcripts form the foundation for the detailed error typology and summarization analysis presented in subsequent sections.

4.3 Typology of ASR Errors and Their Impact on Summary Generation

While WER provides a surface-level indicator of transcription quality, it does not capture the full extent of how recognition errors disrupt the summarization process. In this section, we categorize and analyze the specific types of transcription

[2]Utterance were voiced speech segments in an audio between two adjacent silence/non-voiced segments

errors observed in ASR-generated Bengali speech transcripts and examine their qualitative impact on sentence selection for summarization. But before that, we analyze the ASR-errors based on established hierarchical classification [42]. The errors were broadly grouped as follows:

- **Substitution Errors**: These include both phonological and morphological substitutions, often leading to changes in meaning or part-of-speech.
- **Deletion Errors**: Critical content words were omitted entirely, especially from sentence boundaries. Pitch-based analysis showed these often correspond to low-amplitude segments, which ASR fails to detect (Tables 4.8to 4.9).

Table 4.4: Example of a substitution type transcription error of নেপু

ASR reference	কিন্তু খামোখা নেপুর ঘরে তালা লাগানোর মানে কি	ASR hypothesis	মনিপুর ঘরে তালা লাগানোর মানে কি
transliteration	***kinṭu khāmōkhā nēpur*** *gharē tālā lāgānōr māne ki*	*transliteration*	***Manipur*** *gharē tālā lāgānōr mānē ki*
translation	But what does it mean to put a lock on Nepu's house?	translation	What does it mean to put a lock on the Monipur house?

Table 4.5: Example of a deletion and substitution type transcription error of প্রতিমা

ASR reference	প্রতিমা ধীরস্বরে বলে	ASR hypothesis	বাদশারে বলে
transliteration	***Pratimā dhīrsharē*** *balē*	*transliteration*	***Bādśārē*** *balē*
translation	Protima said in a gentle voice	translation	Tells Emperor

Table 4.6: Example of a morphological substitution type transcription error of কাঙালী

ASR reference	কাঙালী বলিল	ASR hypothesis	বাঙালি বলিল
transliteration	***kāṅgālī balila***	*transliteration*	***bāṅgālī balila***
translation	Kangali said	translation	Bangali said

The occurence of these errors in the ASR-generated transcripts of the Bengali spoken documents were illustrated in Table 4.10. The transliteration of the Bengali words in this paper were done following ISO 15919:2001 standard [3].

[3]This international standard provides tables which enable the transliteration into Latin characters from text in Indic scripts. For more details, visit https://www.iso.org/standard/28333.html

Table 4.7: Example of a substitution type transcription error of মায়াবতী

ASR reference	মায়াবতী ঝেঝে উঠে বলেন	ASR hypothesis	মারুটি সুজুকি বালেনো
transliteration	***māẏābatī jhējhe uṭhē balēn***	*transliteration*	***Māruṭi sujuki bālēno***
translation	Mayaboti said irritably	translation	*(nonsensical sentence)*

Table 4.8: Example of a deletion type transcription error, where আর ,জ্বর and এলো were deleted.

ASR reference	আর সর্বদাই ভয় ওই বুঝি জ্বর এলো	ASR hypothesis	সর্বদাই ভয় ওই বুঝি
transliteration	***ār*** *sarbadāi bhaẏ oi bujhi* ***jwar ēlo***	*transliteration*	*sarbadāi bhaẏ oi bujhi*
translation	And there was always a fear that fever was back	translation	there was always a fear that

Table 4.9: Example of a phonological substitution type transcription error of বৌমা

ASR reference	এই দুঃসময়ে তুমি হাসছ বৌমা	ASR hypothesis	এই দুঃসময়ে তুমি হাসছো বোমা
transliteration	*Ēi duhsamaẏē tumi hāscha* ***baumā***	*transliteration*	*Ēi duhsamaẏē tumi hāscha* ***bomā***
translation	In this difficult time you were smiling, Bouma	translation	*(nonsensical sentence)*

Table 4.10: Types of substitution-type transcription error analysis of some of the terms of documents A, B and C.

Type of substitution	Original word in spoken document	ASR-generated word in transcript
One-to-One	ছেলেটার (chēlēṭār) কাঙালী (kāṅgālī) তাহাকে (tāhākē)	সিলেটের (silētēr) বাঙালি (bāṅgālī) ঢাকে (ḍhākē)
One-to-many	খেপেছিস (khēpēchis) ঘুচিবে (ghucibē) আসামীকে (āsāmīkē)	কি পেয়েছিস (ki pēẏēchis) কচি মেয়ে (kaci mēẏē) আসন কে (āsan kē)
Many-to-one	বিলেত যাওয়ার (bilēt jāōẏār) গায়ে তাহার (gāẏē tāhār) তাহার সেই (tāhār sēi) সে সেই (sē sēi)	ভিলেজার (bhilējār) গাড়িতে (gāṛitē) হাসি (hāsi) শিশি (śiśi)
Many-to-many	জ্বর আসাটা (jar āsāṭā) বৌমা বলে (baumā balē) নিজ হাতে সিন্দুক খুলেছি (nija hātē sinduk khulēchi) শয়তান কে একবার ডেকে (śaẏtān kē ēkbār dēkē)	জোড়া সেটা (jōṛā sēṭā) বোমা গুলো (bōmā gulō) নিশা ফেইসবুক খুলেছে (niśā facebook khulēchē) শতাংশ এক ব্যক্তি কে (śatāṁśa ēk byakti kē)
Morphological	পুকুরের (pukurēr) কাঙালী (kāṅgālī) জোর (jōr)	কুকুরের (kukurēr) বাঙালি (bāṅgālī) (in Table 4.6) জন্য (janya)
Phonological	নেপু (nēpu) বৌমা (baumā) হাতে (hātē) শাসানির (śāsānir)	নিপু (nipu) বোমা (bōmā) (in Table 4.9) সাথে (sāthē) শাসনের (śāsanēr)

Table 4.11: Transcription errors of most frequent terms of documents A, B and C.

Document ID	Word	Frequency of the word in original audio	WER (in %)
	নেপু (nēpu)	21	95.2
A	প্রতিমা (pratimā)	14	57.1
	মায়াবতী (māẏābatī)	12	50
	মা (mā)	54	16.67
B	কাঙালী (kāṅgālī)	56	57.1
	বাবা (bābā)	20	5
	মা (mā)	35	37.1
C	জ্বর (jar)	28	39.2
	হারু (hāru)	28	25

4.3.1 Proposed Error Taxonomy: From Recognition to Summarization Failure

The most frequently occurring terms of a document were unquestionably a part of the core information representing a document, due to which they were sought out to be included in the summary [4]. Thus losing these terms due to recognition errors would be tantamount to losing the core information of the document. Table 4.11 shows the recognition errors of the most frequent terms of spoken documents A, B and C .

To systematically understand how ASR errors affect summarization, we developed a typology of error patterns based on manual inspection of transcription errors between ASR outputs and their reference transcripts. To better comprehend the major types of errors impacting the context of a summary, the existing classification of errors was used as a foundation of our typology. Although this typology was derived from the limited samples of our selected documents, this can provide a useful starting point for comprehension and detailed research on ASR transcription errors for Bengali and languages phonetically similar to Bengali. The main criteria that forms the basis of the categories of this typology,was loss of context in varying degrees.

This typology was based on both the linguistic nature of the error and its affect on the summarization task — particularly in the loss of sentence-level informativeness and context.

The errors were broadly grouped as follows:

4.3.1.1 Pitch-Driven Boundary Deletion

In several cases, deletion of sentence-initial or sentence-final words corresponded with regions of low pitch, indicating that the ASR system failed to recognize speech segments with insufficient amplitude. For example:

1. আর ভাত দেবে না (*ār bhāt dēbē nā*) becomes আর ভাত (*ār bhāt*)
2. বেশ ফুর্তি আছে (*Bēś furti āchē*) becomes ফুর্তি (*furti*)

Table 4.12 and Table 4.13 shows the average and max pitch for each word in such cases.

Table 4.12: Pitch values for আর ভাত দেবে না

Word	Mean pitch (in Hz)	Maximum Pitch (in Hz)
ār	**210.55**	**351.04**
bhāt	**198.80**	**299.65**
dēbē	145.71	147.88
nā	151.74	155.41

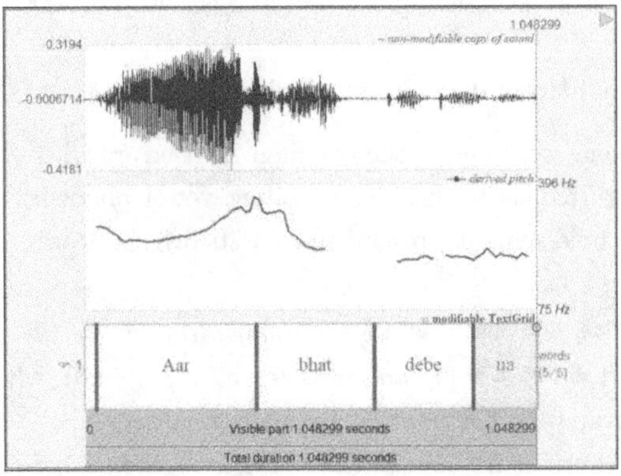

Figure 4-1: Deletion of the last two words of আর ভাত দেবে না

The respective pitch contours can be visualized in Fig. 4-1 and Fig. 4-2. These results suggest that loss of **low-pitch segments due to ASR's energy thresholds** disproportionately affect word boundaries and lead to high deletion rates. In turn, this reduce the likelihood of such sentences being selected by extractive summarization algorithms, even if they contain key information.

Table 4.13: Pitch values for বেশ ফুর্তি আছে

Word	Mean pitch (in Hz)	Maximum Pitch (in Hz)
Bēś	206.26	237.43
furti	**215.49**	**301.35**
āchē	140.65	151.89

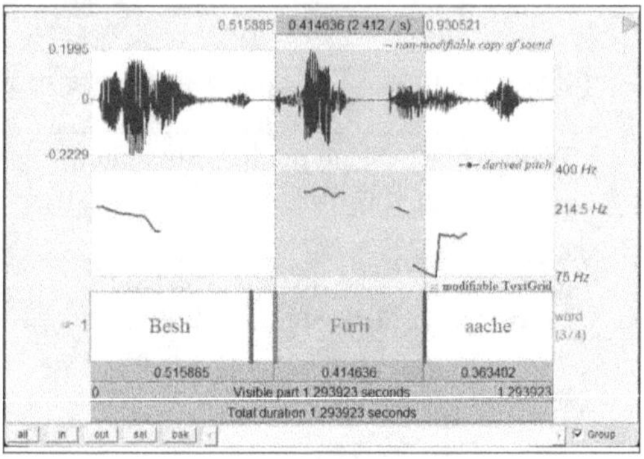

Figure 4-2: Deletion of the first and last word of বেশ ফুর্তি আছে

4.3.1.2 Substitutions due to vowel phoneme error.

Vowel substitutions were one of the common ASR errors where a vowel phoneme can be misrecognized as its nearest sounding vowel phoneme. The word thus changed doesn't hold semantic resemblance to its original words. For the following sentences,

1. কেন মরতে তুই কাল এখানে এলি (*Kēnō mōrtē tui kāl ēkhānē ēli*) becomes কেন মূর্তি তুই কাল এখানে এলি (*Kēnō murti tui kāl ēkhānē ēli*), where মরতে (mōrtē) was substituted by মূর্তি (murti). In the original sentence মরতে was used as an idiomatic expression [4], but in the converted sentence মূর্তি (meaning: statue) was used as a noun. Although it loses context, this change in parts of speech can be identified easily.
2. এই দুঃসময়ে তুমি হাসছ বৌমা (*Ēi duhsamaẏē tumi hāscha baumā*) becomes এই দুঃসময়ে তুমি হাসছো বোমা (*Ēi duhsamaẏē tumi hāscha bomā*), where বৌমা (baumā) was substituted by বোমা (bomā). In the original sentence বৌমা meaning *daughter-in-law* changes to বোমা meaning *explosive* in the converted sentence, thus rendering the sentence nonsensical but not enough to lose con-

[4]The English counterpart of this sentence could be: "Why in heaven's name did you have to come here yesterday!"

text. With the help of the background information from their surrounding sentences, this word can be identified and corrected manually.

4.3.1.3 Substitutions due to consonant error.

Consonant errors generally cascade through the entire sentence, generating a higher word-error rate.

1. নিজ হাতে সিন্দুক খুলেছি (*nija hātē sinduk khulēchi*) becomes নিশা ফেসবুক খুলেছে (*niśā facebuk khulēchē*). The consonants **Ni**(ja hātē sind)**uk** was detected correctly in Ni(śā faceb)uk khulēchē, rendering the entire sentence nonsensical, and 3 out of 4 words were lost. This hinders the context greatly even in the presence of background information.
2. মায়াবতী ঝেঝে উঠে বলেন (*māẏābatī jhējhe uthē balēn*) becomes মারুতি সুজুকি বালেনো (*māruṭi sujuki bālēno*) (shown in Table 4.7. The consonants mā(ẏāba)tī was correctly recognized in mā(ru)ṭi, and then the rest of the words were recognized incorrectly. With 3 out of 3 words lost to errors, the entire sentence was nonsensical and loses context entirely.

4.3.1.4 Misboundary Errors

The hindrance of continuous speech is, there were no clear boundaries between two words. Phoneme-level confusion in continuous speech leads to errors in word boundary recognition, causing malformed phrases or sentence fragments.

1. জ্বর আসাটা যেন ওর মস্ত অপরাধ (*Jar āsātā jēna ōr masta aparādh*) becomes জোড়া সেটা যেন ওর মস্ত অপরাধ (*Jōrā sētā jēna ōr masta aparādh*). The boundary between *Jar āsātā* in the original sentence was changed where the boundary was set between *Jōrā sētā* in the converted sentence, i.e. the boundary was set after the first phoneme ā of আসাটা (āsātā). The collective phonemes of the phrase জ্বর আসাটা were Jar[b]āsātā was converted to Jōrā[b]sētā resulting to জোড়া সেটা, where [*b*] denotes the boundary between two words.
2. রহিল তাহার আচলে বেগুন বাধা (*Rahila tāhār āchalē bēgun bādhā*) becomes রহিলো তাহারা চলে বেগুন বাধা (*Rahila tāhārā chalē bēgun bādhā*). Like the previous example, the phonemes remain same but the word-boundary was shifted to result into a different phrase altogether. The collective phonemes of the phrase তাহার আচলে were tāhār[b]āchalē was converted to tāhārā[b]chalē resulting to তাহারা চলে.
3. ও তোর ভুল কথা (*Ō tōr bhul kōthā*) becomes উত্তর ভুল কথা (*Uttōr bhul kōthā*). The collective phonemes of the phrase ও তোর were ō[b]tōr was converted to uttōr resulting to উত্তর.

4.3.1.5 Misidentification of Dialectal segments

There were five major dialects in Bangla, appearing both spoken and linguistically. The novellas whose audiobook was transcribed using the ASR in this work does not contain purely of standard Bangla. The dialogues were generally in a dialect other than the standard Bangla, differing not only in tone and accents but also in usage of terms. Such dialectal speech segments were highly prone to ASR errors, since it was very likely that the Google ASR we have used has been designed for the standard variety of Bangla.

1. রাধবো'খন রে (*Rādhbō khōn rē*) becomes রাখবো খন্ডে (*Rākhbō khōndē*). The original sentence roughly translates to "will cook now", which in standard Bangla generally was spoken/written as এখন রান্না করবো / এখন রাধবো, which was quite different than in Western Bengali dialect as shown in the example.
2. তুই খেলি নে মা (*Tui khēli nē mā*) becomes সিনেমা (*Sinēmā*, translated to Cinema). The original sentence roughly translates to "you didn't eat, mother", which in standard Bangla generally was spoken/written as তুমি খাওনি মা, which was quite different than in Western Bengali dialect as shown in the example.

4.3.1.6 Segmentation-Induced Substitution Errors

These were the types of substitution errors due to discontinuity introduced by utterance segmentation. The sentence চুপ করিয়া রহিল, কাঙালী তেমনি ধীরে ধীরে was a part of a continuous sentence which was segmented into two utterances চুপ করিয়া রহিল and কাঙালী তেমনি ধীরে ধীরে due to the presence of a silence-segment between them. The two utterances were then converted to text using the ASR, where the second utterance কাঙালী তেমনি ধীরে ধীরে (*kāngāli tēmni dhirē dhirē*)was recognised as বাঙালি তেমনি ধীরে ধীরে (*bāngāli tēmni dhirē dhirē*). However it was observed that when the sentence was left unsegmented it was recognized correctly by the ASR. The same phenomenon was observed for every utterance where কাঙালীwas the first word of utterance, as given in Table 4.14.
All of these utterances when segmented in a manner কাঙালী not at the beginning of an utterance, produces the correct transcription. This leads us to speculate that the error produced was likely due to the discontinuity introduced during utterance segmentation. This was further cemented by experiments carried out with different utterance segmentation boundaries.

Table 4.14: Substitution of কাঙালী due to utterance-segmentation discontinuity

utterances where কাঙালীwas correctly recognized	utterances where কাঙালীwas incorrectly recognized as বাঙালি
সে কাঙালীর মা	কাঙালী মায়ের বুকে ঠেস দিয়া বসিয়া ভাবিতে লাগিল (sentence 64 in Fig. 4-10)
ঊর্ধ্বদৃষ্টে চাহিয়া কাঙালীর মায়ের দুই চোখে (sentence 21 in Fig. 4-10)	কাঙালী কাঁদিয়া কহিল (sentence 116 in Fig. 4-10)
একদিন কাঙালীর মা হইতে বাচিয়া রহিল	কাঙালী বলিল (sentence 132 in Fig. 4-10)
ও শিশুপুত্র কাঙালীকে লইয়া	কাঙালীকেও স্নান করাইয়া ঘরে ফিরিল
কিন্তু ছেলেমানুষ কাঙালীর বুকে গিয়া	কাঙালীর মার জীবনের ইতিহাস ছোট

4.3.2 Sentence-Level Impact on Summary Selection

These transcription errors have direct implications for extractive summarization. Since sentence importance was computed from lexical content (e.g., TF-IDF vectors), any alteration in word identity or count distorts the semantic representation of the sentence.

Key observed effects include:

- **Summary sentence omission**: Important sentences were not selected because crucial keywords were deleted or substituted (e.g., "Protima said softly" transcribed as "Tells Emperor").
- **Distorted sentence ranking**: Sentences with altered morphology or phonology receive lower TF-IDF scores, skewing cosine similarity-based ranking.
- **Loss of summary coherence**: When many-to-many substitutions create nonsensical phrases, selected summaries lack internal coherence (see Table 4.10).

4.3.3 Summary Generation from Clean and Noisy Transcripts

To evaluate how transcription errors affect summary quality, we implemented two simple yet interpretable extractive summarization methods—TF-IDF-based sentence ranking and K-means clustering, as depicted in Fig. 4-3. These methods were intentionally chosen to avoid model complexity, thereby allowing a focused assessment of how ASR errors alone influence summary content.

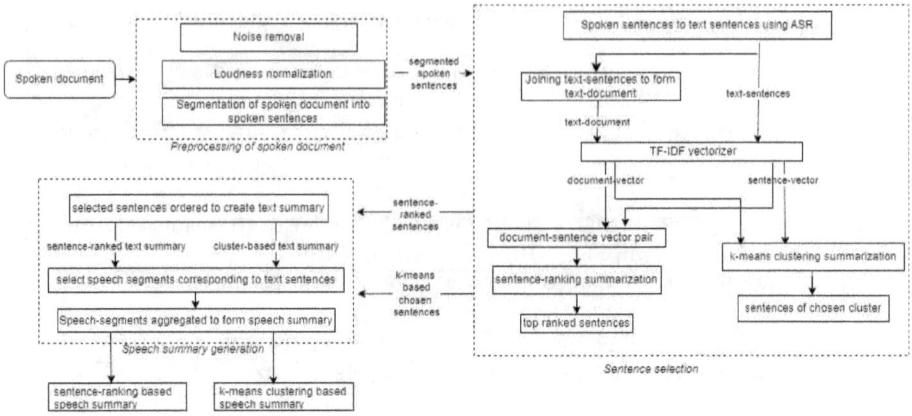

Figure 4-3: The framework for creating text and spoken summaries.

4.3.3.1 Sentence Vector Representation using TF-IDF

Each spoken document was first converted to its corresponding text transcript—either manual (clean) or ASR-generated (noisy). Sentences were then tokenized, stopwords were removed, and the remaining words were transformed into numerical vectors using Term Frequency–Inverse Document Frequency (TF-IDF). TF-IDF scoring assigns higher weights to words that were frequent in a sentence but rare across the full document, capturing the relative importance of words.

Each sentence thus becomes a TF-IDF vector, and the entire document was represented by a single aggregate document-vector created similarly. The vector for a sentence s in document $d$was defined by:

$$\text{tfidf}(t, s, d) = \text{tf}(t, s) \cdot \text{idf}(t, d) \tag{4.2}$$

where

$$\text{tf}(t, s) = \log(1 + \text{freq}(t, s)), \quad \text{idf}(t, d) = \log\left(\frac{N}{\text{count}(s \in d : t \in s)}\right) \tag{4.3}$$

4.3.3.2 Sentence Ranking by Cosine Similarity

In the ranking-based method, we calculate the cosine similarity between each sentence vector and the document vector. Sentences with the highest similarity scores were considered most central and were selected as summary candidates:

$$\cos(\vec{s}, \vec{d}) = \frac{\vec{s} \cdot \vec{d}}{||\vec{s}||\,||\vec{d}||} \tag{4.4}$$

Here, $\vec{s}$ and $\vec{d}$ were the TF-IDF vectors of the sentence and document respectively. The top-ranked sentences based on similarity were selected, and their original order in the document was preserved to maintain coherence.

4.3.3.3 K-Means Clustering of Sentence Vectors

We also implemented a K-means clustering approach. All sentence vectors were grouped into K clusters using cosine distance as the metric. The optimal value of K was determined using the Elbow method, as shown in Fig. 4-4. Sentences belonging to the cluster that contains the document vector were selected, assuming they represent the thematic core of the document.

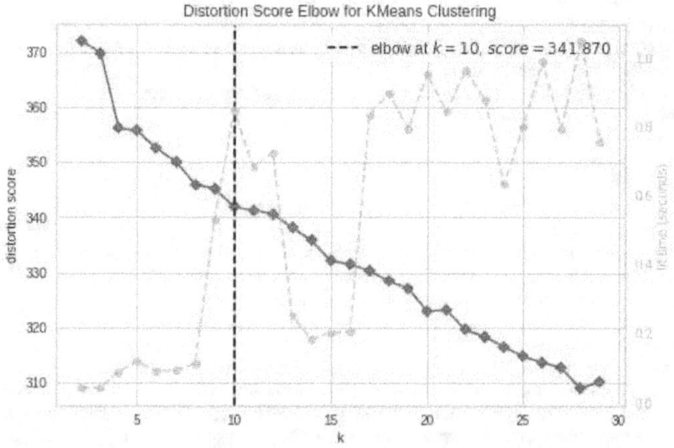

Figure 4-4: Elbow method for obtaining the optimal number of clusters.

Multiple optimal K values were tested to generate alternative summaries ('summary2', 'summary3', 'summary4'), complementing the ranking-based 'summary1'. Figures 4-5 to 4-8 illustrate example summaries from these methods.

4.3.3.4 Speech Summary Reconstruction

For both methods, we additionally constructed speech summaries. The selected text sentences were mapped back to their original speech segments using timestamps obtained during segmentation (Chapter 3). These audio segments were concatenated in order to create a spoken version of the summary. This allowed us to compare summaries in both modalities—text and speech—under identical sentence selection strategies.

The use of unsupervised, lightweight methods was deliberate. By avoiding complex, data-hungry neural architectures, we ensure that any degradation in sum-

231. রাখালের মা বাঙালির হাতে একটা ঘড়ি কি জালা দিয়া তাহারি হাত ধরিয়া মায়ের মুখের স্পর্শ করা ফেলিয়া দিল
77. বাঙালি মাদুর পাতিনি কথা পাতিল মাচার উপর হইতে বালিশটা পারিয়া দিয়া হাত ধরিয়া তাকে বিছানায় টানিয়া লইয়া যাইতে মা কহিল বাঙালি আজ তোরা কাজে গিয়ে কাজ নেই
75. ছেলে হাত দিয়া জল বুঝাইয়া দিয়া বলিল পেদে দেবো মা ছবি
68. বাঙালির মা চুপ করিয়া রহিল বাঙালি তেমনি ধীরে ধীরে করিতে লাগিল বাবা যখন তড়িৎ ছেড়ে দিল কত লোক ধোনিকে করতে সাধাসাধি করলে
21. ঊর্ধ্ব দৃষ্টি চাহিয়া কাঙালীর মায়ের দুই চোখে অশ্রুধারা বহিতে ছিল এ সময়ে একটি বছর 14 15 ছেলে আঁচলে টান দিয়া কহিল তুই দাড়িয়ে আছিস মা ভাতার বিনা
64. বাঙালি মায়ের বুকে ঠেস দিয়া বসিয়া ভাবিতে লাগিল
116. বাঙালি কাঁদিয়া কহিল তুই তো বললি নে মা ফেলে দিলি
10. কাঙালীর মা
56. মা শশব্যস্তে ছেলের মুখে হাত চাপা দিয়া কহিল শিবা মরা পোড়ানো বলতে নেই পাপ হয়
132. বাঙালি বলিল আসবে কেন মা
134. বাঙালি তখনই যাইতে উদ্ধত হইলে সে তাহার হাতটা ধরিয়া ফেলিয়া বলিল একটু কাঁদা কাটা করি বাবা বলিস মা যাচ্ছে
89. সেই রাতে সেই রাঙা দুটি সীতার স্বর্গে যাওয়া কেমন করিয়া শোকার্ত স্বামী শেষ পথ ভোলা দিয়া গা দিয়া বিদায় দিলেন কি করিয়া হরিধ্বনি দিয়া ছেলেরা মা তাকে বহন করিয়া লইয়া গেল তারপরে সন্তানের হাতের আগুন
110. হল মধু আদার সত্য তুলসী পাতার রস বাঙালির মা ছেলের প্রতি রাগ করিয়া বলিল কেন তুই আমাকে না বলে ঘটি বাধা দিতে গেলে বাবা
18. স্বামী পুত্র কন্যা নাতি-নাতনি দাস-দাসী পরিজন সমস্ত সংসার উজ্জ্বল রাখিয়া ডিজে স্বর্গারোহণ দেখিয়া হারবো উড়িয়া ফুলিয়া উঠিতে লাগিল সৌভাগ্যের শে জানুয়ারি আত্মা করিতে পারিল না শুদ্ধ প্রজ্বলিত চিতা অজস্র ধোয়া নীল রংয়ের ছায়া ফেলিয়া ঘুরিয়া ঘুরিয়া আকাশে উঠেছিল কাঙালীর মা ইহারই মধ্যে ছোট একখানি রথের চেহারা স্পষ্ট দেখিতে পাইল
177. বাঙালি না বাবু মশাই বাবা গাছ কাটতে ছিল আমার মা মরেছে বলিতে বলিতে কান্নার চাপিতে পারিল না
107. বাঙালি কিয়া কাদাকাটি করিল হাতে পায়ে পরি লো ঘটি বাধা দিয়া তাহাকে এক টাকা প্রণামী দিল
58. ছেলে সন্দেহ করিয়া কহিল কথা
14. সেখানে পূর্বাহ্নে মাটির ভাঁড় চন্দনের টুকরা মধু ধুপধুনা প্রভৃতি উপকরণ সঞ্চিত হইয়াছিল কাঙালীর মা ছোট যা দুলের মেয়ে বলিয়া কাছে যাইতে সাহস পায়না তফাত একটা উঁচু ঢিবির মধ্যে দাঁড়াইয়া সমস্ত অন্ত্যেষ্টিক্রিয়া প্রথম হতে শেষ পর্যন্ত উৎসুক আগ্রহের চোখ মেলিয়া দেখিতে লাগিল
212. আমি বাঙালি
94. বাঙালি অস্ফুটে শুধু কহিল বলতে নেই

Figure 4-5: Text-summary generated after sentence-ranking method (summary1) of document C

22. মা চমকিয়া ফিরিয়া চাহিয়া কহিল রাখবো খন্ডে
23. হঠাৎ উপরে অঙ্গুলিনির্দেশ করিয়া ব্যাঘ্র শহরে কহিল দেখ দেখ বাবা বামুন মাহোই রথে চড়ে সঙ্গে যাচ্ছে
26. রাগ করিয়া কহিল বেলা দুপুর বাজে আমার খিদে পায় না বুঝি
33. ছেলের হাত ধরিয়া ঘাটে নামিয়া নিজেও স্নান করিনি বাঙালি কেউ স্নান করে ঘরে ফিরল শ্মশান সৎকারের শেষটুকু দেখা আর তার ভাগ্যে ঘটিলো না
44. বাঙালি পুকুর হইতাছে আসিয়া দেখিল তাহার বাতের ভুক্তাবশেষ মাইট্টা মাটির পাত্রে ঢাকিয়া রাখিতেছে আশ্চর্য হইয়া জিজ্ঞাসা করিল সিনেমা
56. মা শশব্যস্তে ছেলের মুখে হাত চাপা দিয়া কহিল শিবা মরা পোড়ানো বলতে নেই পাপ হয়
70. বাঙালি বাসলে আমার দুঃখ বুজবে আবার নিকে করতে যাবো কিসের জন্য
77. বাঙালি মাদুর পাতিনি কথা পাতিল মাচার উপর হইতে বালিশটা পারিয়া দিয়া হাত ধরিয়া তাকে বিছানায় টানিয়া লইয়া যাইতে মা কহিল বাঙালি আজ তোরা কাজে গিয়ে কাজ নেই
80. আর প্রলুব্ধ করিতে হইল না বাঙালি তৎক্ষণাৎ মায়ের বুকে শিয়া শিয়া পড়িয়া কহিল বল তাহলে
94. বাঙালি অস্ফুটে শুধু কহিল বলতে নেই
98. মা কইলো দেখা গাড়ি বাবাকে একবার ধরে আনবি অমনি যেন পায়ের ধুলা মাথায় দিয়ে আমাকে বিদায় দেয়
114. ছেলেমানুষ কাঙ্গালি ব্যতিব্যস্ত হইয়া উঠিতে মাথাকে কাজে টানিয়া লইয়া কহিল কবিরাজের বরিতে কিছু হলো না বাবা ভারতের ওষুধে কাজ হবে
116. বাঙালি কাঁদিয়া কহিল তুই তো বললি নে মা ফেলে দিলি
120. বাঙালি প্রথম অবস্থায় বাত্রা দিতে প্রবৃত্ত হইল
127. সকলে চলিয়া গেলে সে ছেলেকে কহিল এইবার একবার তাকে ডেকে আনতে পারিস বাবা
130. বাঙালি বুঝিয়া কহিল বাবাকে
132. বাঙালি বলিল আসবে কেন মা
133. অভাগীর নিজেরই যথেষ্ট সন্দেহ ছিল আস্তে আস্তে কহিল গিয়ে বলবি মা শুধু তোমার পায়ের ধুলো চাই
134. বাঙালি তখনই যাইতে উদ্ধত হইলে সে তাহার হাতটা ধরিয়া ফেলিয়া বলিল একটু কাঁদা কাটা করি বাবা বলিস মা যাচ্ছে
135. একটু থামিয়া কহিল ফেরবার পথে অমনি নাপতে বৌদির কাছ থেকে একটু আলতা চেহারা নিস কাঙ্গালি আমার নাম করলেই সে দেবে
141. বাঙালি কাঁদিয়া কহিল মাগো বাবা এসেছে পায়ের ধুলো নেবেনা
146. হিন্দির পিসি দাড়ায়া ছিল সে কহিল দাও বাবা রশি অগ্রসর হইয়া আসিল
158. বাবাকে খামোখা তুমি মারলে কেন
166. লোক গুলো যখন হিন্দুস্থানী টির কাছে প্রার্থনা নয় করিতে লাগিল বাঙালি উর্ধশ্বাসে দৌড় একেবারে কাছারিবাড়িতে আসে উপস্থিত হইল
172. বিস্মিত বাকরুদ্ধ হইয়া কহিলেন বাঙালি
174. দারোয়ান জি আমার বাবাকে মেরেছে
177. বাঙালি না বাবু মশাই বাবা গাছ কাটতে ছিল আমার মা মরেছে বলিতে বলিতে কান্নার চাপিতে পারিল না
183. সভায় প্রাঙ্গণে নামে দাঁড়াইয়া কহিল আমরা দুলে
185. বাঙালি বল মাঝে আমাকে আগুন দিতে ভুলে গেছে
190. বাঙালি জানি তো তাও সম্ভব
195. বাঙালি বলিল আমাদের উঠোনের কাজ বাবুমশাই
209. বাঙালি আশিয়া সম্মুখে দাঁড়ায়ে কহিল ঠাকুর মশাই আমার মা মরে গেছে
212. আমি বাঙালি
215. ব্যাপারটা ইতিমধ্যেই মুখে মুখে প্রচারিত হইয়া পড়িয়াছিল একজন কহিল অবউৎ একটা কাজ চাই

Figure 4-6: Text-summary generated after k-means clustering method for $optimal_1$ K of document C (summary2)

12. রহিলো তাহার হাটে যাওয়া রহিলো তাহারা চলে বেগুন বাধা সে চোখের জল মুছতে মুছতে সকল এর পিছনে শ্মশানে আছে উপস্থিত হইল
15. সুস্বাস্থ্য পর্যাপ্ত চিতার পরে যখন সব স্থাপিত করা হইল তখন তাহার রাঙা পা দুখানি দেখিয়া দুচোখ জুড়াইয়া গেল ইচ্ছা হইল ছুটিয়া গিয়া একবিন্দু আলো ছায়া লইয়া মাথায় দেয়
40. জাহিদ বিবাহ হইল তাহার নাম রফিক বাগ বাঘের অন্য বাঘিনী ছিল সে গ্রামান্তরে উঠিয়া গেল অভাগী তাহার অভাগ্য শিশুপুত্র কাঙ্গালি কে লইয়া আমি পড়িয়া রহিল
51. এই বয়সের ছেলে সচারাচার এর কিন্তু শিশুকাল হইতে বহুকাল যাবৎ রুগ্ন ছিল বলিয়া মায়ের কোড ছাড়িয়া বাহিরের সঙ্গী-সাথীদের বেশি বার সুযোগ পায় নাই
64. বাঙালি মায়ের বুকে ঠেস দিয়া বসিয়া ভাবিতে লাগিল
68. বাঙালির মা চুপ করিয়া রহিল বাঙালি তেমনি ধীরে ধীরে করিতে লাগিল বাবা যখন তড়িৎ ছেড়ে দিল কত লোক ধোনিকে করতে সাধাসাধি করলে
74. বস্তুত সেদিন তাহাকে পরামর্শ আমলকি দেয় নাই এবং যখন সে কিছুতেই রাজি হইল না যখন উৎপাত উপদ্রবও তাহার প্রতি সামান্য হয় নাই সে কথা স্মরণ করিয়া অভাগীর চোখ দিয়ে জল পড়িতে লাগিল
80. আর প্রলুব্ধ করিতে হইল না বাঙালি তৎক্ষণাৎ মায়ের বুকে শিয়া শিয়া পড়িয়া কহিল বল তাহলে
105. বোধকরি 30 টা বছর আজও পার হয়েছে কি হয় নাই শিশু হইল তেমনি সামান্য ভাবে
120. বাঙালি প্রথম অবস্থায় বাত্রা দিতে প্রবৃত্ত হইল
122. মুনতাহার জলে না ভিতরে জলপরী আধোয়া হয় ভাটিয়ালিতে চারদিকে ছড়িয়ে পড়ে মায়ের চোখ ছল ছল করিয়া আসিল
126. বাঙালির মা ইহার অর্থ বলছিল কিন্তু তাহার ভয় হইল না
139. পরদিন রশিদুল সময়মতো যখন আসিয়া উপস্থিত হইল যখন অভাগীর আর বড় জ্ঞান নাই
166. লোক গুলো যখন হিন্দুস্থানী টির কাছে প্রার্থনা নয় করিতে লাগিল বাঙালি উর্ধশ্বাসে দৌড় একেবারে কাছারিবাড়িতে আসে উপস্থিত হইল
196. হিজামার মায়ের হাতে পতাকা
200. বাংলা ছাড়িয়া হারাইলো তারপর ধীরে ধীরে বাহির হইয়া গেল
229. নিঃশব্দে ধীরে ধীরে তাহার মরা মায়ের কাছে গিয়ে উপস্থিত হইল

Figure 4-7: Text-summary generated after k-means clustering method for $optimal_2$ K of document C (summary3)

5. মেয়েরা কাদিতে কাদিতে মায়ের দুই পায়ে আলতা এবং মাথায় গনোরিয়া সিন্দুর লেবিয়া দিল বধু রান্না চন্দনে চর্চিত কোরিয়া বহুমূল্য বস্ত্রে শাশুড়ির দেহ আচ্ছাদিত করিয়া দিয়া আঁচল দিয়া তাহার শেষ পদধূলি বুঝাইয়া বইল
8. প্রবল হরিধ্বনি তে প্রভাত আকাশ আলোড়িত কোরিয়া সমস্ত গ্রাম সঙ্গে চলিল
37. ঢাকে জন্ম দিয়া মা মরিয়া ছিল বাঁকড়া উড়িয়া নাকি
64. বাঙালি মায়ের বুকে ঠেস দিয়া বসিয়া ভাবিতে লাগিল
75. ছেলে হাত দিয়া জল বুঝাইয়া দিয়া বলিল পেদে দেবো মা ছবি
81. রাজপুত্তুর কোটালপুত্র রাশি পঙ্খিরাজ ঘোড়া অভাগী রাজপুত্র কোটালপুত্র আর পক্ষীরাজ ঘোড়ার কথা দিয়া গল্প আরম্ভ করিল
85. ধার বিরাম নাই বিচ্ছেদ নয় বাঙালির স্বপ্ন দেহ বারবার রোমাঞ্চিত হইতে লাগিল
86. ভয়ে বিষয়ে পুলকেশীর সজোরে মায়ের গলা জড়াইয়া তার বুকের মধ্যে যেন মিশে যাইতে চাইলো
87. বাহিরের বেলা শেষ হইল সূর্য অস্ত গেল সন্ধ্যার গান ছায়া গারুলিয়া চরাচর ব্যাপ্ত করিল কিন্তু ঘরের মধ্যে আজার দিপজল ইলোনা গৃহস্থের শেষ কর্তব্য সমাধা করিতে কেউ ছিলনা নিবিড় অন্ধকার কেবল রুগ্ন মাথার অবাধ গুঞ্জন নিস্তব্ধ পুত্রের কানের সুধাবর্ষণ করিয়া চলিতে লাগিল
89. সেই রাতে সেই রাঙা দুটি সীতার স্বর্গে যাওয়া কেমন করিয়া শোকার্ত স্বামী শেষ পথ ভোলা দিয়া গা দিয়া বিদায় দিলেন কি করিয়া হরিধ্বনি দিয়া ছেলেরা মা তাকে বহন করিয়া লইয়া গেল তারপরে সন্তানের হাতের আগুন
99. পায়ে আলতা মাথায় সিঁদুর দিয়া কিন্তু কিভাবে
103. অভাগীর জীবন নাটের শেষ অংক পরিসমাপ্ত হইতে চলিল
107. বাঙালি কিয়া কাদাকাটি করিল হাতে পায়ে পরি লো ঘটি বাধা দিয়া তাহাকে এক টাকা প্রণামী দিল
138. জ্বর হওয়া অবধি মায়ের মুখে সেই কয়টা জিনিসের কথা এতবার এত রকম কুরিয়ার শুনি আছে যে শিখন হইতেই কাদিতে কাদিতে যাত্রা করিল
143. মৃত্যুপথযাত্রী তাহার ও বাহুখানি সূর্যের বাহিরে বাড়াইয়া দিয়া হাত পা দিল
155. এটা বোঝা গেল রাত্রি শেষ না হইতেই দুনিয়া সে তেরি আখি আছে
156. রাঙ্গুনিয়া একটা বেল গাছ একটা কুড়ুল চাহিয়া নিয়া রোহিঙ্গাদের ঘাটতি আছে কি দেয় নাই জমিদারের গাড়োয়ান কোথা হইতে ছুটিয়া আসিয়া গালি সশব্দে খাচ্চর কষাইয়া দিল
160. কিন্তু সে নাকি তার জননীর মৃতদেহ স্পর্শ করিয়া বসিয়া ছিল অশৌচের ভয় গায়ে হাত দিল
180. হামাক দিয়া বলিলেন মা পরিচিত যা এনেবেল
199. রাশিয়া গলা ধাক্কা দিল এমন কথা উচ্চারণ করিল যাহা কেবল জমিদারের কর্মচারীরাই পারে
229. নিঃশব্দে ধীরে ধীরে তাহার মরা মায়ের কাছে গিয়ে উপস্থিত হইল
231. রাখালের মা বাঙালির হাতে একটা ঘড়ি কি জালা দিয়া তাহারি হাত ধরিয়া মায়ের মুখের স্পর্শ করা ফেলিয়া দিল
232. তারপরে সকলে মিলিয়া মাটিচাপা দেয়া কাঙালীর মায়ের শেষ চিহ্ন বিলুপ্ত করিয়া দিল

Figure 4-8: Text-summary generated after k-means clustering method for $optimal_3$ K of document C (summary4)

mary quality can be attributed more directly to transcription errors rather than model brittleness. This design choice also makes the methods more applicable to low-resource settings, where computational efficiency and interpretability were essential.

4.3.4 Evaluation Strategy

To systematically assess the impact of ASR-induced transcription errors on summary quality, due to the subjective nature of the quality of a summary, we employed a subjective evaluation protocol grounded in the Mean Opinion Score (MOS) framework. This widely adopted metric in speech and multimedia evaluation offers a direct, human-centered estimate of perceptual quality.

4.3.4.1 Subjective Evaluation using MOS

10. সে কাঙালীর মা
21. উর্ধদৃষ্টে চাহিয়া কাঙালীর মায়ের দুই চোখে অশ্রুর ধারা বহিতেছিল এমন সময়ে একটি বছর চোদ্দ-পনরর ছেলে তাহার আঁচলে টান দিয়া কহিল হেথায় তুই দাড়িয়ে আছিস মা ভাত রাধবি নে
56. মা শশব্যস্তে ছেলের মুখে হাত চাপা দিয়া কহিল ছি বাবা মড়া-পোড়ানো বলতে নেই পাপ হয়
60. মা বলিল আমি যে চোখে দেখনু কাঙালী বামুন-মা রথের উপরে বসে
77. কাঙালী মাদুর পাতিল কাঁথা পাতিল মাচার উপর হইতে ছোট বালিশটি পাড়িয়া দিয়া হাত ধরিয়া তাহাকে বিছানায় টানিয়া লইয়া যাইতে মা কহিল কাঙালী আজ তোর আর কাজে গিয়ে কাজ নেই
92. কেন মা
107. কাঙালী গিয়া কাদাকাটি করিল হাতে-পায়ে পড়িল শেষে ঘটি বাধা দিয়া তাহাকে একটাকা প্রণামী দিল
116. কাঙালী কাঁদিয়া কহিল তুই বড়ি ত খেলি নে মা উনুনে ফেলে দিলি
185. কাঙালী বলিল মা যে আমাকে আগুন দিতে বলে গেছে
231. রাখালের মা কাঙালীর হাতে একটা খড়ের আঁটি জ্বালিয়া দিয়া তাহারই হাত ধরিয়া মায়ের মুখে স্পর্শ করাইয়া ফেলিয়া দিল

Figure 4-9: Summary from manual transcription of document C

10. কাঙালীর মা
21. উর্ধ্ব দৃষ্টি চাহিয়া কাঙালীর মায়ের দুই চোখে অশ্রুধারা বহিতে ছিল এ সময়ে একটি বছর 14 15 ছেলে আঁচলে টান দিয়া কহিল তুই দাড়িয়ে আছিস মা ভাতার বিনা
56. মা শশব্যস্তে ছেলের মুখে হাত চাপা দিয়া কহিল শিবা মরা পোড়ানো বলতে নেই পাপ হয়
64. বাঙালি মায়ের বুকে ঠেস দিয়া বসিয়া ভাবিতে লাগিল
68. বাঙালির মা চুপ করিয়া রহিল বাঙালি তেমনি ধীরে ধীরে করিতে লাগিল বাবা যখন তড়িৎ ছেড়ে দিল কত লোক ধোনিকে করতে সাধাসাধি করলে
75. ছেলে হাত দিয়া জল বুঝাইয়া দিয়া বলিল দেবো মা ছবি
77. বাঙালি মাদুর পাতিনি কথা পাতিল মাচার উপর হইতে বালিশটা পারিয়া দিয়া হাত ধরিয়া তাকে বিছানায় টানিয়া লইয়া যাইতে মা কহিল বাঙালি আজ তোরা কাজে গিয়ে কাজ নেই
116. বাঙালি কাঁদিয়া কহিল তুই তো বললি নে মা ফেলে দিলি
132. বাঙালি বলিল আসবে কেন মা
231. রাখালের মা বাঙালির হাতে একটা ঘড়ি কি জালা দিয়া তাহারি হাত ধরিয়া মায়ের মুখের স্পর্শ করা ফেলিয়া দিল

Figure 4-10: Summary from ASR transcription of document C

The evaluation protocol was carefully designed to compare the perceived quality of summaries generated from clean (manual) and noisy (ASR-based) transcripts (referred in Fig. 4-9 and Fig. 4-10, respectively). Specifically, both text and speech summaries were evaluated using the following procedure:

1. **Evaluation Scale:** A 5-point Likert scale (see Fig. 4-11) was used to grade each summary. The ratings ranged from 5 (Excellent) to 1 (Poor), with higher values reflecting better perceived quality.

5: Excellent

4: Good

3: Could be better

2: Bad

1: Poor

Figure 4-11: The Mean opinion score (MOS) scale for evaluating the subjective quality of the summaries.

2. **Participants:** Five independent human raters participated in the subjective evaluation [5]. All raters were native Bengali speakers with active engagement in Bengali literary communities. The evaluation panel consisted of five native Bengali speakers with professional backgrounds in Bengali literature. One rater is a practicing news columnist, two are literature educators, and two hold formal academic degrees in Bengali literature. All raters are actively engaged in literary activities and have experience in reading and evaluating narrative texts. Their experience in reading, writing, and analyzing literary texts made them well suited to judge the quality, coherence, and meaning of summaries generated from Bengali novels. The raters were not involved in developing the system and worked independently. Before the evaluation, they were given clear written instructions about how to score the summaries. Each rater reviewed the original spoken document along with the generated summaries and rated them based on informativeness and coherence. All ratings were collected separately and then combined for analysis.
3. **Criteria:** Each summary was rated based on two core aspects:
   - **Relevance:** How well the summary captured the main theme of the original document.
   - **Coverage:** Whether the summary included all the important subtopics or themes.
4. **Aggregation:** The final score for each summary $S(x)$ was computed as the

[5] While a larger number of raters is generally recommended for mean opinion score evaluations, the present study employs a limited panel to provide qualitative and indicative human judgments rather than statistically conclusive ratings.

mean of the five individual scores:

$$S(x) = \frac{1}{n}\sum_{i=1}^{n} sc(x_i) \tag{4.5}$$

where $sc(x_i)$was the score given by the ith evaluator and $n = 5$(refer to Table 4.15.

4.3.4.2 Comparative Evaluation: ASR vs Manual Transcripts

To isolate the effect of ASR errors on perceived quality, we compared summaries derived from ASR transcripts with those derived from manually corrected transcripts. For each document, summaries were generated using the same sentence selection strategies (ranking and clustering), and speech summaries were reconstructed by concatenating original spoken segments corresponding to the selected sentences.

The final MOS for text and speech summaries were reported in Table 4.15. For each pair, we compute a score difference:

$$D(t,u) = S(u) - S(t) \tag{4.6}$$

Table 4.15: Summary quality comparison between the text summaries and their corresponding speech summaries of the spoken documents A, B and C based on their Mean opinion scores (MOS)

Document ID d	Summary ID	Final MOS of text summary $S(t)$	Final MOS of speech summary $S(u)$	$D(t,u) = S(u) - S(t)$	Quality score of text summary $Q(t,d)$	Quality score of speech summary $Q(u,d)$
A	1	2.5	3.8	1.3	2	2.95
	2	3	3	0		
	3	1.25	2	0.75		
	4	1.25	3	1.75		
B	1	2.5	2.6	0.1	2.375	3.45
	2	3.5	3.6	0.1		
	3	1.5	3.2	1.7		
	4	2	4.4	2.4		
C	1	2	3	1	2	2.9
	2	1.6	3	1.4		
	3	2.6	3.6	1		
	4	1.8	2	0.2		

Here, $S(t)$ and $S(u)$ represent the final MOS scores for the text and speech summaries respectively. The difference D acts as a proxy for quantifying the effect of transcription errors: a large positive D suggests the text summary's readability suffered due to ASR errors, while the speech version (being error-free) retained listener clarity.

Observations and Interpretation: The data reveals consistent trends:

- **Speech summaries outperform text summaries** in most cases, especially when ASR errors severely degrade text readability.
- In some cases, low $S(u)$ and $S(t)$ together imply that poor sentence selection (due to ASR errors) led to low-quality summaries in both modalities.
- The threshold $D = 1.0$ was used to flag significant readability degradation due to ASR errors.

The score difference sheds light on how the ASR-errors played on the reader's perception of the quality of a summary. In our work, we consider two criteria based on which the effect of ASR errors on the quality of a summary was analyzed: the quality of sentence selection during summarization, and the readability of the summary created.

1. For $D >= 1.0$, it indicates the score achieved of speech summary i.e. $S(u)$ was quite higher than the score of text summary i.e. $S(t)$. The threshold value for D was set as 1, based on the mean value calculated from all the D instances (which can be observed from Table 4.15), ensuring that any D with a score below this threshold was considered below average. It must be kept in mind that speech summary represents the perfect error-less transcription of the summary represented by the error-full text summary. High $S(u)$ indicates sentence-selection in the summarization process doesn't suffer significantly due to presence of ASR errors. The only possible cause of low $S(t)$ was poor readability due to the presence of ASR errors.
2. The case of $D < 1.0$, suggests two possible scenarios.
    (a) Scores of both text summary $S(t)$ and speech summary $S(u)$ were < 3. For distinguishing between a *good* summary and a *bad* summary, the score of 3 was chosen as a threshold, due to its position between 1 and 5 on the MOS scale. In this case, the perfect error-less transcription represented by speech summary scores as bad as error-full text summary. This indicates that the sentence-selection in summarization process suffers due to the presence of ASR errors. This results in overall poor quality summary in both mediums.
    (b) Scores of both text summary $S(t)$ and speech summary $S(u)$ were $>= 3$. In other words, both the perfect error-less transcription rep-

resented by speech summary and error-full text summary perform favourably. This indicates that the sentence-selection in summarization process does not suffer due to the presence of ASR errors. Additionally, readability was also unaffected significantly as seen by favourable score of text summary. This can possibly mean ASR errors were relatively less in these summaries.

This analysis was encapsulated in Table 4.16, where ✓ indicates that summary quality was unaffected by ASR errors, while × indicate the summary quality affected by ASR errors. The score difference D was thus a quantitative metric adopted to analyze the effects of ASR errors on quality of a summary, based on the scores obtained using subjective evaluation by MOS scale.

These findings highlight the dual impact of transcription errors: they degrade sentence selection (summary content) and hinder readability (summary form). Hence, even when summary-worthy sentences were present in the transcript, ASR noise may render them unreadable in text form—while the speech version remains intelligible.

Table 4.16: Effect of ASR errors on two criteria of summary quality.

Summary quality	$D >= 1$	$D < 1$	
		$S(t) and S(u) >= 3$	$S(t) and S(u) < 3$
Sentence selection	✓	✓	×
Readability	×	✓	×

A more direct representation of the perceived quality of the text summaries and their counterpart speech summaries were made in Fig. 4-15 where all the scores received by each summary were averaged and compared. Overall summary quality $Q(x, Y)$ of a summary-medium x (either text, or speech) was given by

$$Q(x, Y) = \frac{\sum_{i=1}^{n_Y} S(x)}{n_Y} \quad \text{where } x \in \{t, u\} \tag{4.7}$$

where n_Y was the number of summaries (four for text-summaries and four for speech summaries) for document Y; t and u indicates text and speech summary respectively; $S(x)$ indicates the score for the summary in medium x. The detailed scores were presented in Table 4.15.

4.4 Discussion and Implications

This chapter set out to understand a core problem in speech-based summarization for low-resource languages: *how do ASR errors distort the extractive summa-*

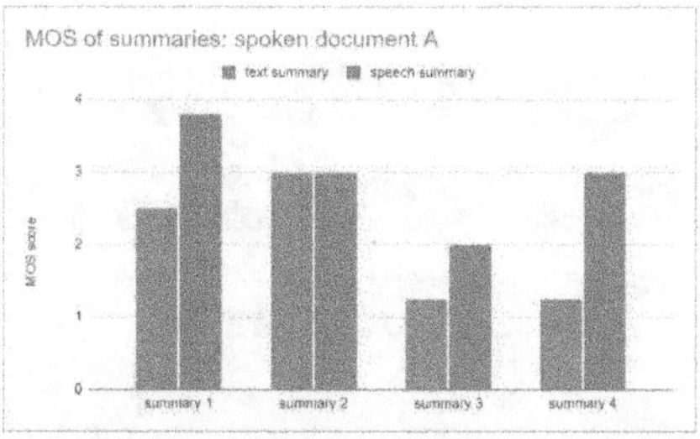

Figure 4-12: Mean opinion score for the summaries of spoken document A.

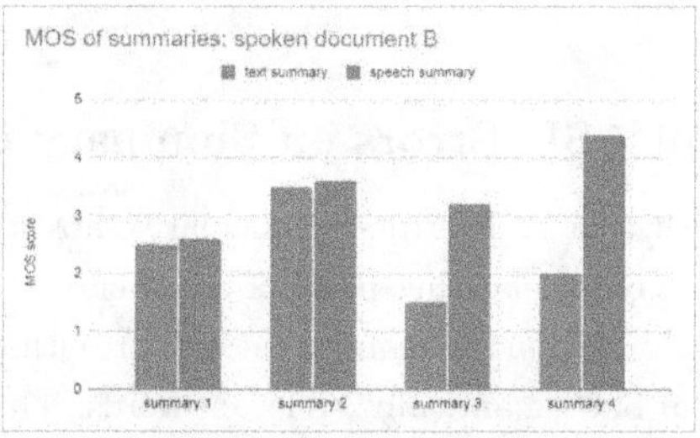

Figure 4-13: Mean opinion score for the summaries of spoken document B.

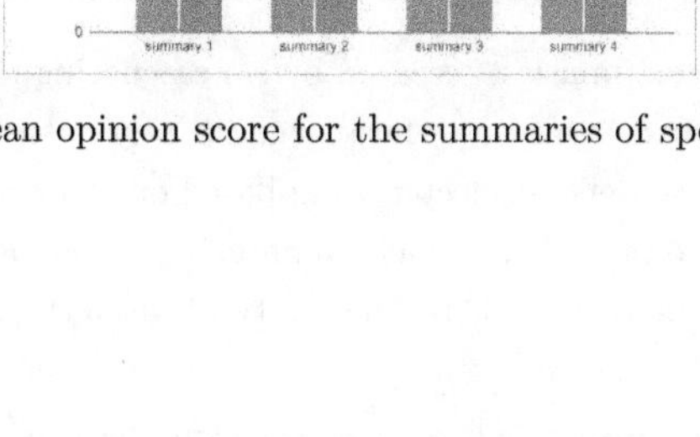

Figure 4-14: Mean opinion score for the summaries of spoken document C.

rization process? Through a focused case study on Bengali speech documents and widely-used unsupervised techniques, this analysis provides empirical evidence that such errors significantly degrade the informativeness and readability of summaries—both in their textual and spoken forms.

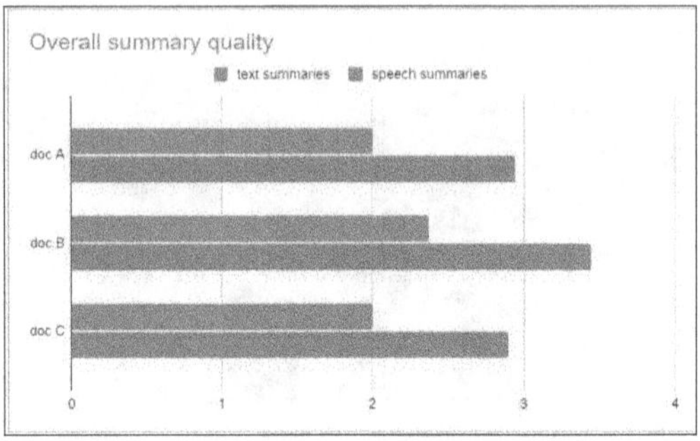

Figure 4-15: The perceived quality of the summaries in both text and speech medium after evaluation.

4.4.1 Impact of ASR Errors on Summary Quality

The results make clear that ASR errors, particularly substitutions and deletions, often affect the most content-bearing parts of a sentence. In many cases, words that carried crucial information for summarization were either omitted or replaced by phonetically similar but semantically irrelevant words. This had a direct impact on sentence selection during summarization.

As shown in Figures 4-9 and 4-10, and Tables 4.15, 4.17, the summaries generated from ASR-transcripts consistently scored lower on Mean Opinion Score (MOS) evaluations. This degradation occurred even when the same summarization method (sentence-ranking or k-means clustering) was used across both manual and ASR transcripts, as seen in Tables 4.17.

4.4.2 Speech Summaries as a Reference Standard

Interestingly, speech summaries—created by concatenating the corresponding audio segments of the text-summary—fared significantly better in subjective evaluation. Although the sentences selected were based on error-prone transcripts, the spoken form preserved prosody and natural phrasing. This suggests that while sentence selection may be distorted, the modality of delivery plays a compensatory role in human comprehension.

However, it also reinforces a key insight: speech summarization pipelines that rely exclusively on ASR outputs were inherently vulnerable in low-resource contexts.

Table 4.17: Performance comparison of sentence-ranking and k-means clustering methods for generating text summary and speech summary for spoken documents A, B and C based on their Mean-opinion scores (MOS)

Summary Method	MOS of speech summary			MOS of text summary		
	A	B	C	A	B	C
Sentence-ranking	**3.8**	2.6	3	2.5	2.5	2
K-means for $optimal_1$ clusters	3	3.6	3	**3**	**3.5**	1.6
K-means for $optimal_2$ clusters	2	3.2	**3.6**	1.25	1.5	**2.6**
K-means for $optimal_3$ clusters	3	**4.4**	2	1.25	2	1.8

4.4.3 Why the Problem Isn't the Model

One might argue that more sophisticated summarization models could correct for transcription noise. However, the methods used in this study—TF-IDF based ranking and clustering—were intentionally simple and interpretable. This was by design: to isolate the effect of ASR quality from the modeling sophistication. Therefore, the observed degradation was not due to weak summarization methods, but to the quality of input representations themselves.

This has broader implications. Even if a neural summarizer were used, if it was trained or deployed on faulty transcripts, its input representations were already compromised. Garbage in, garbage out.

4.4.4 Implications for Low-Resource Speech Technology

The findings of this chapter underscore a harsh but important truth: conventional speech summarization pipelines, which work well in high-resource languages like English, do not directly transfer to languages like Bengali. Without reliable ASR, these pipelines collapse at the very first stage.

Thus, future efforts must explore alternatives. One path was the development of ASR-robust or ASR-free summarization systems—such as those relying on acoustic-prosodic cues (see Chapter 6). Another direction was the incorporation of error-aware learning mechanisms that can infer summary-worthiness from noisy inputs.

4.5 Chapter Summary

To summarize, this chapter presented a detailed empirical analysis of how ASR-induced transcription errors compromise extractive summarization in Bengali speech. The chapter used unsupervised summarization methods to isolate the effect of transcript quality, and a subjective human evaluation to quantify the impact. The analysis in this chapter has shown that transcription errors—particularly deletions and substitutions—significantly harm the quality of extractive summaries when generated from ASR-transcribed speech. These effects were observed consistently across multiple evaluation settings and summarization methods. These insights motivate the need for text-independent or robust approaches to summarization in low-resource settings—precisely the focus of the upcoming chapters.

Chapter 5

Evaluating text-based extractive speech summarization methods in low-resource language

Automatic speech recognition (ASR) systems often introduce transcription errors that distort the original context and reduce the salience of spoken content. The observations made in the previous chapter (Chapter 4) motivate the need to explore alternative directions. One of them, addressed in this chapter, was to test a wider range of extractive summarization strategies that may be more robust to noisy transcriptions. This chapter evaluates several widely-used summarization algorithms—including graph-based, topic-model-based, and redundancy-aware techniques—combined with different types of sentence embeddings, to determine whether some methods degrade more gracefully than others in the presence of ASR noise.

5.1 Introduction

Text-based methods for speech summarization typically rely on transcriptions generated by Automatic Speech Recognition (ASR) systems. These methods have become the foundation of most modern summarization systems due to their simplicity and reliance on established natural language processing (NLP) techniques, including extractive summarization and abstractive summarization [14]. In extractive summarization, sentences or segments deemed most relevant to the main topics of the speech are selected, based on a variety of features derived from the ASR-transcribed text. These features often include lexical content, syntactic structure, and semantic analysis.

5.1.1 Limitations in Low-Resource ASR Settings

However, the effectiveness of text-based summarization is directly tied to the quality of the ASR system and the availability of clean, reliable transcriptions. In high-resource languages like English, where large-scale datasets for training ASR models are readily available, text-based methods have been largely successful. But in low-resource languages, the situation is quite different. The lack of substantial linguistic resources, training data, and sophisticated ASR models creates substantial barriers for implementing these methods effectively.

One of the major challenges is the high word error rate (WER) typically associated with ASR outputs in low-resource languages. Inaccurate or noisy transcriptions degrade the quality of the summaries generated by these systems. Even when advanced ASR systems are available, they often struggle with mispronunciations, code-switching, and other language-specific nuances, resulting in transcriptions that poorly reflect the intended meaning of the speech. This, in turn, leads to reduced summarization performance, as text-based summarization models rely heavily on accurate text input.

Another key limitation is the linguistic diversity and complex sentence structures present in many low-resource languages, which complicate the extraction of relevant information from ASR outputs. For example, in languages like Bengali and other Indic languages, regional dialects, morphological variation, and syntactic complexity present significant hurdles for standard ASR systems. Furthermore, the use of prosodic elements such as pitch, rhythm, and pauses to convey meaning—common in these languages—remains largely unaccounted for in text-based summarization methods.

In response to these limitations, research has explored using richer embeddings or additional textual features to improve the quality of text-based summarization. Approaches such as embedding-based sentence representations, including pre-trained models like BERT or transformers, have shown promise in boosting performance in more resource-rich languages [39, 90]. These techniques, however, still rely fundamentally on the availability of clean, accurate ASR transcriptions, which remain a significant bottleneck in low-resource contexts.

Moreover, while significant progress has been made in the development of deep learning-based models for extractive summarization in high-resource languages, such models were often computationally expensive and may not be viable in resource-constrained environments. This further limits the applicability of text-based methods in low-resource settings, where computational resources and annotated data were scarce.

5.1.2 Motivation

In summary, while text-based methods have proven successful in high-resource contexts, their reliance on accurate ASR systems and clean transcriptions makes them less practical in low-resource settings. The limitations discussed above—high WER, insufficient training data, and the lack of prosodic features—highlight the need for alternative approaches. Accordingly, this chapter evaluates how a set of widely-used extractive summarization techniques—including frequency-based, graph-based, topic modeling, and redundancy-aware methods—perform when paired with different sentence embeddings under noisy ASR conditions, with the goal of identifying combinations that are more resilient to transcription errors in low-resource settings.

5.2 Comparative Setup

In speech summarization pipelines, extractive summarization typically follows an ASR step that converts speech into text. The summarization system then identifies and selects the most salient sentences from the transcript based on content relevance. This process assumes the availability of high-quality textual input, which becomes a limiting factor in low-resource ASR settings where errors are common. Understanding how summarization methods interact with such noisy transcriptions is critical for building robust speech summarization systems.

Despite the rise of neural approaches, traditional extractive summarization methods remain relevant in low-resource contexts due to their low computational cost, interpretability, and minimal data requirements. These methods—such as TextRank, Latent Semantic Analysis, and Maximal Marginal Relevance—require no task-specific fine-tuning and can be quickly adapted using off-the-shelf NLP toolkits. Evaluating their robustness in the presence of ASR errors helps determine whether these lightweight strategies can still serve as viable baselines in low-resource speech settings.

5.3 Text-Based Extractive Speech Summarization

Text-based extractive summarization is a widely used approach in spoken document processing pipelines, particularly due to its simplicity, interpretability, and minimal training requirements. These methods function by selecting a subset of sentences from the input document that are considered most representative of its overall content. When applied to spoken documents, this process typically follows automatic transcription by an ASR system, treating the resulting text as input for standard summarization algorithms. An overview of the most popular methods that has been the foundation of text-based extractive summarization is given in Table 5.1.

Table 5.1: Overview of Popular Text-Based Extractive Summarization Methods for Speech

Method	Category	Core Mechanism	Typical Input	Limitations in Noisy ASR Settings
Luhn (1958) [58], Edmundson (1969) [19]	Statistical	Cue words, word frequency	Word counts, TF-IDF	Ignores semantic content; highly sensitive to ASR distortion
TextRank (2004) [71], LexRank (2004) [21]	Graph-based	Centrality in sentence graph	TF-IDF, GloVe	Sentence similarity reduced by transcription errors
LSA (2001) [30], Gong & Liu	Latent semantic	Topic extraction via SVD	TF-IDF matrix	Co-occurrence stats distorted by ASR noise
LDA (2003), Malioutov	Topic-aware	Topic distributions	Bag-of-words, TF-IDF	Weak with short-/noisy utterances
MMR (1998), Zhu et al.	Redundancy-aware	Relevance–novelty balance	TF-IDF, embeddings	Sensitive to similarity distortion from noise
BERT-based models [39, 60, 90] (2019–)	Contextual embeddings	Transformer-based sentence vectors	BERT, XLM-R	Require large data; prone to performance drop in low-resource noisy ASR

Extractive summarization techniques have evolved across three broad categories:

- **Statistical methods**, such as sentence ranking based on term frequency or TF-IDF scores, operate on surface-level lexical information.
- **Graph-based methods**, such as TextRank, represent sentences as nodes in a graph and rank them using centrality measures derived from inter-sentence similarity [71].
- **Topic-aware methods**, such as Latent Semantic Analysis (LSA) and Latent Dirichlet Allocation (LDA), leverage latent topics to guide sentence selection toward thematic coherence [30].

Despite their design for well-formed text, these methods are often deployed in speech settings without adaptation, assuming the transcription is sufficiently accurate. However, in low-resource languages—where ASR systems are typically trained on limited and noisy data—transcriptions often suffer from high word error rates, omissions, or distorted syntactic structures. These limitations significantly affect the performance of extractive methods, which rely heavily on the integrity of lexical and semantic cues.

This study evaluates how representative summarization strategies from each of these three categories perform when used with transcriptions that contain ASR errors. The goal is to empirically assess whether certain summarization methods are inherently more resilient to noise and to understand how their performance varies with different sentence representations.

5.4 Methodology

5.4.1 Representing sentences using word-embedding methods

Text embeddings are a foundational component of many natural language processing (NLP) tasks. They transform words or sentences into dense vector representations that encode semantic and syntactic properties of the text. In this work, four embedding methods were used to represent sentences: TF-IDF [5], FastText [112], XLM-R [60], and GloVe [85]. Except for TF-IDF, all embeddings were derived from pretrained word vectors specific to Bengali. Sentence representations were obtained by aggregating word-level vectors, typically through averaging. The following sections describe each embedding method in detail.

1. **TF-IDF** (Term Frequency-Inverse Document Frequency) [5]is a statistical measure used to evaluate the importance of a word in a document relative to a collection of documents (corpus). It is widely used in information retrieval and text mining to transform raw text into a numerical representation. The TF-IDF value for a term t in a document d within a corpus D s the product of two components: Term Frequency (TF) which indicates the relevance of a term within a document, and Inverse Document Frequency (IDF) which reduces the weight of common words that appear in many documents and increases the weight of rare words. TF measures how often a term t appears in a document d. It can be defined as:

$$\mathrm{TF}(t,d) = \frac{f_{t,d}}{\sum_{t' \in d} f_{t',d}} \tag{5.1}$$

where $f_{t,d}$ was the frequency of term t in a document d, and the denominator was the sum of frequencies of all terms in d.

IDF measures how unique or rare a term was across the entire corpus D. It is defined as:

$$\text{IDF}(t, D) = \log\left(\frac{N}{|\{d \in D : t \in d\}|}\right) \tag{5.2}$$

where N was the total number of documents in the corpus, and $|\{d \in D : t \in d\}|$ was the number of documents containing the term t. The TF-IDF score for a term t in a document d is given by:

$$\text{TF-IDF}(t, d, D) = \text{TF}(t, d) \times \text{IDF}(t, D) \tag{5.3}$$

The resulting TF-IDF score helps in identifying terms that were significant for a particular document but not common across all documents.

2. **FastText** [112] is an extension of the Word2Vec model developed by Facebook AI Research that enhances the handling of rare and out-of-vocabulary (OOV) words through subword information. Unlike traditional word embeddings that map entire words to vectors, FastText breaks down words into character-level n-grams, allowing it to capture subword structures and morphological variations. FastText represents each word as a bag of character n-grams. Given a word w, FastText represents it using the set of its subwords (character n-grams). Let $G(w)$ be the set of all n-grams for the word w. The vector representation of the word w, denoted as v_{word}, is then defined as:

$$v_{\text{word}} = \sum_{g \in G(w)} v_g \tag{5.4}$$

where v_g represents the embedding vector for the n-gram g. This approach allows FastText to construct robust representations that capture morphological information, making it well-suited for languages with rich morphology or complex word forms.
FastText uses the Skip-gram model with negative sampling for training, similar to Word2Vec. The main difference lies in the inclusion of subword units. The objective of the Skip-gram model was to maximize the probability of context words given the central word:

$$\sum_{w \in V} \sum_{c \in C(w)} \log P(c|w) \tag{5.5}$$

where V was the vocabulary, $C(w)$ was the context of the word w, and $P(c|w)$ was defined using the softmax function:

$$P(c|w) = \frac{\exp(\mathbf{v}_c \cdot \mathbf{v}_w)}{\sum_{w' \in V} \exp(\mathbf{v}_{w'} \cdot \mathbf{v}_w)} \tag{5.6}$$

For negative sampling, this objective can be simplified to:

$$\log \sigma(\mathbf{v}_c \cdot \mathbf{v}_w) + \sum_{k=1}^{K} \mathbb{E}_{w_k \sim P_n(w)}[\log \sigma(-\mathbf{v}_{w_k} \cdot \mathbf{v}_w)] \tag{5.7}$$

where σ was the sigmoid function, K was the number of negative samples, and $P_n(w)$ was a noise distribution. The subword-based representation enables FastText to generalize better to morphologically rich languages and noisy ASR outputs.

3. **XLM-R (XLM-RoBERTa)** [60] is a multilingual variant of the RoBERTa model, which itself is an optimized version of BERT (Bidirectional Encoder Representations from Transformers). XLM-R was designed to handle multiple languages effectively, providing high performance on a range of natural language processing (NLP) tasks across various languages, including those with limited training data. It was pre-trained on a massive multilingual corpus using a masked language modeling (MLM) objective. XLM-R uses subword tokenization (Byte-Pair Encoding, BPE) to represent input sequences. Given an input sentence S, it was tokenized into a sequence of subwords $(x_1, x_2, ..., x_n)$. Each subword was embedded into a vector space using an embedding matrix E. The MLM training objective involves randomly masking a subset of the input tokens and predicting the masked tokens based on their surrounding context. Let X be the input sequence of subword embeddings, with M as the masked tokens:

$$X_{masked} = (x_1, M_2, ..., x_n) \tag{5.8}$$

The goal was to maximize the likelihood of the masked tokens given their context:

$$\mathcal{L}_{MLM} = - \sum_{i \in \text{masked}} \log P(x_i \mid X_{\text{masked}}) \tag{5.9}$$

XLM-R uses a stack of transformer encoder layers, each composed of multi-head self-attention mechanisms and position-wise feed-forward networks. For an input $H^{(l)}$ at layer l, the self-attention mechanism computes:

$$\text{Attention}(Q, K, V) = \text{softmax}\left(\frac{QK^T}{\sqrt{d_k}}\right) V \tag{5.10}$$

where Q, K and V were the query, key, and value matrices, respectively, and d_k was the dimension of the key vectors.

XLM-R was pre-trained on CommonCrawl data in 100 languages, using more than 2 terabytes of text data. This extensive training enables it to learn cross-lingual representations, making it highly effective for multilingual tasks.

4. **GloVe** (Global Vectors for Word Representation) [85] create vector representations of words based on the global statistical information of a corpus, such as the frequency with which words co-occur within a specified context. GloVe constructs word embeddings by factorizing a word co-occurrence matrix. The core idea was that word relationships can be captured by examining how frequently pairs of words appear within a defined context window in a large corpus. GloVe was based on the principle that the relationships between words in a corpus can be captured by a word-to-word co-occurrence matrix, where each element of the matrix indicates the frequency of one word appearing in the context of another. Let X be a co-occurrence matrix where each entry X_{ij} represents the number of times word j appears in the context of word i. The goal was to learn word vectors w_i and context vectors c_j for each word and context, respectively. GloVe attempts to factorize the matrix X into two lower-dimensional matrices:

$$X_{ij} \approx \mathbf{w}_i^T \mathbf{c}_j \tag{5.11}$$

where w_i was the word vector for word i, and c_j was the context vector for word j. The GloVe model optimizes a cost function based on the weighted least squares objective. The objective function is:

$$J = \sum_{i,j=1}^{V} f(X_{ij}) \left(\mathbf{w}_i^T \mathbf{c}_j + b_i + b_j - \log X_{ij} \right)^2 \tag{5.12}$$

where X_{ij} was the co-occurrence count of words i and j, b_i and b_j were biases for the word and context vectors, $f(X_{ij})$ was a weighting function that down-weights the importance of very frequent word pairs and prevents the model from overfitting to these common co-occurrences. Typically,

$$f(X_{ij}) = \begin{cases} \left(\frac{x_{\max}}{X_{ij}} \right)^{\alpha}, & \text{if } X_{ij} < x_{\max} \\ 1, & \text{otherwise} \end{cases} \tag{5.13}$$

GloVe embeddings effectively capture both syntactic and semantic word relationships, making them useful for various NLP tasks.

5.4.2 Summarization Methods

This section details the extractive summarization techniques evaluated in this study. All methods operate on sentence-level representations and select a subset of sentences from the input transcript to form the summary. The methods differ in how they compute sentence importance, ranging from graph-based centrality to topic modeling and relevance-redundancy balancing. We provide the mathematical formulation for each technique below.

5.4.2.1 Ranking-Based Method

This is a simple unsupervised baseline where sentence scores were computed as the mean of their constituent word embeddings. Let a sentence $S = \{w_1, w_2, ..., w_n\}$ be represented by word vectors $v(w_i) \in \mathbb{R}^d$. The sentence embedding $v(S)$ was computed as:

$$v(S) = \frac{1}{n} \sum_{i=1}^{n} v(w_i) \tag{5.14}$$

Sentence scores were calculated using cosine similarity between $v(S)$ and the centroid vector v_{doc} of the full document:

$$v_{\text{doc}} = \frac{1}{m} \sum_{j=1}^{m} v(S_j) \tag{5.15}$$

$$\text{Score}(S) = \cos(v(S), v_{\text{doc}}) = \frac{v(S) \cdot v_{\text{doc}}}{\|v(S)\| \cdot \|v_{\text{doc}}\|} \tag{5.16}$$

Sentences were ranked by this score, and the top k were selected for the summary.

5.4.2.2 TextRank

TextRank is an unsupervised graph-based ranking algorithm inspired by PageRank [71]. Sentences were nodes in a graph, and edges denote similarity. Let $G = (V, E)$ be an undirected graph where each vertex v_i corresponds to sentence S_i. Edge weights were given by pairwise sentence similarity, typically cosine similarity:

$$w_{ij} = \cos(v(S_i), v(S_j)) \tag{5.17}$$

Let $R(S_i)$ denote the score of sentence S_i. The recursive update rule is:

$$R(S_i) = (1 - d) + d \sum_{j \in \text{Adj}(i)} \frac{w_{ji}}{\sum_{k \in \text{Adj}(j)} w_{jk}} R(S_j) \tag{5.18}$$

where d was a damping factor (typically 0.85), and $\text{Adj}(i)$ was the set of sentences adjacent to S_i. Scores were iteratively updated until convergence, and top-scoring sentences were selected.

5.4.2.3 Latent Semantic Analysis (LSA)

LSA performs dimensionality reduction on the sentence-term matrix to identify latent topics [30]. Let $A \in \mathbb{R}^{m \times n}$ be a term-sentence matrix, where A_{ij} was the TF-IDF weight of term i in sentence j. Singular Value Decomposition (SVD) factorizes A as:

$$A = U \Sigma V^T \tag{5.19}$$

Here, U and V were orthogonal matrices, and Σ was a diagonal matrix of singular values. LSA approximates A using the top-k singular values:

$$A_k \approx U_k \Sigma_k V_k^T \tag{5.20}$$

The rows of V_k^T represent sentences in the reduced topic space. Sentence scores were calculated using the L_2 norm of these representations:

$$\text{Score}(S_j) = \|V_k^T[j,:]\| \tag{5.21}$$

5.4.2.4 Latent Dirichlet Allocation (LDA)

LDA is a generative probabilistic model that assigns topics to sentences based on a Dirichlet prior. For a corpus of D documents and K topics:

- For each document d, draw a topic distribution $\theta_d \sim \text{Dir}(\alpha)$
- For each word w_n in document d:
  - Choose a topic $z_n \sim \text{Multinomial}(\theta_d)$
  - Choose a word $w_n \sim \text{Multinomial}(\beta_{z_n})$

LDA infers the topic distribution θ_d for each sentence. To score a sentence S_i, we compute the entropy of its topic distribution:

$$\text{Score}(S_i) = -\sum_{k=1}^{K} \theta_{ik} \log \theta_{ik} \tag{5.22}$$

Low entropy implies strong topic alignment and higher informativeness. Top-k low-entropy sentences were selected.

5.4.2.5 Maximal Marginal Relevance (MMR)

MMR balances relevance to the document and redundancy with already-selected sentences. Let S be the set of selected sentences, and R the set of remaining candidates. At each step, MMR selects sentence s^* that maximizes:

$$s^* = \arg\max_{s \in R} \left[\lambda \cdot \mathrm{Sim}(s, Q) - (1 - \lambda) \cdot \max_{s' \in S} \mathrm{Sim}(s, s') \right] \tag{5.23}$$

Here, Q was the document vector (or centroid), Sim was cosine similarity, and $\lambda \in [0, 1]$ balances relevance and redundancy. This iterative process continues until the desired number of summary sentences was selected.

Table 5.2: Summary of Extractive Summarization Methods Evaluated

Method	**Category**	**Core Idea**	**Notes / Limitations**
Sentence Ranking	Statistical	Ranks sentences by global scores	Sensitive to surface-level features; prone to redundancy
TextRank	Graph-based	Builds sentence similarity graph	Ignores topic structure; struggles with ASR noise
Latent Semantic Analysis (LSA)	Statistical	Captures latent topics via matrix decomposition (SVD)	Limited semantic richness; susceptible to noisy data
Latent Dirichlet Allocation (LDA)	Topic-aware	Models document as a mixture of latent topics	Ineffective for short sentences or sparse input
Maximal Marginal Relevance (MMR)	Graph-based	Selects sentences balancing relevance and diversity	Redundancy-aware but depends heavily on similarity threshold

A summary of these text-based methods is given in Table 5.2.

5.5 Experimental setup

5.5.1 Data description

The experiments were conducted on a subset of a larger manually curated speech summarization corpus developed in a previous chapter (Chapter 3). This portion of the dataset consists of Bengali audiobook recordings, as detailed in Chapter 3. The audiobooks include narrated fictional content, segmented into sentence-level utterances for analysis. On average, each spoken sentence spans approximately 45 seconds. The corresponding transcriptions were generated using Google Speech

API ASR system and exhibit moderate word error rates typical of low-resource settings (detailed in Chapter 4). Handwritten extractive summaries were prepared by five independent annotators, following a standard summarization protocol. These reference summaries were used to evaluate extractive outputs generated under different experimental conditions.

The text transcriptions of the spoken documents were generated using the Bengali ASR of Google Cloud Speech API [1]. The vocabulary difference between manual and ASR transcriptions in Table 5.3 is mainly due to recognition errors introduced by the ASR system. ASR outputs may contain substitutions, deletions, or incorrect word forms caused by noise, speaker variability, or pronunciation differences. These errors introduce vocabulary items that do not appear in manual transcriptions, leading to a mismatch in vocabulary despite similar underlying content.

Table 5.3: Metadata of the corpus used.

No. of sentences	685
No. of words in manual transcription	31246
No. of words in ASR transcription	29381
Size of vocabulary in manual transcription	5126
Size of vocabulary in ASR transcription	4768

5.5.2 Summary Generation

Each summarization method produced extractive summaries by selecting a fixed proportion (i.e., top 20%) of sentences based on internal ranking or scoring. The summary length was kept constant across methods and embeddings for comparability.

5.5.3 Evaluation Metrics

To quantitatively evaluate the similarity between system-generated and human-generated (reference) summaries, the widely-used ROUGE (Recall-Oriented Understudy for Gisting Evaluation) metrics [52] was adopted. ROUGE computes the overlap of units such as n-grams, word sequences, or word pairs between the candidate and reference summaries. The following variants were considered:

- **ROUGE-1:** Measures unigram (i.e., single word) overlap between the candidate summary and the reference summary. It captures basic lexical similarity.

[1]This API was used through Google API client library for Python language, which was a part of the package SpeechRecognition 3.8.1 to be installed in platforms supporting Python. For more details of this package, check https://pypi.org/project/SpeechRecognition/

$$\text{ROUGE-1 Recall} = \frac{\sum_{w \in \text{Ref}} \min(\text{Count}_{\text{Cand}}(w), \text{Count}_{\text{Ref}}(w))}{\sum_{w \in \text{Ref}} \text{Count}_{\text{Ref}}(w)} \tag{5.24}$$

where w was a unigram, $\text{Count}_{\text{Cand}}(w)$ was its frequency in the candidate summary, and $\text{Count}_{\text{Ref}}(w)$ was its frequency in the reference summary.

- **ROUGE-2:** Measures bigram (two-word sequence) overlap. This metric was more sensitive to word ordering and syntactic patterns than ROUGE-1.

$$\text{ROUGE-2 Recall} = \frac{\sum_{b \in \text{Ref}} \min(\text{Count}_{\text{Cand}}(b), \text{Count}_{\text{Ref}}(b))}{\sum_{b \in \text{Ref}} \text{Count}_{\text{Ref}}(b)} \tag{5.25}$$

where b denotes a bigram.

- **ROUGE-L:** Based on the Longest Common Subsequence (LCS), ROUGE-L evaluates the fluency and sentence-level similarity between summaries. Unlike ROUGE-1/2, LCS does not require consecutive matches but does preserve the original order of words.

  Let $LCS(X,Y)$ denote the length of the longest common subsequence between the reference X and candidate Y:

$$\text{ROUGE-L Recall} = \frac{LCS(X,Y)}{\text{Length}(X)} \qquad \text{ROUGE-L Precision} = \frac{LCS(X,Y)}{\text{Length}(Y)} \tag{5.26}$$

  The F1 score was computed as:

$$\text{ROUGE-L F1} = \frac{(1+\beta^2) \cdot \text{Precision} \cdot \text{Recall}}{\beta^2 \cdot \text{Precision} + \text{Recall}} \tag{5.27}$$

  where β was typically set to 1 to give equal weight to recall and precision.

All ROUGE scores reported in this thesis were computed using recall and F1 measures, averaged across all documents in the test set. While ROUGE was a useful baseline, its reliance on lexical overlap can underrepresent the quality of summaries derived from prosodic or non-lexical cues, especially in low-resource language scenarios.

For each summarization method and embedding combination, average ROUGE scores were reported over all sessions in the test set.

5.6 Results and Analysis

We are conducting two kinds of comparisons in this analysis: method-wise and embedding-wise. The method-wise analysis evaluates the performance of different unsupervised summarization techniques, highlighting how various approaches handle the challenges posed by noisy ASR-generated transcripts. In contrast, the embedding-wise analysis examines the effectiveness of different text representations in capturing semantic and contextual relationships, especially when transitioning from clean manual transcripts to noisy ASR outputs. Together, these perspectives provide a comprehensive understanding of the factors influencing summarization performance, setting the stage for deeper insights into the interplay between summarization methods and embedding quality. The subsequent sections delve into these analyses to explore how these factors contribute to the observed trends and performance degradations.

5.6.1 Performance Degradation Across Summarization Methods in ASR-Generated Transcripts

Table 5.4: Performance Comparison for TF-IDF Embedding: Manual vs. ASR Transcripts

Method	Manual Transcripts			ASR Transcripts		
	R1	R2	RL	R1	R2	RL
Ranking	0.563	0.397	0.278	0.426	0.184	0.146
TextRank	0.501	0.318	0.215	0.424	0.177	0.133
LSA	0.444	0.247	0.206	0.374	0.144	0.155
LDA	0.506	0.305	0.362	0.398	0.150	0.216
MMR	0.545	0.338	0.311	0.351	0.097	0.136

Table 5.5: Performance Comparison for FastText Embedding: Manual vs. ASR Transcripts

Method	Manual Transcripts			ASR Transcripts		
	R1	R2	RL	R1	R2	RL
Ranking	0.604	0.458	0.304	0.442	0.218	0.149
TextRank	0.585	0.414	0.264	0.441	0.212	0.167
LSA	0.383	0.179	0.174	0.328	0.101	0.123
LDA	0.473	0.295	0.409	0.338	0.113	0.179
MMR	0.585	0.414	0.280	0.444	0.210	0.206

The method-wise analysis of summarization performance for each embedding—TF-IDF, FastText, XLM-R, and GloVe—provides an in-depth view of how various

Table 5.6: Performance Comparison for XLM-R Embedding: Manual vs. ASR Transcripts

Method	Manual Transcripts			ASR Transcripts		
	R1	R2	RL	R1	R2	RL
Ranking	0.581	0.423	0.334	0.425	0.190	0.157
TextRank	0.480	0.262	0.158	0.397	0.138	0.125
LSA	0.285	0.041	0.109	0.253	0.029	0.086
LDA	0.593	0.408	0.450	0.389	0.146	0.275
MMR	0.596	0.431	0.306	0.430	0.194	0.164

Table 5.7: Performance Comparison for GloVe Embedding: Manual vs. ASR Transcripts

Method	Manual Transcripts			ASR Transcripts		
	R1	R2	RL	R1	R2	RL
Ranking	0.630	0.466	0.307	0.620	0.449	0.308
TextRank	0.627	0.459	0.325	0.446	0.207	0.175
LSA	0.348	0.129	0.127	0.295	0.081	0.114
LDA	0.467	0.274	0.361	0.375	0.137	0.252
MMR	0.612	0.429	0.339	0.457	0.219	0.189

methods perform when applied to manual transcripts versus ASR-generated transcripts, as shown in Tables 5.4-5.7. Across all embeddings, methods like Ranking and TextRank consistently show better performance for manual transcripts compared to ASR-based transcripts, as reflected in higher ROUGE-1 (R1), ROUGE-2 (R2), and ROUGE-L (RL) scores. Notably, Ranking shows superior results with embeddings like FastText and GloVe for manual transcripts, achieving R1 scores of 0.604 and 0.63, respectively, whereas the performance drops significantly for ASR-generated transcripts, with reductions of up to 0.162 in R1 scores for FastText. This trend highlights how manual transcripts allow the models to fully leverage embedding representations, whereas ASR errors lead to information loss and inconsistencies that degrade summarization quality.

Among embeddings, FastText and GloVe perform better overall in terms of R1, R2, and RL scores, indicating that they were more effective in capturing contextual and semantic relationships in spoken documents. However, embeddings like XLM-R, which rely heavily on pre-trained multilingual contexts, also exhibit potential, though their performance for ASR transcripts was hindered, as seen in Figure 5-1. For example, TextRank combined with GloVe achieves an R1 score of 0.627 for manual transcripts, which drops to 0.446 for ASR-based transcripts. Similarly, MMR using FastText suffers a sharp decline in R2 scores, going from 0.414 (manual) to 0.21 (ASR). These discrepancies indicate that embeddings optimized for contextual learning were more adversely affected by ASR errors compared to

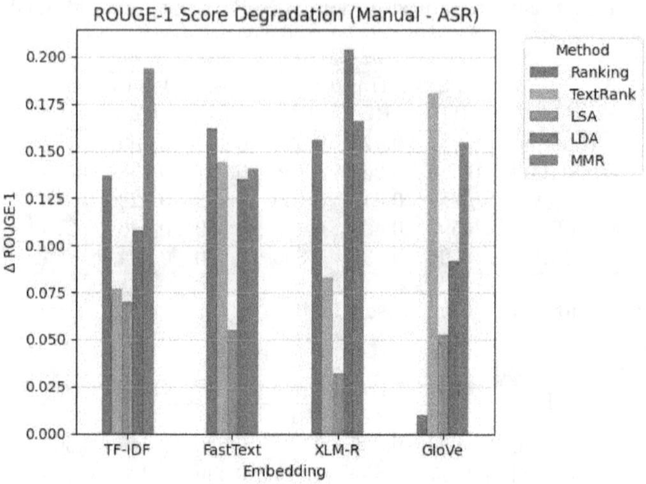

Figure 5-1: Absolute degradation in ROUGE-1 scores ($\Delta = Manual - ASR$) for each summarization method and embedding.
Higher delta values indicate greater sensitivity to ASR errors. Methods relying on contextual embeddings suffer more, confirming the impact of transcription noise on deep embedding-based summarization.

simpler methods like TF-IDF, which rely on keyword frequency rather than deep contextual understanding.

The overall analysis underscores the critical impact of ASR transcription quality on summarization performance. While manual transcripts enable state-of-the-art methods to operate at near-optimal performance, ASR-generated transcripts consistently result in substantial reductions in ROUGE scores across all methods and embeddings. This performance drop was attributed to the propagation of ASR errors—such as word substitutions, deletions, and insertions—into the embeddings, which disrupts the semantic and structural coherence of the input. Consequently, the summarization models struggle to identify and prioritize relevant content accurately.

While summarization methods using higher-representation embeddings such as XLM-R or FastText have shown strong resilience to transcription noise in high-resource languages, the same robustness does not extend well to low-resource settings. In languages like Bengali, where ASR errors were frequent and often severe, these embeddings struggle to recover semantic context. This leads to a noticeable drop in extractive summarization quality when applied to ASR-transcribed speech. As shown in Figure 5-2, the degradation was not just statistical but affects the overall informativeness and coherence of the summaries produced.

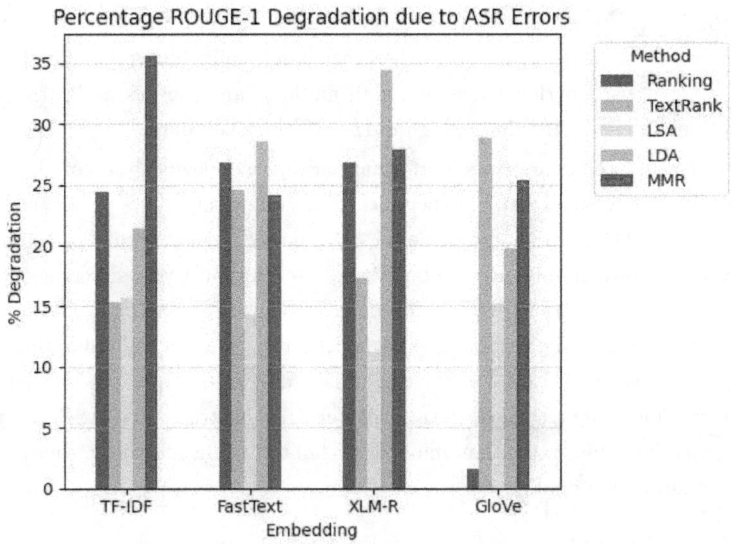

Figure 5-2: Percentage drop in ROUGE-1 scores across summarization methods and embeddings.
The scores quantify the relative degradation due to ASR errors.
Embedding-method pairs like MMR with XLM-R show severe proportional losses, highlighting the vulnerability of context-sensitive models in noisy ASR settings.

5.6.2 Embedding-Based Comparison of Summarization Methods

The embedding-wise values for the unsupervised methods, Ranking, TextRank, LSA, LDA, and MMR reveal significant variations in performance across different embeddings (TF-IDF, FastText, XLM-R, and GloVe) for both manual and ASR-generated transcripts. For manual transcripts, embeddings like GloVe consistently deliver higher performance metrics (R1, R2, RL), indicating their effectiveness in capturing meaningful sentence representations for summarization tasks. For instance, GloVe achieves the best scores with Ranking (R1: 0.63, RL: 0.307) and TextRank (R1: 0.627, RL: 0.325), suggesting its capability to capture semantic and syntactic nuances in text. On the other hand, embeddings like TF-IDF and LSA struggle with performance across all methods and metrics, indicating their limitations in processing dense, high-dimensional spoken data.

For ASR-generated transcripts, performance drops were evident across all embeddings. FastText, for example, experiences a decline of over 50% in R2 scores for Ranking and MMR methods, while TF-IDF shows a decrease of approximately 24.2% in R1 for Ranking. Even XLM-R, despite its robustness, suffers significant reductions in all metrics, with a 55% decrease in R2 for Ranking. GloVe, however, appears relatively less impacted by ASR errors, showing only marginal drops (e.g., R1 decreases by 1.6% for Ranking), likely due to its strong pre-trained word representations. Nevertheless, the overall trend demonstrates that ASR-generated transcripts introduce noise that embeddings fail to handle effectively, thus degrading summarization quality.

5.6.3 Discussion: Impact of ASR Transcriptions on Summarization

This chapter highlight key insights into the summarization performance across manual and ASR-generated transcripts using various embeddings (TF-IDF, FastText, XLM-R, GloVe) and methods (Ranking, TextRank, LSA, LDA, and MMR). For high-resource embeddings such as GloVe and XLM-R, coupled with robust unsupervised methods like MMR or Ranking, the performance drop due to ASR transcription errors was relatively minimal, especially in metrics like ROUGE-1 and ROUGE-L. This indicates that high-quality embeddings can retain semantic coherence even in the presence of transcription noise, resulting in summaries that were close to those generated from manual transcripts. For example, the GloVe embedding with the Ranking method shows only a negligible decrease of 1.6% in ROUGE-1, and in some cases, such as ROUGE-L, even a slight improvement was observed (+0.3%). Similarly, XLM-R maintains a strong performance despite ASR errors, demonstrating the robustness of contextual embeddings in mitigating transcription noise.

On the other hand, low-resource embeddings such as TF-IDF and FastText, which rely on shallow representations of text, show significant performance degradation across all methods when ASR transcriptions were used. This was particularly evident for methods like LDA and LSA, where ROUGE-2 and ROUGE-L scores drop drastically, often exceeding 50%. For instance, the performance of LDA with FastText embedding shows a 61.7% drop in ROUGE-2 and a 56.2% drop in ROUGE-L. This reflects the vulnerability of low-resource embeddings to the inaccuracies introduced by ASR systems, as they lack the sophisticated contextual understanding required to recover semantic relationships from noisy input.

5.6.3.1 Behavior of ROUGE-L in Low-resource Extractive Summarization

ROUGE-L evaluates summary quality based on the longest common subsequence between the system-generated summary and the reference summary. This makes the metric highly sensitive to the continuity and ordering of words. In extractive summarization, although sentences are directly selected from the source text, the exact sentences and their order may differ between the system output and the reference summary.

In the extractive Bengali summaries, the sentences selected by the system and the reference summary did not come from the same position in the original text or appear in the same order. As a result, although both summaries contained similar information, the words do not form long continuous sequences. Since ROUGE-L relies on matching long word sequences in the same order, this leads to lower ROUGE-L scores despite reasonable content overlap.

Hence, lower ROUGE-L scores reflect sensitivity to sequence alignment rather than lack of content overlap, which is still captured by ROUGE-1 and ROUGE-2.

5.6.3.2 High vs. Low Resource Languages: Embedding Impact and ASR Challenges

The better performance of GloVe and FastText can be attributed to their stability and ability to capture local context in limited-data settings. In contrast, contextual embeddings like XLM-R often overfit or fail to generalize when trained on small or noisy datasets, especially without fine-tuning. LSA performed poorly with ASR transcripts, as it relies heavily on lexical overlap and fails to handle disfluencies or ASR-specific distortions. Ranking-based methods were more resilient to moderate ASR errors because they rely on sentence-level features and can still prioritize relatively informative units.

Among all combinations, the highest ROUGE-1 score (0.630) was achieved by the Ranking method using GloVe embeddings on manual transcripts. In contrast, the lowest R2 score (0.029) was recorded by LSA with XLM-R on ASR transcripts, reflecting a severe breakdown of semantic coherence in noisy input conditions. These patterns were consistent with the error types discussed in Chapter 4—ASR transcripts often include substitution and insertion errors, especially in proper names and key content. This noise affects sentence meaning and makes it harder for models to identify important content.

Contextual models like XLM-R, which rely on sentence-level semantics, were especially sensitive to such distortions. Even strong models can select irrelevant or confusing sentences when the input was flawed. While pretrained embeddings like GloVe can still support stable performance in high-resource settings with clean text, this stability breaks down in low-resource languages where both ASR and embeddings were weaker. Even large multilingual models like XLM-R perform poorly without fine-tuning, which was often not feasible due to lack of labeled data. The issue was not only the quality of embeddings but the entire assumption that text was a reliable intermediate. In low-resource settings, ASR transcripts are often too noisy for effective summarization, regardless of the embedding used. This makes text-based methods inherently fragile under real-world constraints.

In conclusion, while higher embeddings and advanced methods can largely ignore ASR errors in high-resource languages, low-resource embeddings and languages suffer immensely.

5.7 Chapter Summary

The analysis underscores how heavily summarization performance depends on ASR quality. While manual transcripts enable high ROUGE scores, ASR-generated transcripts cause significant drops across all methods due to errors like substitutions, deletions, and insertions. These distortions degrade embeddings and make it harder for models to detect relevant content.

This exposes a major limitation of text-based summarization: its reliance on clean, coherent input. In low-resource languages with weak ASR and undertrained embeddings, even advanced models struggle. Many well-known methods—effective for English—fail to generalize under such conditions. Their dependence on lexical quality and pretrained models becomes a bottleneck.

To move forward, summarization methods must reduce dependence on text.

Prosody-aware or multimodal strategies—drawing on acoustic and speaker cues—offer more robust alternatives, particularly in low-resource settings. Without such shifts, scalable and reliable speech summarization will remain out of reach in real-world deployments.

Chapter 6

A Text-Independent Prosody-Driven Framework for Extractive Speech Summarization in Low-Resource Languages

Many state-of-the-art summarization systems rely on text derived from Automatic Speech Recognition (ASR). While effective in high-resource languages, such systems become problematic in low-resource contexts, where annotated corpora were scarce, ASR models were undertrained, and linguistic diversity was high. Even when an ASR system exists, high word error rates can severely degrade summarization quality. Complex sentence structures, code-switching, and pronunciation variability further challenge ASR reliability in low-resource languages like Assamese and Bengali. These limitations make fully text-dependent approaches less practical. Consequently, exploring speech-based cues—particularly prosody, which encodes emphasis, information structure, and salience directly in the audio—offers an alternative to unreliable ASR transcriptions.

6.1 Introduction

The impact of ASR errors on extractive speech summarization was found to be dire in case of low-resource languages, where advanced embedding techniques failed to reduce degradation caused by erroneous transcriptions. In response, this chapter shifts focus towards a text-independent approach, leveraging acoustic-prosodic features directly from the speech signal. These features, such as intonation patterns, speaking rate, and pause dynamics, offer a promising alternative to ASR-dependent summarization systems, particularly in low-resource languages like Assamese and Bengali.

This chapter investigates whether acoustic-prosodic features alone can support extractive summarization in noisy or text-limited environments. While text-based methods dominate the literature, their success depends on accurate ASR systems or clean transcripts, which were often unavailable in low-resource settings. The goal was not to outperform text-based models but to explore the feasibility of a text-independent approach that operates under resource constraints. To address this, a combined approach was used—testing both lexical and prosody-based features—especially in situations where the text was either limited or unreliable. The goal was to explore whether speech summarization could work even without depending on clean, accurate transcriptions.

6.2 Text-independent methods

In contrast to text-based methods that rely heavily on Automatic Speech Recognition (ASR) transcriptions, text-independent methods for speech summarization aim to extract relevant information directly from the audio signal, bypassing the need for precise and error-prone transcriptions. These methods leverage acoustic and prosodic features, which convey critical information such as emphasis, sentence boundaries, and speaker intent, directly from the speech signal [75, 78, 109]. This was especially important in low-resource language settings, where ASR models were undertrained and often prone to high word error rates (WER) [34], leading to unreliable textual input for summarization.

The primary advantage of text-independent methods is their ability to operate without the intermediary step of transcription, which is prone to errors in languages with limited resources and complex linguistic features. By focusing on the raw audio signal, these methods make summarization possible even when high-quality transcriptions are not available, providing a solution that is more robust under low-resource conditions.

Acoustic features, such as pitch, intensity, speaking rate, and duration, provide valuable cues for determining sentence boundaries, identifying key phrases, and detecting emphasis. For example, changes in pitch can indicate a shift in focus or the presence of a new topic, while variations in intensity and speaking rate can signal important information or emphasize specific parts of the speech. Similarly, prosodic features, such as pauses, rhythm, and stress patterns, can be utilized to assess the structure and informativeness of speech [81]. These features have been shown to correlate with the salience of spoken content, enabling the identification of significant segments within the audio that were crucial for summarization [11].

While lexical content was often used in text-based summarization methods, these methods were dependent on accurate transcriptions. However, in the absence of such reliable transcriptions, acoustic-prosodic features offer a promising alternative for segmenting and summarizing speech. In particular, these features can help to segment the speech into coherent units and rank these units by importance without the need for a precise textual representation of the content. This is critical in languages with high variability in pronunciation, syntax, and morphology, such as Assamese and Bengali, where ASR errors are frequent and substantial.

In this chapter, we explored the potential of these text-independent summarization methods by evaluating the effectiveness of acoustic-prosodic features in speech summarization tasks. By focusing on prosody-based cues, we aim to determine whether these features can serve as reliable indicators of sentence relevance, even in the absence of accurate transcriptions. This approach aligns with the need for flexible and robust summarization systems that can operate effectively in low-resource settings, offering a pathway to meaningful summarization that does not depend on high-quality textual transcriptions.

Ultimately, text-independent methods offer a promising direction for improving speech summarization systems in low-resource languages, where ASR errors are prevalent, and high-quality textual data is scarce. By relying on features inherent to the speech signal itself, such methods provide a potential solution for addressing the challenges posed by resource constraints, and can help in creating more robust, scalable systems for speech summarization. This approach reduces the reliance on costly and error-prone ASR systems, making it more feasible in real-world applications where accurate transcription is not always available.

6.3 Feature-vector of the spoken sentence

The sentence audios were represented by their feature-vector [67, 69]. A feature-vector comprises the following feature-sets: acoustic-prosodic features, lexical features, and relevance features. These features were discussed below:

6.3.1 Acoustic-prosodic features

The acoustic-prosodic features used here to represent the sentence audios are pitch (minimum, maximum, mean, range), energy (minimum, maximum, root mean square), duration of the audio segment, and mel-frequency cepstral coefficients (MFCC). These features were selected because they capture essential characteristics of prosody, which plays a key role in conveying meaning, emphasis, and structure in spoken language, as detailed below [37].

1. **Pitch (minimum, maximum, mean, range)**: Pitch is a fundamental attribute of speech prosody that reflects the perceived frequency of the speaker's voice. Variations in pitch can signal different emotions, emphasis, or intentions, and are essential in distinguishing questions from statements or highlighting key points. By analyzing minimum, maximum, mean, range, and slope, we can capture the overall pitch pattern and dynamic changes within the speech, providing insights into the speaker's intent and focus. Pitch is a core prosodic feature that directly influences intonation and emphasis in speech. Variations in pitch help convey the underlying structure of speech, such as questioning versus statement intonation, or the focus on specific words or phrases. In this study, features such as pitch range and slope were used to capture the variation in intonation patterns over the course of a sentence. These pitch-related features help detect sentence-level emphasis, which was critical for identifying salient or informative sentences for extractive summarization. The justification for using pitch is supported by extensive literature, which links pitch variations to prosodic marking of focus and salience in speech.
2. **Energy (minimum, maximum, root mean square)**: In the context of this work, energy should be interpreted as short-time energy rather than absolute signal energy. It is sensitive to recording conditions such as microphone placement and excitation mode. In this work, energy features are computed at the frame level and summarized using statistical measures (minimum, maximum, and RMS), which correspond to short-time energy representations.

   Energy reflects the loudness or intensity of the audio signal, which can vary based on the speaker's stress, emotion, or emphasis on certain words. Higher energy levels often correspond to emphasis on key points, while lower energy may indicate less important parts of the speech. By including minimum, maximum, root mean square energy measures, the model can better understand how emphasis was distributed across the spoken sentences, thus aiding in identifying segments that were more likely to be relevant to the summary.

   Energy is another acoustic feature that has prosodic relevance. It reflects the loudness or intensity of speech, and higher energy is often correlated with stressed syllables or emphasized words. Stressed syllables tend to have higher energy in many languages, and this feature plays a crucial role in marking the importance or salience of words in a sentence. While energy is often considered an acoustic feature, it directly reflects the prosodic characteristic of stress, and its variation can help identify prominent parts of the sentence. By leveraging energy, we aim to capture the stress patterns in speech, which are essential for identifying the most informative parts of the speech signal.

3. **Duration of the audio segment**: The duration of a spoken sentence or segment can provide clues about its importance. For instance, longer pauses or extended segments may be indicative of more detailed explanations or critical information. By including duration as a feature, the model can better assess the rhythm and pacing of speech, which often correlates with the speaker's intentions and the relative importance of different parts of the content. Variations in duration can help identify pauses that segment speech into meaningful chunks, marking sentence boundaries or shifts in topic. Duration also captures the pacing of speech, which was often slower in more important or emphasized segments. In prosodic terms, the lengthening of syllables or pauses can be an indicator of emphasis or importance. While duration is more often discussed in terms of speech rhythm rather than traditional prosody, it is a valuable feature for identifying parts of the speech that carry higher informativeness or focus, especially when text-based methods fail due to poor ASR quality.
4. **Mel-Frequency Cepstral Coefficients (MFCC)**: MFCCs are widely used in speech processing as they provide a compact representation of the speech signal that closely mimics how the human ear perceives sound. MFCCs capture the spectral characteristics of the audio signal, which include information about the timbre and overall quality of the speech. These coefficients are effective in identifying phonetic and tonal elements, making them particularly useful for understanding how different parts of the speech sound and how they contribute to the overall prosodic pattern. MFCCs are typically used in speech recognition and speaker identification, as they capture the spectral envelope of the speech signal. Although MFCCs are generally not considered directly prosodic, they can capture acoustic properties related to voice quality and timbre, which can indirectly reflect prosodic aspects such as emotional tone, focus, and intonation. While MFCCs do not represent prosody in the traditional sense (such as stress or intonation), they can be useful in identifying tonal characteristics and variability in the speaker's delivery. These features contribute to the overall expressiveness of speech, and in combination with other prosodic features, they can provide insight into the relative importance or salience of sentences within the speech signal.

Together, these features provide a comprehensive representation of the prosodic characteristics of spoken sentences. By capturing variations in pitch, energy, duration, and spectral properties, the model can identify patterns that are associated with emphasis, emotion, and the structural flow of information, ultimately helping to determine which sentences were likely to be most relevant in a summarized version of the spoken content. All the acoustic-prosodic features were extracted with the help of Praat[1].

Table 6.1: Feature-set description

Feature-set	Feature-type	Feature	Attribute in dataset
Acoustic-prosodic features	Fundamental frequency (F_0)	Mean of F_0	Pitch
		Maximum of F_0	MaxPitch
		Minimum of F_0	MinPitch
		Range of F_0	PitchRange
	Energy (E)	Maximum value of E	MaxIntensity
		Minimum value of E	MinIntensity
		Mean value of E	Intensity
	Duration	Sentence duration	sentDuration
	Spectral feature	Mel-Frequency Cepstral Coefficients (MFCC)	M1 - M39
Lexical features	Number of Named entities	No. of organization-names	NE1
		No. of person-names	NE2
		No. of place-names	NE3
		No. of remaining named entities	NE4
	Number of words	No. of words in current sentence	NW1
		No. of words in previous sentence	NW2
		No. of words in following sentence	NW3
Relevance feature	Prosodic score	Sentence importance score	stressFactor

[1]Praat was a free computer software package for speech analysis in phonetics. For more information, visit https://www.fon.hum.uva.nl/praat/

6.3.2 Lexical features

The lexical features were derived from the textual transcripts of the audio segments[2], capturing key linguistic attributes that contribute to sentence importance. These features play a crucial role in assessing the informativeness and relevance of a sentence within the overall discourse, which is essential for extractive summarization [67].

One key aspect of lexical analysis is **Named Entity Recognition (NER)**, which helps identify sentences that contain significant information, such as proper nouns and domain-specific terms. Sentences containing named entities are often more informative and tend to appear in summaries. To quantify this, four different named entity counts were used:

- **NEI**: Number of organization names and titles in the sentence (e.g., company names, governmental bodies, institutions). Sentences mentioning organizations are likely to contain critical information about events or affiliations.
- **NEII**: Number of person names, capturing references to key individuals in the discourse. Since news and conversational data often revolve around people, this feature helps prioritize sentences that introduce or discuss prominent figures.
- **NEIII**: Number of location names, which are crucial for understanding event context. Summaries typically preserve sentences mentioning geographic locations, as they provide essential background details.
- **NEIV**: Number of other miscellaneous named entities (e.g., dates, numerical expressions, product names). These elements often indicate specific details that are crucial for comprehending key facts.

Beyond named entities, **word count-based features** provide additional context for sentence importance:

- **NWI**: The number of words in the current sentence, which helps gauge sentence complexity and information density. Longer sentences may contain richer information, but excessively long ones might be redundant.
- **NWII**: The number of words in the preceding sentence, which helps model contextual dependencies. If the prior sentence was lengthy and information-

[2]While lexical features are included in this chapter, their role is primarily comparative. They are used to benchmark performance and highlight scenarios where lexical cues may still be informative, especially when partial or noisy transcripts are available. However, the main contribution lies in demonstrating that effective extractive summarization is achievable even when lexical input is minimal or unreliable. This aligns with the broader motivation of this thesis—to explore alternative, prosody-driven strategies in low-resource settings where clean transcriptions and pretrained text models may not be feasible.

rich, the current sentence might serve as an elaboration or conclusion.

- **NWIII**: The number of words in the subsequent sentence, which helps determine if a sentence is introductory, transitional, or concluding within a segment.

By incorporating these lexical attributes, the model can better identify sentences that are contextually rich, information-dense, and relevant to the overall content, complementing acoustic and prosodic features in the summarization process. This ensures that extracted summaries retain key factual details while minimizing redundancy.

6.3.3 Prosody-based Importance Feature

Many extractive summarization methods in the literature rely on computing a sentence relevance score—typically based on lexical or semantic similarity, frequency statistics, or contextual embeddings—to rank sentences by their informativeness. In contrast, this work proposes a novel, prosody-based sentence importance score, which serves as a relevance feature derived entirely from acoustic-prosodic features such as pitch and intensity. This feature aims to capture how a sentence is *spoken*—reflecting emphasis and prominence—rather than what is said. In the absence of reliable transcriptions, such prosodic cues offer a viable and interpretable alternative for guiding extractive summarization in low-resource speech settings.
For low-resource languages which do not have an ASR, or have one with a high word error rate, the textual features extracted would be full of errors and most of the information will be lost. Thus, we propose a sentence-scoring method that would be text-independent. Here, a sentence-segment is considered to be an aggregation of word-unit segments w. This prosody-based sentence-importance score $I(S)$ indicates the degree of prosodic emphasis in a sentence, i.e. lexical units of the speech have been emphasised. In spoken communication, the speaker indicates informativeness by 'emphasising' certain lexical segments – it could be a word-unit or a phrasal-unit – which can be considered prosodically important.
In broadcast news, the spoken document is mainly comprised of facts and information, and the speakers are trained in relaying the most informative segments using prosody. A sentence being more informative, represented by the prosodic score, would have higher likelihood of being selected to be a part of the summary [40]. The prosodic score of sentence $S = w_1, w_2, ..., w_n$ was thus represented as

$$I(S) = \frac{n_p}{\sum_{i=1}^{n} w_i} \tag{6.1}$$

where n_p is the number of word-units given prosodic 'emphasis'. The words which have higher pitch and higher intensity compared to the speaker's overall pitch and intensity, those words were considered to be 'emphasised'.

Importance, Emphasis and Prosody of a *Spoken* sentence

To estimate how important a sentence is—based only on how it was spoken—we developed a prosody-based score that captures how much emphasis a speaker placed on the words in that sentence. In natural speech, speakers tend to raise their pitch and loudness when highlighting key ideas or introducing important information. When a speaker wants to draw the listener's attention to specific information—such as new facts, names, or emotionally significant details—they naturally adjust the acoustic properties of their voice. These adjustments were most commonly observed as rises in pitch (the perceived frequency of the voice) and intensity (the loudness of the speech signal), often accompanied by slower or more deliberate articulation. These changes serve as auditory cues for listeners, helping them identify which parts of the message are most salient.

We used this linguistic intuition to identify "emphasized" words in each sentence. Our approach taps into this human-like perception by automatically identifying these emphasized moments in the audio. For each word in a sentence, we measure how strongly it stands out in terms of pitch and loudness, compared to the speaker's own average values. This way, we were not just detecting loud speech or high pitch in general—we were detecting *relative emphasis* that reflects intentional highlighting.

A word was marked as emphasized if both its pitch and intensity (loudness) were higher than the average pitch and intensity of the speaker across the entire recording. This allowed us to detect emphasis relative to each speaker's typical speaking style, rather than using fixed thresholds.

Once each word was evaluated for emphasis, we calculated how many emphasized words occurred in a sentence. By counting the number of such emphasized words in a sentence, we generated an importance score that reflects how much emphasis the speaker placed on that sentence. This score was then used by our summarization model to identify potentially key sentences, even without relying on the actual words being spoken. This value was then used as a feature to help the summarization model decide which sentences to include in the final summary.

Figure 6-1 and 6-2 further illustrates how words were 'emphasised', where the words were annotated as 1 indicating emphasis if its pitch and intensity values were higher than the average of the speaker's, or otherwise 0. The number of emphasised segments in a sentence were then counted, represented by n_p, and then divided by the total words in that sentence, to find the importance score of the sentence.

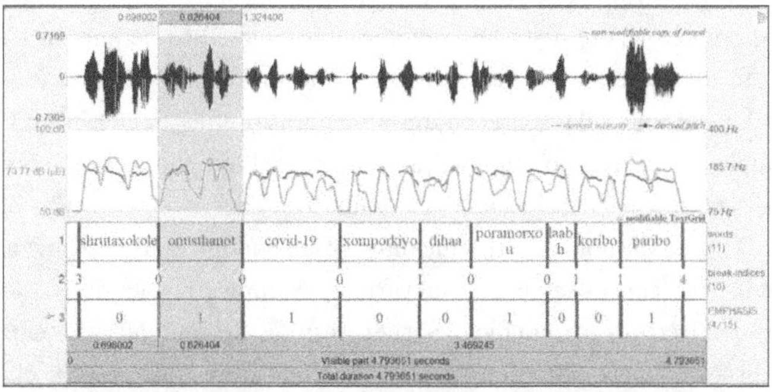

Figure 6-1: Prosodic Annotation: Word-units annotated as 1 for 'emphasized' words, based on the speaker's pitch and intensity characteristics.

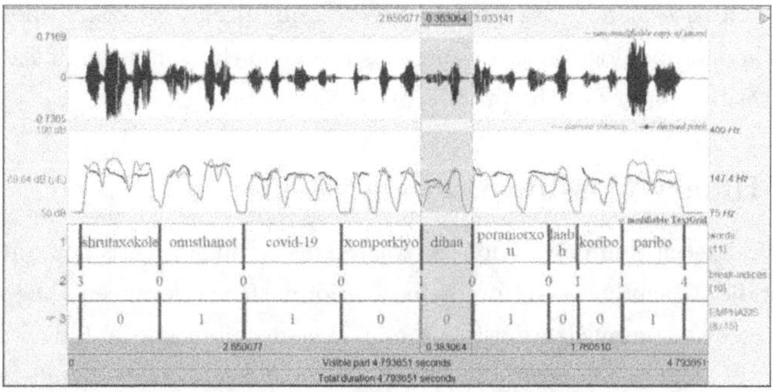

Figure 6-2: Prosodic Annotation: Words labeled as 'no-emphasize' who exhibit no significant acoustic prominence

6.4 Methodology

Extractive summarization aims to identify and aggregate the most informative content units from a document to form a condensed version that reflects the central theme. In contrast to abstractive methods—which generate novel text using natural language generation—extractive summarization selects existing segments based on relevance. The following subsections outline the formulation of extractive summarization as a binary classification task and describe the classification models considered in this work, including both base learners and ensemble approaches.

6.4.1 Extractive summarization as binary classification problem

Spoken summary from a spoken document in this work was created in an extractive approach, where a speech segment was selected to be part of a summary according to its relevance to the document. The spoken document was segmented as per its lexical unit, like sentence-units or phrasal-units, which would encapsulate a complete information. In our framework, we have considered sentences as a unit for speech segment to consider in summarization. A sentence was considered 'important' based on not only the meaning of its content but also how a sentence was spoken. We can observe this in various examples in our daily life through conversations, lectures or monologues that despite the content, a listener's attention was directed to the sentences/phrases having significant prosodic change. We base our text-independent speech summarization framework on this observation. In this work, the problem of extractive speech summarization can be defined as a binary classification problem, where a classification model is trained on handcrafted summaries, and then used to predict summaries for other spoken documents. The methodology in this paper was based on this rendition of the problem, and the various phases of the process are discussed as follows.

6.4.2 Binary classification algorithms

Extractive speech summarization is treated as a binary classification problem where candidate sentences are predicted based on their relevance to the summary. Since extractive summarization was modeled as a sentence-level binary classification task, classifiers commonly used for general-purpose text classification were also applicable. Each sentence or utterance was treated as an independent instance, with the label indicating whether it should be included in the summary. This framing allows the use of standard classifiers such as Support Vector Machines (SVM), Logistic Regression, Random Forest, etc. which have been widely adopted in text classification literature.

In our work, the performances of base classifiers were analyzed, which were also used for building ensemble methods.

- The following base classifiers were used:
  1. **K nearest neighbour (KNN)** [73, 96, 99]. KNN is a classification algorithm which works by measuring the similarity between feature vectors in a multidimensional space.
  2. **Support vector machine (SVM)** [16, 57, 101, 103]. SVMs are effective in high-dimensional spaces and are versatile due to their ability

to use different kernel functions.

3. **Gaussian naive bayes (GB)** [23, 44]. Gaussian naive bayes is a probabilistic classification algorithm based on Bayes' Theorem with the assumption of independence between features.
4. **Logistic regression (LR)** [63, 89, 96]. Logistic regression is a supervised machine learning algorithm used for classification tasks. The goal was to predict the probability that a data point belongs to a given class or not, using a logistic function.
5. **Decision tree (DT)**[86]. A decision tree was a tree-like model used for making decisions based on input features. It recursively partitions the feature space into regions and assigns a prediction to each region.

- Ensemble methods can be divided into bagging [10], boosting [24], stacking and voting. The major techniques explored in this paper were as follows.
  1. **Random forest (RF)**[86, 96]. Bagging combines predictions from multiple base models trained on different subsets of the training data. Each base model is trained independently using the same learning algorithm. Random forest is a type of bagging method which utilizes decision trees as base learners to improve the performance.
  2. **Extra trees (ET)** [27]. Extra trees is another bagging method, and like RF, uses decision trees as their base learners. The only difference from RF is the splitting value for feature was randomly selected, which further randomizes the construction of the decision trees.
  3. **Gradient boost (GBM)**. Gradient boosting is a type of boosting method. Boosting follows the principle that, for certain problems a single base performing models may not work well. In that case, various such base learners are combined to make a powerful and better performing model.
  4. **Extreme gradient boost/ XGBoost (XGB)** [15]. XGBoost is another boosting technique. XGBoost improves the efficacy of gradient boosting, by several factors. While GBM may suffer from overfitting, XGB incorporates both L1 and L2 regularization to prevent overfitting.
  5. **Adaptive Boost / AdaBoost (ADA)** [24]. AdaBoost is a type of boosting method. Contrary to gradient boosting fitting the base learners to the residual errors made by the previous learners, AdaBoost aims to improve the performance of a base learner by iteratively focusing on the data points which were hardest to classify.
  6. **Light gradient boost / LightGBM (LGB)** [43]. Another variant of gradient boosting, LightGBM optimizes memory usage and train-

ing time by selectively retaining instances with large gradients during training.

- Additionally, meta-ensemble or cross-model ensembling was also used.
  1. **Stacking**. Stacked generalization, or stacking, combines the predictions from base learners, like bagging and boosting. However, unlike bagging, models were diverse in stacking.
  2. **Hard voting**. Voting ensemble combines the predictions from multiple base learners. There were two approaches of voting, one of them is hard voting. Hard voting predicts the class with the largest sum of votes from its base learners. It sums the predictions for each class and predicts the class label with most votes.
  3. **Soft voting**. In contrast to hard voting, soft voting sums the predicted probabilities for each class, and then predicts that class label with the highest probability. In other words, in soft voting the final prediction is made based on the weighted average of predicted probabilities from multiple base classifiers.

6.5 Experimental setup

This chapter investigates whether acoustic-prosodic features can effectively support extractive summarization in low-resource speech settings. The main aim was to evaluate the extent to which pitch, energy, pause duration, and related prosodic patterns contribute to identifying summary-worthy content—particularly when lexical information was sparse or unavailable. To operationalize this, a prosodic importance score (I) was proposed, capturing sentence-level relevance based on pitch, pause, and duration features. This score was used as a relevance feature within a supervised binary classification framework that predicts whether each sentence should be included in the summary.

The study was conducted on the Assamese broadcast news subset of the corpus. Sentence-level feature vectors include both acoustic-prosodic attributes and basic lexical indicators. Evaluation was performed in two phases: first, classifiers were trained and tested to assess sentence-level prediction accuracy; second, extractive summaries generated from predicted sentences were evaluated using ROUGE scores against human-written references. The full methodology is detailed in the following subsections.

6.5.1 Dataset description

To support extractive summarization via binary classification, the speech corpus (the Assamese segment of the Broadcast News subcorpus, referenced in Chapter 3 serves as the chosen corpus for the summarization classifiers/models) was transformed into a structured dataset where each sentence-level audio segment was represented by a feature vector. This dataset includes the following components:

- **Attributes**. The spoken sentences were represented by their corresponding feature-vectors, which encapsulate key characteristics derived from the speech data. These feature-vectors include attributes such as acoustic-prosodic features (e.g., pitch, intensity, rhythm) and lexical features (e.g., word frequency, semantic content). Together, these feature-vectors form the attributes of the dataset, serving as the input for machine learning algorithms to classify and identify which sentences were relevant for summarization. A description of the attributes were given in Table 6.1.
- **Class/label**. In this study, the process of generating a summary involves selecting sentences considered relevant to the content of the spoken document. To achieve this, a binary classification algorithm was trained to distinguish between summary-worthy and non-summary-worthy sentences. Each sentence was represented by a feature-vector derived from its audio, encapsulating various acoustic-prosodic and lexical attributes. The "relevance" or summary-worthiness of a sentence was determined by comparing it to handcrafted summaries created by human annotators. Specifically, five annotators independently review each spoken document and select the sentences that they believe should be included in the final summary. These human-generated summaries serve as the gold standard for training the classification models, providing a benchmark for evaluating the algorithm's performance in accurately identifying key information within the spoken content.

6.5.1.1 Language used in the experiment

The experiments in this chapter were conducted on the Assamese broadcast news portion of the corpus. While the corpus also includes audiobook recordings and data in Bangla, this particular subset was chosen because it offers consistent audio quality, clearer sentence boundaries, and more uniform prosodic structure—all of which support focused evaluation of prosody-based summarization methods. The speech style in broadcast news, with its deliberate pacing and minimal disfluencies, allows clearer identification of acoustic-prosodic patterns linked to sentence salience [97]. This makes it a suitable and stable testbed for validating the proposed approach. Although the method was designed to generalize to more variable domains, such as audiobooks or conversational speech, this initial evaluation on broadcast news establishes a strong proof of concept within a controlled setting.

Additionally, while both Bengali and Assamese were low-resource languages, their current NLP tool ecosystems differ significantly. Assamese, in particular, lacks robust pretrained contextual embedding models and named entity recognizers [84]. As such, the experiments in this chapter were designed under stricter constraints — without access to reliable high-level textual representations — to explore the feasibility of text-independent summarization in more challenging conditions. This contrast also reflects a broader point made throughout the thesis — that low-resource languages differ widely in what tools and data were available. They do not all face the same limitations, and summarization systems must be adapted accordingly.

Out of the 14 available sessions[3] in the Assamese section of the Broadcast news sub-corpus (detailed in Chapter 3), 11 were used for classifier training and evaluation via 10-fold stratified cross-validation. The remaining 3 sessions were held out entirely and used exclusively for summary-level evaluation using ROUGE. This split offers a reasonable balance between robust model tuning and independent assessment of generalizability.

6.5.1.2 Utterance Segmentation and Duration Estimation

Utterance-level segmentation was performed manually for all spoken documents to ensure precise alignment between linguistic units and their corresponding acoustic realizations. The segmentation process was guided by the source text of the spoken material, where each sentence in the text was treated as a target utterance. Using this textual reference, sentence boundaries were carefully mapped onto the audio signal, and start and end time markers were annotated accordingly.

Once segmentation was completed, the duration of each utterance was calculated as the time difference between its annotated start and end boundaries. This computation was performed automatically using a custom script implemented in the Praat software[4]. This approach ensures accurate duration estimation while preserving consistency across the corpus. Manual segmentation was preferred over automatic methods to avoid boundary errors caused by ASR inaccuracies and to maintain reliable ground truth for downstream analysis involving prosodic features and sentence-level summarization.

[3] Each session refers to a full spoken broadcast segment, approximately 15 minutes in duration, taken from Assamese All India Radio news bulletins (morning or evening editions). Each session was treated as a distinct spoken document for summarization, with sentences segmented and labeled for summary inclusion.

[4] A Praat script was developed to extract utterance durations from the annotated TextGrid files.

6.5.2 Evaluation Strategy

This chapter adopts a two-phase evaluation strategy to assess the effectiveness of acoustic-prosodic features for extractive summarization in low-resource settings. The evaluation was conducted at both the sentence level (via classification performance) and the summary level (via ROUGE-based similarity to human-written summaries), as shown in Table 6.2. These two phases serve complementary goals: classification assesses how well models can distinguish relevant from irrelevant sentences, while ROUGE evaluation measures the actual informativeness and coherence of the final summaries.

6.5.2.1 Sentence-level Classification-Based Evaluation

Classification is treated as a practical way to test whether the feature helps models distinguish important content. The first phase involves a supervised binary classification task to predict whether each sentence-level speech segment should be included in the summary. The goal was to evaluate the predictive ability of different classifiers across multiple feature combinations using cross-validation.

To evaluate the predictive performance of individual classifiers, a 10-fold stratified cross-validation was conducted on a subset of 11 sessions from the Assamese broadcast news dataset. Stratified sampling ensured a balanced distribution of summary and non-summary sentences across all folds. In each fold, classifiers were trained on 90% of the data and tested on the remaining 10%. The average accuracy and macro F1-score across folds were computed, and their standard deviations were reported to assess consistency.

The results of this evaluation served three key purposes:

- These metrics provide an objective basis for comparing models and feature combinations, and
- In addition to identifying the most effective individual models, the classification results were used to guide ensemble construction. Top-performing models from distinct algorithmic families (e.g., tree-based, distance-based, linear) were selected to serve as base learners in ensemble methods such as voting and stacking.
- Additionally, the top four classifiers—based on cross-validation accuracy and F1-score—are retrained on the full dataset and used to generate extractive summaries for held-out sessions. These summaries were evaluated using ROUGE metrics (detailed in section 2.7).

6.5.2.2 Summary-Level Evaluation Using Held-Out Sessions with ROUGE

The second evaluation phase examines the actual quality of the summaries generated by the trained classifiers and ensembles. For this, three sessions from the Assamese broadcast news dataset were held out entirely—unused during both training and cross-validation. The top-performing classifiers from the first phase were retrained on the full dataset and used to generate predictions on three held-out sessions. The final models were used to predict sentence importance in these sessions, and extractive summaries were generated based on predicted labels. Additionally, To ensure consistent summary lengths and fair ROUGE evaluation, sentences were ranked by predicted probability, and the top-n were selected [22], where n matches the number of sentences in the human-written reference.

The resulting machine-generated summaries were then compared against human-annotated reference summaries using ROUGE-1, ROUGE-2, and ROUGE-L metrics [8]. This summary-level evaluation assesses whether improvements in classification performance correspond to meaningful gains in summary informativeness and coherence. By isolating this evaluation on held-out sessions, the results reflect realistic generalization to unseen data and help validate the practical utility of the summarization models.

Table 6.2: Evaluation Summary Table

Evaluation Type	**Purpose**	**Data Used**	**Metric(s)**	**Models Used**
Sentence Classification	Measure classifier performance	12 sessions (CV folds)	Accuracy, Macro F1-score	All base + ensemble classifiers
Summary-Level Evaluation	Measure summary quality (ROUGE)	3 held-out sessions	ROUGE-1, ROUGE-2, ROUGE-L	The top four performing models (based on classifier performance) trained on 12 sessions

6.5.3 Evaluation metrics

The evaluation of the proposed summarization framework was conducted at two levels: sentence classification and summary-level quality. Each level uses appropriate metrics to measure different aspects of system performance.

6.5.3.1 Classification Metrics

For the classification task, the primary metrics reported were accuracy, macro-averaged precision, recall, and F1-score. These were calculated over ten-fold cross-validation to ensure robustness across partitions and to account for class imbalance. To evaluate the performance of the extractive summarization approach, stratified 10-fold cross-validation was employed. In each fold, the dataset was split so that 90% of the data was used for training, and the remaining 10% was used for testing. This procedure was repeated across all ten folds, with the final performance reported as the average across these repetitions.

Stratification was used to ensure that the distribution of the two target classes—summary-relevant and non-relevant sentences—was preserved within each fold. This was crucial in extractive summarization tasks, where class imbalance was common, as relevant sentences tend to be fewer than non-relevant ones. By maintaining proportional representation of both classes, stratified sampling reduces the risk of biased training or evaluation, which could result from uneven class splits.

This evaluation setup ensures a robust and generalizable assessment of performance while making efficient use of the available annotated data. It was particularly relevant for low-resource scenarios, where datasets were often small, and annotated examples were limited.

F1-score, in particular, was treated as the central metric due to the binary nature of the classification task and the relatively sparse positive class (informative segments).

For each classifier, the mean and standard deviation of both accuracy and macro F1-score were reported across the 10 folds. This provides a robust estimate of performance and helps assess the stability of each model. The cross-validation scores also informed the selection of estimators for the ensemble models.

6.5.3.2 ROUGE Metrics for Summary Evaluation

To evaluate the quality of the generated summaries, the ROUGE (Recall-Oriented Understudy for Gisting Evaluation) metric suite was used (detailed in section 2.7). Specifically, ROUGE-1, ROUGE-2, and ROUGE-L scores were computed to capture unigram overlap, bigram overlap, and longest common subsequence between the model-generated and human reference summaries.

This evaluation was performed on three held-out sessions that were not used in any part of model training or cross-validation. By using these unseen sessions, the ROUGE evaluation reflects the generalization performance of the summarization system in realistic, low-resource settings. Scores were reported in terms of ROUGE recall, aligning with the extractive nature of the task and the goal of preserving key content from the original speech.

6.6 Results and Analysis

6.6.1 Sufficiency of Acoustic Features (A) as a Strong Baseline

Table 6.3 presents the performance of all classifiers when trained exclusively on the acoustic-prosodic feature set (A). The results demonstrate that acoustic features alone yield consistent summarization performance across a wide range of models, supporting their effectiveness in identifying important spoken content without relying on lexical information.

Among the individual classifiers, Random Forest (RF), Extra Trees (ET), and Gradient Boosting (GB) deliver the strongest overall results, with F1-scores exceeding 0.62 and accuracies in the 63–65% range. These results indicate that ensemble-based models, particularly tree-based learners, were well-suited for acoustic summarization tasks. LightGBM and XGBoost also perform competitively, though slightly lower than GB and ET.

Logistic Regression and K-Nearest Neighbors show moderate performance, suggesting that even relatively simple models can capture prosodic regularities that correlate with sentence-level importance. In contrast, Support Vector Machines and Gaussian Naive Bayes perform less effectively, indicating a limitation in capturing the variability of prosodic cues with more rigid or generative assumptions.

The ensemble strategies—Soft Voting, Hard Voting, and Stacking—perform worse than their constituent base models, especially in terms of F1-score. This suggests that the ensembling approach may dilute the strengths of individual classifiers when only acoustic inputs were available. In particular, the low F1-score of the Stacking model suggests overfitting or poor calibration of the meta-learner when lexical information was absent.

Overall, these findings affirm that acoustic-prosodic features alone provide a meaningful signal for extractive summarization. This has strong implications for low-resource scenarios, where reliable transcriptions or linguistic annotations may not be available, yet speech-based summarization remains necessary.

Table 6.3: Performance of all models using the acoustic feature set (A).

Model	Accuracy (%)	F1-Score
K-Nearest Neighbors	62.03 ± 4.97	0.6164 ± 0.0522
Support Vector Machine	55.46 ± 2.09	0.4883 ± 0.0219
Gaussian Naive Bayes	58.43 ± 4.25	0.5810 ± 0.0435
Logistic Regression	61.01 ± 3.69	0.6034 ± 0.0362
Decision Tree	58.24 ± 4.78	0.5787 ± 0.0463
Random Forest	**65.12 ± 4.24**	**0.6445 ± 0.0446**
Extra Trees	64.30 ± 3.44	0.6342 ± 0.0370
AdaBoost	60.90 ± 3.18	0.6003 ± 0.0321
Gradient Boosting	63.16 ± 3.99	**0.6222 ± 0.0423**
XGBoost	61.00 ± 4.51	0.6051 ± 0.0474
LightGBM	61.93 ± 4.06	0.6139 ± 0.0434
Stacking Ensemble	51.03 ± 7.26	0.3189 ± 0.1852
Hard Voting Ensemble	53.30 ± 10.14	0.4448 ± 0.2038
Soft Voting Ensemble	54.33 ± 11.05	0.4532 ± 0.1917

6.6.2 Feature Ablation Study for Assessing the Significance of Acoustic Features

To assess the contribution of individual acoustic feature groups, a feature ablation study was conducted using pitch, intensity, and duration features in different combinations. The experiments were evaluated using five classification algorithms, and performance was analyzed using both accuracy and F-score to provide a balanced assessment of classification effectiveness.

Across both metrics, the combined feature set consisting of pitch, intensity, and duration consistently achieved the best or near-best performance across classifiers. This trend indicates that these features capture complementary prosodic information that is beneficial for sentence-level classification. The consistency of this observation across accuracy and F-score suggests that the improvement is not limited to overall correctness but also reflects better class-wise balance.

When individual feature groups were removed, a clear reduction in performance was observed in both accuracy and F-score. In particular, configurations using pitch alone or intensity alone resulted in lower values across most classifiers, indicating that single-feature representations are insufficient to capture the prosodic variability required for the task. Feature combinations that excluded intensity or duration also showed degraded performance compared to the full feature set, highlighting the importance of these features alongside pitch.

Overall, the ablation results demonstrate that the effectiveness of acoustic features arises from their joint modeling rather than from any single feature in isolation. The agreement between accuracy- and F-score-based analyses strengthens

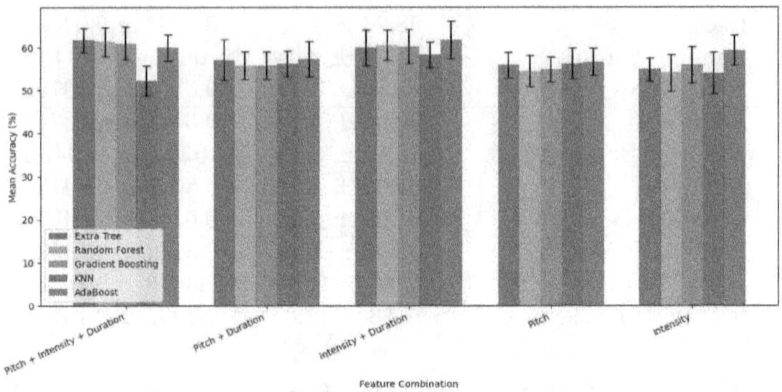

Figure 6-3: Mean Accuracy (%) across combination of acoustic features using binary classifiers.

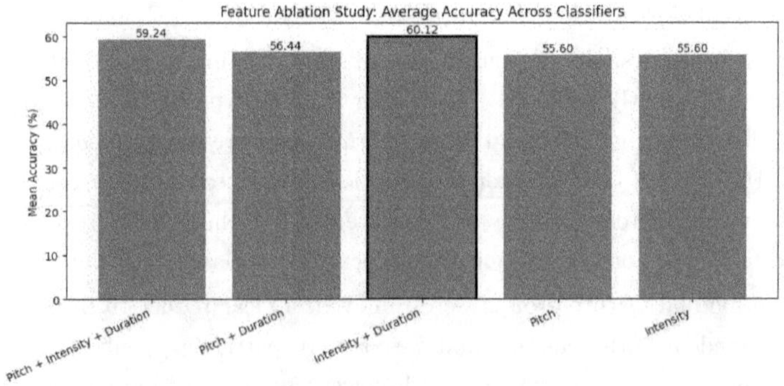

Figure 6-4: Average of Accuracy (%) for all 5 binary classifiers across combination of acoustic features.

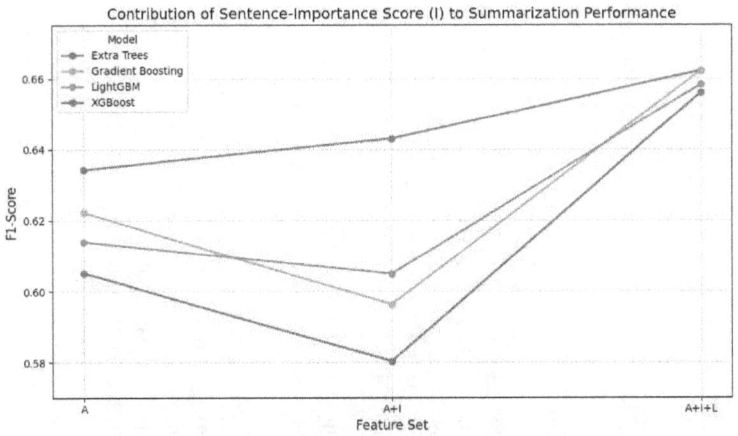

Figure 6-5: Effect of adding the sentence-importance score (I) on summarization performance.
Each line tracks F1-score progression for a classifier across feature combinations (A → A+I → A+I+L). Most models show stability or minor gains from A to A+I, and significant, consistent gains from A+I to A+I+L, confirming the complementary contribution of I alongside lexical features.

the conclusion that pitch, intensity, and duration are significant and complementary acoustic features for the summarization task considered in this thesis.

6.6.3 Contribution of Prosodic Sentence-importance score (I) to Enhanced Summarization Performance

In the Table 6.6 the results clearly show that while acoustic features (A) alone provide a strong baseline for extractive summarization as seen in Table 6.3, the addition of the proposed prosodic importance score (I) leads to consistent improvements across nearly all models. This supports the score's utility as a simple and interpretable relevance feature that helps identify important spoken content beyond what raw acoustic or lexical features provide. When comparing the A and A+I feature sets, we observe noticeable gains in both F1-score and accuracy for most classifiers. For example, Extra Trees improves from 64.12% (A) to 65.22% (A+I) in accuracy, while its F1-score increases from 0.6325 to 0.6430. Logistic Regression also shows a clear benefit, rising from 59.46% to 60.80% in accuracy with a corresponding F1-score improvement. These gains were achieved without introducing lexical information, demonstrating that the importance score contributes meaningfully even in low-resource settings where transcripts may be unavailable or unreliable.

Table 6.4: Mean classification accuracy (%) obtained from the feature ablation study, showing the impact of removing individual feature groups.

Model	Pitch + Intensity + Duration	Pitch + Duration	Intensity + Duration	Pitch	Intensity
Extra Tree	61.67% ± 2.81%	57.12% ± 4.82%	59.94% ± 4.18%	55.88% ± 3.03%	54.80% ± 2.78%
Random Forest	61.34% ± 3.30%	55.80% ± 3.30%	60.52% ± 3.51%	54.47% ± 3.63%	54.06% ± 4.30%
Gradient Boosting	61.01% ± 3.88%	55.80% ± 3.27%	60.19% ± 3.94%	54.80% ± 2.95%	55.88% ± 4.21%
K Nearest Neighbour	52.24% ± 3.49%	56.21% ± 2.99%	58.27% ± 2.91%	56.20% ± 3.64%	53.98% ± 4.87%
AdaBoost	59.93% ± 3.01%	57.29% ± 4.10%	61.67% ± 4.37%	56.63% ± 3.15%	59.27% ± 3.52%

Table 6.5: Mean classification F-score obtained from the feature ablation study, showing the impact of removing individual feature groups.

Model	Pitch + Intensity + Duration	Pitch + Duration	Intensity + Duration	Pitch	Intensity
Extra Tree	0.5844 ± 0.0258	0.5417 ± 0.0528	0.5786 ± 0.0467	0.5371 ± 0.0358	0.5238 ± 0.0316
Random Forest	0.5868 ± 0.0346	0.5316 ± 0.0364	0.5857 ± 0.0391	0.5210 ± 0.0372	0.5156 ± 0.0452
Gradient Boosting	0.5838 ± 0.0380	0.5291 ± 0.0329	0.5704 ± 0.0493	0.4972 ± 0.0313	0.5216 ± 0.0424
K Nearest Neighbour	0.5022 ± 0.0386	0.5433 ± 0.0315	0.5648 ± 0.0306	0.5427 ± 0.0393	0.5167 ± 0.0522
AdaBoost	0.5838 ± 0.0380	0.5291 ± 0.0329	0.5704 ± 0.0493	0.4972 ± 0.0313	0.5216 ± 0.0424

Table 6.6: Performance comparison of all models using acoustic + importance (A+I) and acoustic + importance + lexical (A+I+L) features. Best F1-scores in each feature group were highlighted in bold.

Model	A+I		A+I+L	
	Accuracy (%)	**F1-Score**	**Accuracy (%)**	**F1-Score**
K-Nearest Neighbors	62.03 ± 4.97	0.6164 ± 0.0522	62.34 ± 5.18	0.6190 ± 0.0549
Support Vector Machine	55.46 ± 2.09	0.4883 ± 0.0219	55.66 ± 2.20	0.4919 ± 0.0224
Gaussian Naive Bayes	58.12 ± 3.95	0.5799 ± 0.0397	62.76 ± 3.67	0.6167 ± 0.0385
Logistic Regression	60.80 ± 3.34	0.6016 ± 0.0321	61.41 ± 4.32	0.6072 ± 0.0452
Decision Tree	60.39 ± 4.60	0.5975 ± 0.0475	63.88 ± 5.51	0.6325 ± 0.0541
Random Forest	64.40 ± 2.75	0.6354 ± 0.0295	66.46 ± 3.13	0.6571 ± 0.0313
Extra Trees	**65.22 ± 3.50**	**0.6430 ± 0.0364**	66.25 ± 3.52	0.6621 ± 0.0505
AdaBoost	63.16 ± 4.40	0.6235 ± 0.0454	64.82 ± 4.18	0.6400 ± 0.0424
Gradient Boosting	60.09 ± 5.73	0.5963 ± 0.0575	**66.56 ± 2.81**	**0.6621 ± 0.0266**
XGBoost	58.63 ± 5.03	0.5803 ± 0.0508	66.15 ± 4.24	0.6559 ± 0.0424
LightGBM	61.11 ± 4.28	0.6049 ± 0.0418	66.36 ± 4.51	0.6582 ± 0.0461
Stacking Ensemble	50.52 ± 8.98	0.2904 ± 0.1928	57.72 ± 8.35	0.4931 ± 0.1387
Hard Voting Ensemble	55.67 ± 11.09	0.5567 ± 0.1109	56.28 ± 8.48	0.4582 ± 0.1616
Soft Voting Ensemble	56.07 ± 12.30	0.5607 ± 0.1230	58.23 ± 9.10	0.5137 ± 0.1736

Moreover, *I* contributes even in the presence of strong lexical cues, for the full feature combination (A+I+L), where the inclusion of *I* further improves already strong performance. For instance, LightGBM achieves its best results—66.36% accuracy and 0.6582 F1-score—when I was added to A+L, outperforming both the A+I and A+L combinations. Extra Trees and Gradient Boosting follow a similar pattern, showing that the score provides complementary cues that enhance the impact of lexical and acoustic features together. This is further illustrated in Figure 6-5.

Interestingly, ensembling methods also benefit from the addition of I. The Soft Voting model, for example, improves its F1-score from 0.5607 (A+I) to 0.6137 (A+I+L), recovering from a weaker baseline and gaining better stability. Although ensemble variants still underperform compared to their best individual classifiers, the presence of I tends to moderate this effect and improve consistency.

Overall, these results suggest that the proposed importance score (I) functions effectively as a relevance feature within a classification-based summarization setup. The improvements it brings were modest but consistent, reinforcing its value as a lightweight prosodic indicator of sentence-level importance. Especially in low-resource contexts, where lexical features may be limited or noisy, I offers a practical and interpretable signal to support extractive summarization. It is further represented in Figure 6-6.

To better illustrate the sentence-level decisions made by the classifiers, Table 6.7 presents a comparison between the sentences selected by the classifier, and those in the human-generated summary for a representative broadcast news segment. Correctly identified utterances were marked as matches, while spurious selections were shown as misses.

Given the imbalanced nature of the sentence selection task, model performance

Table 6.7: Extractive Summary Comparison: Acoustic-Based Model vs. Reference

#	**System Summary (Classifier-selected**	**Human Summary (Reference)**
	Original Assamese Sentences	
	(1) দেশৰ ১৬খন ৰাজ্য অচিৰেই কৰ'নামুক্ত হোৱাৰ দিশত ✓ (2) ২০ মে'ৰ ভিতৰত ভাৰতত নোহোৱা হ'ব সংক্ৰমণ শিৰোনামৰ এটা বাতৰি দৈনিক জনমভূমি কাকতে প্ৰধান বাতৰি হিচাপে প্ৰথম পৃষ্ঠাত প্ৰকাশ কৰিছে ✗ (3) ৮জন ৰোগীক কালি চিকিৎসালয়ৰ পৰা যাবলৈ দিয়া হয় ✓ (4) অৱশ্যে চৰকাৰী কৰ্মচাৰীসকলে যিহেতু সম্পূৰ্ণ দৰমহা লাভ কৰিছে ✗ (5) কেতিয়া খুলিব লকডাউন, উদ্বিগ্ন জনতা ✗	(1) দেশৰ ১৬খন ৰাজ্য অচিৰেই কৰ'নামুক্ত হোৱাৰ দিশত (2) স্বাস্থ্যমন্ত্ৰীগৰাকীৰ সৈতে স্বাস্থ্য ৰাজ্য মহৰী পিযুষ হাজৰিকাও উপস্থিত থাকে । (3) ৮জন ৰোগীক কালি চিকিৎসালয়ৰ পৰা যাবলৈ দিয়া হয় (4) কোভিড-19ৰ আক্ৰমণত ক্ষত-বিক্ষত বিশ্ব (5) কৰণাত দুই লক্ষাধিকৰ মৃত্যু শীৰ্ষক এটা বাতৰি দৈনিক অগ্ৰদূত কাকতে প্ৰধান বাতৰি হিচাপে প্ৰথম পৃষ্ঠাত প্ৰকাশ কৰিছে
	English Translation of the corresponding Assamese summary-sentences	
1	16 states in the country were on the verge of becoming free of the virus soon ✓	*(Match)*
2	The Daily Janambhumi made a front page headline with the headline ‘Infection will disappear from India by May’ ✗	*(Miss)* The Health Minister was accompanied by State Health Mohari Piyush Hazarika.
3	Eight patients were discharged from the hospital yesterday ✓	*(Match)*
4	However, government employees have received their full salaries ✗	*(Miss)* The world was wounded by the onslaught of COVID-19
5	When will the lockdown be reopened, people were worried ✗	*(Miss)* The Daily ’Agradut’ headlined in its first page that more than 2 lakh died due to Corona

✓ *Match:* Semantically aligned utterance in both summaries (highlighted in green).
✗ *Miss:* System-selected utterance not found in reference summary (highlighted in red).
Extractive Summary Comparison (short excerpt): System-generated summary using Gradient Boosting classifier trained on acoustic feature-set vs. Human-generated (gold-standard) summary. For this qualitative illustration, we showcase the output of the Gradient Boosting classifier, which was trained solely on acoustic feature-set and performed reliably in the quantitative evaluation.

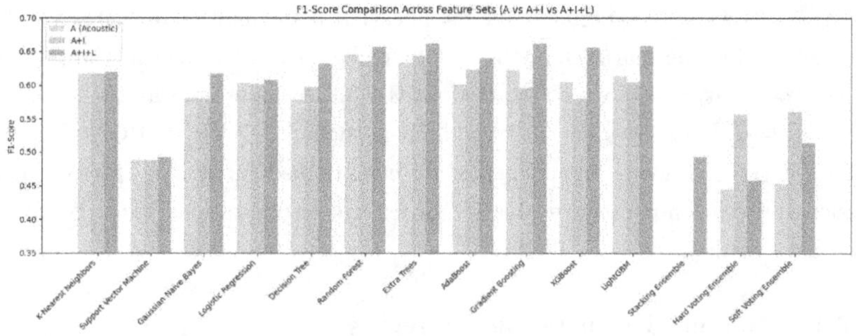

Figure 6-6: F1-score comparison across three feature sets — acoustic-only (A), acoustic + importance (A+I), and full combination (A+I+L).
The consistent upward trend across models demonstrates the additive value of the proposed prosodic importance score (I), both in isolation and in combination with lexical features.

was prioritized based on mean F1-score rather than mean accuracy. Accordingly, the model achieving the highest mean F1-score was selected for summary generation and ROUGE-based evaluation. For ensemble methods such as stacking and voting, multiple base learners with complementary strengths—including models with higher mean accuracy—were incorporated to promote diversity and enhance generalization.

6.6.4 ROUGE-Based Summary Evaluation

Given the imbalanced nature of the sentence selection task, model performance was prioritized based on mean F1-score rather than mean accuracy. Accordingly, the model achieving the highest mean F1-score was selected for summary generation and ROUGE-based evaluation. For ensemble methods such as stacking and voting, multiple base learners with complementary strengths—including models with higher mean accuracy—were incorporated to promote diversity and enhance generalization.

While classifier performance offers insight into the accuracy of sentence-level importance prediction, it does not directly reflect the quality of the generated summaries. In this section, we evaluate the summarization capability of the top performing classifiers using ROUGE metrics, which compare the content of generated summaries with human-written references. This phase complements the classification results by assessing the final outputs in terms of content coverage and redundancy. The evaluation was conducted on held-out sessions using summaries generated from classifier predictions, following a length-controlled strategy to ensure fair comparison.

To evaluate whether sentence-level classification performance translates to effective extractive summarization, the top four classifiers identified in the previous phase (per feature set) were retrained on the full training data and used to generate ranked summaries for three held-out sessions. ROUGE-1, ROUGE-2, and ROUGE-L scores were then computed for each ranked summary. This two-phase design enables comparative evaluation of feature configurations in the context of summary quality.

6.6.4.1 Summary Generation Strategy

In a text-independent extractive speech summarization setting, sentence importance was predicted using only acoustic features, including both prosodic cues (e.g., pitch, duration, energy) and MFCCs, without relying on any lexical or syntactic information. As a result, the classifier outputs were based on non-textual cues such as pitch variation, duration, and energy levels. While this approach was crucial in low-resource scenarios where ASR systems may be unreliable or unavailable, it presents specific challenges during evaluation.

One key issue arises from the variability in classifier predictions when summaries were generated directly from binary outputs. Depending on classifier thresholds and prediction confidence, the classifier may label too many or too few sentences as summary-worthy. This leads to inconsistent summary lengths, which can skew ROUGE scores: overly short summaries penalize recall, and overly long summaries inflate precision. This was especially problematic when evaluating across a dataset with varying content density and sentence structure.

To address this, we adopt a ranking-based summary generation strategy during ROUGE evaluation. Instead of using binary predictions, the classifier's predicted probabilities were treated as *confidence scores*, and sentences were ranked accordingly. For each document, we select the top-n sentences, where n was the number of sentences in the corresponding human-written reference summary. This ensures that summary lengths were consistent across all documents and that the evaluation was not affected by threshold sensitivity or class imbalance.

To mitigate the impact of threshold-based variability in binary classification outputs, we compare ROUGE scores obtained from both direct binary predictions and ranked summaries, across three held-out sessions. Results were reported for two key feature configurations: the acoustic baseline (A) and its extension with the proposed importance score (A+I). Both strategies are compared in Tables 6.8 and 6.9.

As seen in Tables 6.8 and 6.9, binary-generated summaries tend to yield variable performance across sessions, likely due to inconsistent summary lengths. The

Table 6.8: ROUGE scores for summaries generated using Feature Set A (Acoustic Baseline)

Session [5]	Summary Type	ROUGE-1	ROUGE-2	ROUGE-L
20	Binary	0.398	0.271	0.356
	Ranked	0.395	0.267	0.351
28	Binary	0.427	0.302	0.388
	Ranked	0.420	0.298	0.382
35	Binary	0.411	0.282	0.371
	Ranked	0.408	0.279	0.368

Table 6.9: ROUGE scores for summaries generated using Feature Set A+I (Acoustic + Importance Score)

Session	Summary Type	ROUGE-1	ROUGE-2	ROUGE-L
20	Binary	0.431	0.297	0.389
	Ranked	0.437	0.306	0.397
28	Binary	0.451	0.314	0.406
	Ranked	0.456	0.320	0.411
35	Binary	0.438	0.301	0.391
	Ranked	0.445	0.309	0.398

ranking-based approach provides more stable and competitive ROUGE scores, and was therefore adopted for all subsequent evaluation and analysis in this chapter.

6.6.4.2 Feature-based analysis of the summaries

Table 6.10: ROUGE Scores for Ranked Summaries using Acoustic Features (A)

Session	Model	ROUGE-1	ROUGE-2	ROUGE-L
20	ET	0.4999	0.3086	0.2187
	GBM	0.6013	0.4287	0.2979
	KNN	0.4887	0.2499	0.2090
	RF	0.5094	0.3080	0.2228
28	ET	0.6482	0.5545	0.2809
	GBM	0.5072	0.4006	0.2912
	KNN	0.6453	0.5178	0.2434
	RF	0.4611	0.3289	0.2367
35	ET	0.3588	0.1855	0.2093
	GBM	0.4198	0.3004	0.2179
	KNN	0.3469	0.2128	0.2105
	RF	0.3767	0.2120	0.2640

Henceforth, we evaluate the summaries based on the ranked sentences from each model. This lets us compare feature sets more fairly, based on how informative the selected sentences actually are. We organize the analysis into a series of structured observations across sessions and feature sets.

Table 6.11: ROUGE Scores for Ranked Summaries using Acoustic + Importance Features (A+I)

Session	Model	ROUGE-1	ROUGE-2	ROUGE-L
20	ADA	0.5020	0.3249	0.2550
	ET	0.5083	0.3213	0.2166
	KNN	0.4887	0.2499	0.2090
	RF	0.5013	0.3067	0.2246
28	ADA	0.4541	0.2938	0.2342
	ET	0.5151	0.3733	0.2998
	KNN	0.6453	0.5178	0.2434
	RF	0.5508	0.4446	0.2754
35	ADA	0.4207	0.3130	0.2537
	ET	0.5488	0.4192	0.2710
	KNN	0.3469	0.2128	0.2105
	RF	0.5042	0.3749	0.2964

Table 6.12: ROUGE Scores for Ranked Summaries using Acoustic + Importance + Lexical Features (A+I+L)

Session	Model	ROUGE-1	ROUGE-2	ROUGE-L
20	ET	0.5330	0.3760	0.2777
	GBM	0.4638	0.2824	0.2646
	LGB	0.5362	0.3476	0.2954
	RF	0.5436	0.3364	0.2441
28	ET	0.4999	0.3631	0.2354
	GBM	0.5091	0.3923	0.2557
	LGB	0.6240	0.5289	0.3194
	RF	0.5388	0.4087	0.3882
35	ET	0.4500	0.2496	0.2165
	GBM	0.4341	0.2570	0.2206
	LGB	0.4755	0.3018	0.2202
	RF	0.3964	0.2048	0.1415

1. **Summary Quality was Consistently Higher for A+I than A.** Across most sessions, classifiers using the A+I feature set (Acoustic + Importance) generate summaries with higher ROUGE scores than those using A (Acoustic) alone, as seen in Table 6.10 and 6.11. For example, in Session 35, ROUGE-2 improves from 0.30 (ADA with A+I) to only 0.18–0.21 (A-only models). ROUGE-L similarly rises from approximately 0.21–0.26 (A-only) to 0.25–0.29 (A+I).

   This supports the hypothesis that the prosody-based importance score adds meaningful information for ranking sentences by their summarization value, as seen in Figure 6-7. In sessions where this gain was not dramatic (e.g., Session 28), the performance was at least maintained or mildly improved.

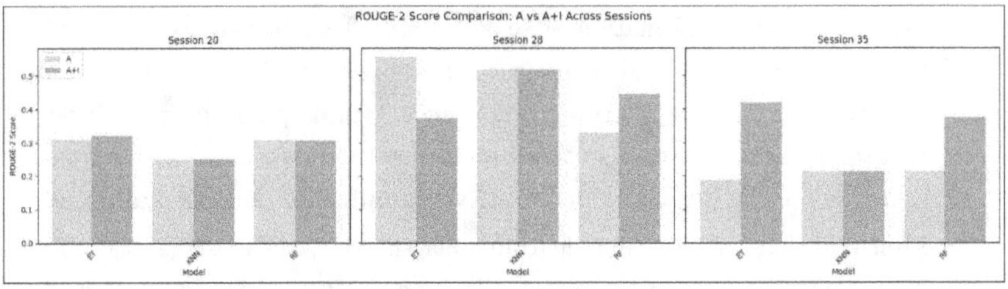

Figure 6-7: ROUGE-2 and ROUGE-L of models ET, KNN and RF, for both A and A+I feature sets across all sessions.A+I performs better than A across sessions.

2. **Performance Gains from Lexical Features (A+I+L) were Mixed and Session-Dependent.** While lexical features such as named entity counts and local word counts can offer useful cues, their contribution was not consistent across sessions. This may depend on document-specific factors such as redundancy or topical diversity. In some cases, these features provide meaningful signals; in others, they may introduce noise or irrelevant variance that does not help summary quality. It can be seen from Table 6.12 that, adding lexical features to create the A+I+L set leads to session-dependent changes: In Session 28, A+I+L yields substantial gains (e.g., ROUGE-2 of 0.52 for LGB, the highest across all sessions). In Session 20, gains were modest or comparable to A+I (e.g., ET model gets 0.32 with A+I vs. 0.38 with A+I+L). In Session 35, performance dips slightly, and models with A+I (e.g., ET, RF) maintain higher ROUGE-2 than A+I+L counterparts. Their utility appears non-uniform, depending on document characteristics such as vocabulary diversity or redundancy, as seen in Figure 6-8.

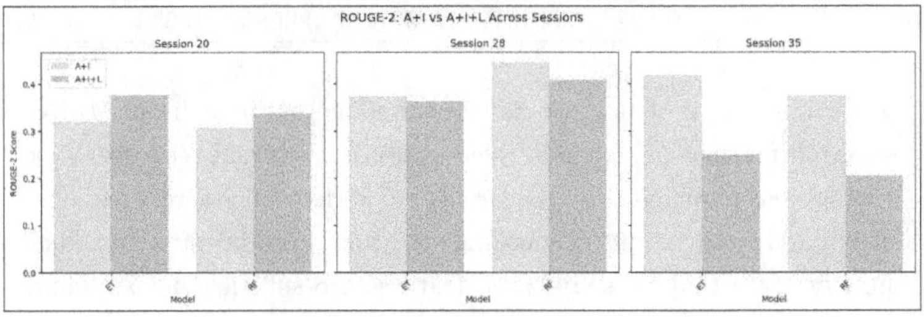

Figure 6-8: Session-wise bar plots comparing A+I vs. A+I+L for each model *This show that lexical features (L) help inconsistently; especially on Session 28 (clear gain), Session 20 (modest), Session 35 (drop).*

3. **Effect of Prosodic Features Excluding MFCCs on Summary Generation.** To explicitly analyse the contribution of prosodic features indepen-

dent of spectral information, a separate set of experiments was conducted using only prosody-based acoustic features, excluding MFCCs. The prosodic feature set comprises suprasegmental cues such as pitch, energy, duration, and their derived statistics, which are commonly associated with emphasis, sentence boundaries, and discourse-level prominence in spoken language.

Multiple classical machine learning classifiers—AdaBoost (ADA), Extra Trees (ET), Gradient Boosting Machine (GBM), k-Nearest Neighbour (KNN), and Random Forest (RF)—were trained and evaluated on two representative broadcast news sessions (Session 20 and Session 28). The performance of these models, measured using ROUGE-1, ROUGE-2, and ROUGE-L metrics, is presented in Table 6.13. The results indicate that prosodic features alone are effective in capturing sentence importance, with tree-based ensemble models such as Extra Trees and Random Forest achieving consistently strong performance across both sessions.

Table 6.13: ROUGE performance of machine learning models using prosodic acoustic features only (excluding MFCCs) on two broadcast news sessions.

Models	Session 20			Session 28		
	R1	R2	R3	R1	R2	R3
ADA	0.3721	0.1866	0.2057	0.5395	0.439	0.2589
ET	0.8217	0.721	0.3593	0.952	0.9449	0.4676
GBM	0.6448	0.4917	0.2814	0.7793	0.738	0.4107
KNN	0.5085	0.3227	0.2301	0.7257	0.6661	0.3547
RF	0.8217	0.7135	0.337	0.9589	0.954	0.4251

The results show that prosodic features alone, without using MFCC-based spectral information, can effectively capture important sentences for extractive speech summarization. Differences in performance across sessions can be attributed to variations in speaking style and prosodic patterns. These findings indicate that prosody-based features are sufficient for summarization and support the thesis goal of developing ASR-independent speech summarization methods using acoustic–prosodic information.

4. **Ensemble Methods Consistently Outperform Simpler Classifiers.** Ensemble models like Extra Trees (ET), Random Forests (RF), and LightGBM (LGB) generally outperform KNN, both in absolute ROUGE scores and consistency across sessions. For example, ET and LGB frequently top

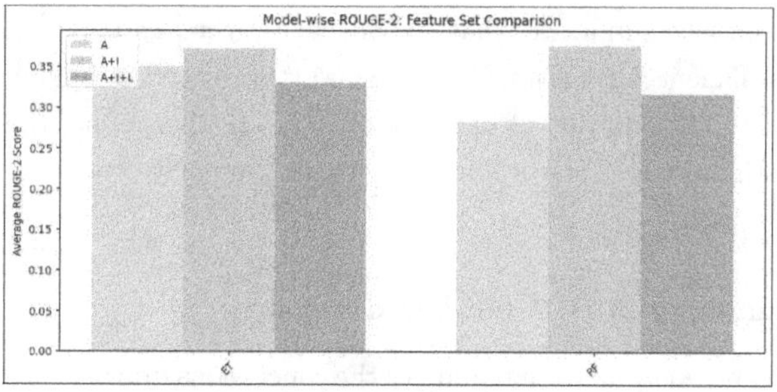

Figure 6-9: Grouped bar chart showing model-wise ROUGE-2 across feature sets.
This emphasize how acoustic features alone (A), A+I, and A+I+L perform. Supports that acoustic-prosodic features were robust even without text.

the ROUGE-2 scores across feature sets (shown in Figure 6-9, while KNN trails in most sessions, especially when lexical features were added.

This aligns with prior classification-phase results where KNN showed higher variance and weaker generalization. Here, its ranking ability was similarly less robust, likely due to its sensitivity to sparse or unevenly distributed feature spaces.

5. **ROUGE-2 was a More Discriminative Metric than ROUGE-1 or ROUGE-L.** ROUGE-2 (bigrams) better highlights meaningful performance differences between models than ROUGE-1 or ROUGE-L. While ROUGE-1 and ROUGE-L remain relatively flat across feature sets (especially in Sessions 20 and 35), ROUGE-2 captures sharper gains—for instance, LGB's ROUGE-2 of 0.52 in Session 28 (A+I+L) compared to 0.30 or lower in other settings.

   This reinforces the need to evaluate content-level informativeness rather than relying only on unigram overlap or length-sensitive metrics like ROUGE-L. In this chapter, ROUGE-2 consistently distinguished high-quality summaries more clearly than ROUGE-1 or ROUGE-L. This suggests that ROUGE-2 may serve as a more sensitive evaluation metric for future work involving ranked extractive summarization in speech-based settings.

6. **Overall Trends Validate Acoustic-Prosodic Features for Summary Generation.** The consistent performance of the A and A+I feature sets—despite excluding any textual input—supports the feasibility of text-independent speech summarization in low-resource contexts. Even when lexical features were available, their marginal benefit was not always guaranteed.

This robustness indicates that prosodic cues, when appropriately quantified, were sufficient for learning summary-worthy sentence rankings, as seen in Fig. 6-9. The addition of importance scores further refines these estimates, suggesting a viable feature-driven path for summary generation without full transcription.

6.6.4.3 Summary of ROUGE-based findings

The ROUGE-based evaluation reinforces the conclusions drawn from classifier performance: acoustic-prosodic features, even without textual content, can support meaningful extractive summarization in low-resource speech domains. Models trained solely on these features produced summaries that consistently covered core content as measured by ROUGE scores.

Adding shallow lexical features—limited to named entity counts and word length statistics—provided further improvements in some sessions. However, the gains were modest and inconsistent, indicating that such content-level cues, while beneficial, may depend on document-specific characteristics such as redundancy or sentence structure.

Importantly, the results validate the two-phase evaluation setup. Classifier-based sentence selection, when paired with ranked summary generation, yields coherent summaries that reflect the relative informativeness of spoken content. This supports the broader thesis that full-text transcriptions are not strictly necessary for summarization, provided prosodic cues are well-captured.

6.6.4.4 Limitations of ROUGE in Low-Resource Language Evaluation

While this approach improves comparability and reliability of ROUGE scoring, there were important limitations that must be acknowledged—particularly in the context of evaluating summaries in low-resource languages such as Assamese. ROUGE, as a metric, relies on surface-level n-gram overlap and does not account for semantic similarity or linguistic nuance. Its effectiveness was therefore reduced in languages where:

- Preprocessing tools (e.g., tokenizers, lemmatizers) were underdeveloped or error-prone.
- Word order was more flexible, leading to mismatched n-grams despite semantic similarity.
- Morphological variation increases surface mismatch even for equivalent content.

In this work, although system summaries were generated without textual information, they were ultimately evaluated in text form by retrieving the corresponding transcriptions of selected sentences. However, due to ROUGE's dependence on accurate string-level overlap, its scores should be interpreted with caution, especially in Assamese, where robust NLP pipelines were still lacking. This limitation highlights the need for more linguistically informed and language-agnostic evaluation metrics in future work.

6.6.5 Discussion

The two-phase evaluation was designed to assess summarization quality from complementary perspectives: sentence-level classification accuracy and final summary informativeness. Together, these analyses provide a holistic picture of how well the proposed models and feature sets support extractive summarization under resource constraints. One of the key contributions of this study was the introduction of a prosody-based sentence importance score. While it was not used directly for summary generation, it served as a relevance feature in the classification models and consistently improved performance—demonstrating its value as a linguistically informed indicator in low-resource speech summarization.

In the classification phase (Sections 6.6.1 to 6.6.3), acoustic and prosodic features (A and I) proved effective in identifying informative sentences, with shallow lexical cues (L) offering occasional but session-dependent improvements. Classifier performance varied across models, but ensemble methods generally provided more robust outcomes.

The ROUGE-based summary evaluation (Section 6.6.4) confirmed that sentence-level predictions can be translated into summaries with reasonable content coverage. Feature sets that improved F1-score in classification also tended to yield higher ROUGE scores, reinforcing the connection between accurate importance prediction and effective summary generation.

Crucially, these results demonstrate that even in the absence of full-text input or high-resource ASR systems, summarization from speech was viable using well-chosen acoustic-prosodic and basic lexical features. The combined findings establish a strong baseline for low-resource summarization and point toward avenues for more semantically aware evaluation and modeling in future work.

Taken together, the findings validate the feasibility of extractive speech summarization in low-resource settings using minimal resources. This aligns with the broader objective of the thesis—to explore viable summarization pipelines in the absence of accurate transcriptions or pretrained language models. The outcomes may inform future development of lightweight speech processing tools suited for under-resourced languages.

6.7 Chapter Summary

This chapter proposed a two-stage framework for extractive speech summarization in low-resource settings using only acoustic-prosodic and shallow lexical features. It showed that sentence importance can be predicted without transcriptions, and these predictions can form coherent summaries with competitive ROUGE scores. Prosodic cues like pitch and intensity emerged as reliable indicators of salience. While the models were simple and interpretable, they assume ideal conditions like clean segmentation and speaker normalization. ROUGE also has known limitations, especially in morphologically rich languages. Still, the work demonstrates that text-independent summarization was feasible, offering a lightweight, language-independent alternative for under-resourced languages.

Chapter 7

A Lightweight Neural Approach for Extractive Speech Summarization in Low-Resource Settings

Chapter 6 demonstrated the feasibility of using traditional machine learning classifiers for prosody-based extractive summarization in low-resource speech corpora. Building on that foundation, this chapter introduces a neural formulation to assess whether a lightweight deep learning model can better capture prosodic sentence importance without relying on transcript. While CNNs have shown promise in extractive summarization of spoken content using textual embeddings [105], their applicability in a purely speech-driven, low-resource setting remains underexplored. This motivates our investigation of CNNs trained solely on acoustic-prosodic inputs.

7.1 Introduction

Neural models for extractive speech summarization are typically data-hungry and resource-intensive, limiting their applicability to low-resourced languages. While much progress has been made in speech summarization through large-scale models, low-resource environments demand simpler, robust alternatives. To explore a more feasible alternative, this chapter introduces a streamlined neural framework built on prosodic and shallow acoustic cues. Building upon the classifier-based framework developed in Chapter 6, we extended the idea of text-independent summarization using a trainable deep learning model. The central question was whether a minimal neural architecture—trained solely on acoustic-prosodic features—can approximate or outperform traditional classifiers in selecting summary-worthy sentences from speech.

The motivation stems from two interlinked challenges in low-resource speech processing: the absence of high-quality automatic speech recognition (ASR) systems, and the lack of large-scale parallel corpora to train text-based summarizers. Most existing extractive summarization methods operate on transcripts, which were either unavailable or highly error-prone in languages like Assamese. In such contexts, speech-driven summarization offers a viable alternative, provided we can effectively model prosodic cues such as pitch variation, energy contours, and pause duration.

To this end, we proposed a simple yet effective one-dimensional Convolutional Neural Network (1D-CNN) architecture that operates directly on handcrafted acoustic-prosodic features. The model was intentionally kept minimal in depth and parameter count, in line with the limited size of annotated data and the real-world need for low-complexity deployment. By avoiding text-based inputs entirely, our approach emphasizes prosody as a standalone modality for summarization—a relatively underexplored avenue in Indian language speech processing.

Unlike prior studies that leverage rich textual or hybrid input modalities, our method represents one of the few fully speech-only neural models in the literature. It does not aim to compete with transformer-based summarizers trained on high-resource English corpora, but rather to demonstrate feasibility in severely constrained settings.

Experiments were conducted on the manually segmented and annotated Assamese broadcast news corpus introduced earlier. We evaluate model performance both in terms of classification metrics and ROUGE scores on generated summaries. Comparative analysis was presented against a suite of classifier-based baselines and neural ablations (dropout, recurrent units, attention). Our findings suggest that even with limited features and no textual input, neural models can offer competitive performance—validating the proposed approach as a viable alternative in low-resource summarization.

7.2 Methodology

Conventional models often assume the availability of rich linguistic input. In contrast, the following approach is designed to work directly with prosodic and acoustic cues, enabling summarization without reliance on transcribed text. This section presents the complete neural architecture and experimental framework designed for text-independent extractive summarization in low-resource speech corpora. Building on prior classifier-based baselines (Chapter 6), this chapter formalizes the task as a binary classification problem over spoken sentences, using only acoustic-prosodic features. The primary research question was whether a lightweight 1D-CNN architecture, trained solely on handcrafted prosodic features, can learn to distinguish summary-worthy sentences without relying on transcriptions.

The methodology was designed with the following constraints in mind:

- **Low-Resource Feasibility:** Models must perform reasonably with limited labeled data.
- **Text Independence:** All models must operate purely on acoustic-prosodic inputs.
- **Interpretability:** Simpler architectures were favored over black-box models for diagnostic and practical reasons.

7.2.1 Model Overview

We explore a family of neural architectures ranging from a minimalist 1D-CNN to more expressive models such as CNN+BiGRU and CNN+Attention. The proposed 1D-CNN serves as the reference model, with all comparative architectures trained under the same conditions for fairness.

7.2.2 Proposed Architecture: Lightweight 1D-CNN

The core idea was to use 1D convolutional layers to extract sequential prosodic patterns over sentence-level speech segments. The input to the model was a fixed-length feature vector of 47dimensions per sentence. These were treated as a 1D sequence with shape $(47, 1)$ to suit convolutional input requirements.

The architecture was defined as follows:

- **Input:** $\mathbf{x} \in \mathbb{R}^{47\times 1}$
- **Conv1D Layer 1:** 64 filters, kernel size 3, ReLU activation
- **Conv1D Layer 2:** 128 filters, kernel size 3, ReLU activation
- **GlobalAveragePooling1D**
- **Dense Layer:** 64 units, ReLU activation
- **Output:** 1 unit, Sigmoid activation (binary prediction)

Mathematically, the convolutional operation at layer l was defined as:

$$h_i^{(l)} = \sigma\left(\sum_{j=0}^{k-1} W_j^{(l)} x_{i+j} + b^{(l)}\right)$$

where k was the kernel size, σ was the ReLU function, and $W^{(l)}$ were learnable weights.

The final sigmoid layer outputs a probability score $\hat{y} \in [0, 1]$, interpreted as the likelihood of a sentence being summary-worthy.

7.2.3 Input Features

Each sentence-level input was a time-aligned acoustic-prosodic feature vector comprising:

- **Pitch:** Minimum, maximum, mean, range
- **Energy:** Minimum, maximum, mean
- **Duration:** Length of audio segment in milliseconds
- **MFCCs:** 39 Mel-Frequency Cepstral Coefficients

Although handcrafted, these features reflect linguistically relevant patterns such as pitch prominence and duration-based phrasing. Despite their simplicity, we show that these low-cost features provide strong performance when used with a suitable neural architecture.

7.2.4 Comparative Architectures

To contextualize the performance of the proposed 1D-CNN architecture, we implemented and evaluated a set of comparative neural models with increasing architectural complexity. These comparative baselines were chosen not only to assess the benefits of additional depth or recurrence, but also to test whether architectural complexity could improve sentence-level summary detection in the absence of textual input and with highly limited data.

All models were trained under identical conditions—using the same input features, class weighting strategy, and brute-force 400-epoch training plan—to ensure a fair comparison. The following subsections detail each architecture's structure, rationale, and specific differences from the proposed CNN baseline.

7.2.4.1 CNN with Dropout Regularization

This variant of the baseline CNN architecture introduces dropout regularization to mitigate potential overfitting. Dropout was applied after the dense layers to randomly deactivate a fraction of neurons during training, thereby encouraging the model to learn robust, distributed representations.

Formally, given a hidden layer activation $h^{(l)} \in \mathbb{R}^n$, dropout applies a binary mask $m \sim \text{Bernoulli}(p)$, where p was the probability of retaining a neuron. The regularized output becomes:

$$\tilde{h}^{(l)} = m \odot h^{(l)}$$

where $\odot$ denotes element-wise multiplication.

The model architecture was as follows:

- `Input`: $(47, 1)$ feature vector
- `Conv1D (filters=64, kernel=3, activation='relu')`
- `Conv1D (filters=128, kernel=3, activation='relu')`
- `GlobalMaxPooling1D`
- `Dense (units=64, activation='relu')`
- `Dropout (rate=0.3)`
- `Dense (units=1, activation='sigmoid')`

Despite the theoretical benefits of dropout, this model underperformed in F1-score for class 1. We hypothesize that in a low-data regime with imbalanced labels, dropout may hinder the model's ability to consistently learn rare patterns associated with summary-worthy sentences.

7.2.4.2 CNN + BiGRU Hybrid Model

This architecture combines the convolutional front-end of the base CNN with a Bidirectional GRU (BiGRU) layer. The motivation was to retain CNN's local feature extraction while adding recurrent modeling to capture temporal dependencies across feature sequences. The BiGRU processes the sequence in both forward and backward directions, potentially enabling richer context aggregation.

Mathematically, a GRU cell operates as:

$$z_t = \sigma(W_z x_t + U_z h_{t-1}), \quad r_t = \sigma(W_r x_t + U_r h_{t-1})$$

$$\tilde{h}_t = \tanh(W_h x_t + U_h(r_t \odot h_{t-1})), \quad h_t = (1 - z_t) \odot h_{t-1} + z_t \odot \tilde{h}_t$$

The BiGRU outputs were then concatenated and passed to a dense layer. The model architecture is:

- `Input`: $(47, 1)$
- `Conv1D (filters=64, kernel=3, activation='relu')`
- `Conv1D (filters=128, kernel=3, activation='relu')`
- `BiGRU (units=64, return_sequences=False)`
- `Dense (units=64, activation='relu')`
- `Dense (units=1, activation='sigmoid')`

This model adds significant complexity and parameter count. Empirical results showed degraded performance on minority class prediction, likely due to overfitting and the added challenge of learning temporal structures from sparse prosodic cues.

7.2.4.3 CNN with Attention Mechanism

To allow the model to dynamically focus on relevant parts of the input feature sequence, we implemented an attention mechanism on top of the CNN layers. This architecture introduces a learnable attention layer that computes weights over the CNN outputs, thereby allowing the model to highlight salient regions contributing to the summary-worthiness of a sentence.

Let $H = [h_1, h_2, \ldots, h_T]$ denote the CNN feature maps. The attention score α_t for timestep t was computed as:

$$e_t = \tanh(Wh_t + b), \quad \alpha_t = \frac{\exp(e_t)}{\sum_{k=1}^{T} \exp(e_k)}$$

The final representation was the weighted sum:

$$c = \sum_{t=1}^{T} \alpha_t h_t$$

Model architecture:

- `Input:` $(47, 1)$
- `Conv1D (filters=64, kernel=3, activation='relu')`
- `Conv1D (filters=128, kernel=3, activation='relu')`
- `Attention Layer`
- `Dense (units=64, activation='relu')`
- `Dense (units=1, activation='sigmoid')`

This model aimed to improve interpretability and dynamic focus, but in practice, the limited size of the dataset hindered effective attention learning. Nonetheless, it serves as an important comparative point in architectural diversity.

7.2.4.4 Multilayer Perceptron (MLP)

As a non-convolutional baseline, the MLP model tests whether simple feedforward dense layers were sufficient to learn discriminative patterns from static prosodic feature vectors. This model lacks any sequential or local connectivity biases.

The structure is:

- `Input:` $(47, 1)$ reshaped to flat $(47,)$
- `Dense (units=64, activation='relu')`

- `Dense (units=128, activation='relu')`
- `Dropout (rate=0.3)`
- `Dense (units=64, activation='relu')`
- `Dense (units=1, activation='sigmoid')`

Although computationally efficient, the MLP underperformed compared to the convolutional models, likely due to the absence of inductive biases that help exploit local feature correlations in acoustic data.

Each of these comparative architectures reveals different failure modes or trade-offs in text-independent summarization. These comparative architectures serve to evaluate whether deeper or recurrent structures can outperform the proposed minimal CNN in the same text-independent setting. Their inclusion allows for a controlled assessment of how architectural variation affects sentence-level summarization performance in prosody-only, low-resource scenarios.

7.2.5 Training Strategy

The training strategy plays a central role in ensuring that our neural summarization models learn to accurately detect summary-worthy sentences, particularly in the presence of severe class imbalance. Since the proposed approach treats extractive summarization as a binary classification task over spoken sentences, it was essential to design the training protocol with attention to both the nature of the data and the goals of the summarization task. This section describes the key considerations and empirical decisions that shape the training process for all neural architectures discussed in this chapter.

7.2.5.1 Framing Summarization as an Imbalanced Classification Task

In the context of extractive summarization, each sentence was assigned a binary label: `label=1` if the sentence was selected for inclusion in the summary, and `label=0` otherwise. However, in natural discourse—especially in broadcast speech, interviews, or spoken news—the number of summary-worthy sentences was typically a small fraction of the total number of sentences in the document. Human-generated summaries include 20% of all sentences.

This leads to a highly imbalanced classification setting where the positive class (label $= 1$) was underrepresented. Such imbalance introduces a core challenge: a naïve classifier could achieve deceptively high accuracy by simply predicting all sentences as non-summary (label $= 0$), thereby ignoring the minority class altogether. While this might result in a high overall accuracy, it entirely defeats the purpose of summarization, which was to correctly detect the small number of sentences that carry essential information.

In this work, we treat the class imbalance not as a secondary problem but as an inherent and defining feature of the summarization task. Accordingly, the training strategy was designed to directly counteract the tendency of the model to bias toward the majority class. This required adjustments to both the loss function and the evaluation procedure.

7.2.5.2 Loss Function and Class Weighting

To mitigate the effects of class imbalance, we apply a class-weighted binary cross-entropy loss during training. This approach increases the contribution of the minority class (label = 1) to the overall loss, thereby encouraging the model to allocate sufficient attention to summary-worthy sentences.

Let $y_i \in \{0, 1\}$ be the ground-truth label for the ith input sentence, and $\hat{y}_i \in [0, 1]$ be the predicted probability of it belonging to class 1. The weighted binary cross-entropy loss was defined as:

$$\mathcal{L}_{\text{weighted}} = -\sum_{i=1}^{N} w_{y_i} \left[y_i \log(\hat{y}_i) + (1 - y_i) \log(1 - \hat{y}_i) \right], \tag{7.1}$$

where w_{y_i} was the weight assigned to the ground-truth class of the ith sample. The weights were computed inversely proportional to the class frequencies in the training data. This ensures that errors on the minority class were penalized more heavily than those on the majority class.

In practical terms, using class weights communicates the following to the model: "A mistake on class 1 was more costly than a mistake on class 0. Pay closer attention to the underrepresented but crucial class." This adjustment was essential for extractive summarization, where the true signal lies precisely in these minority instances.

7.2.5.3 Empirical Epoch Selection: Class-Imbalance Aware Validation

Rather than adopting a fixed number of training epochs based on heuristics or external benchmarks, we adopted a data-driven approach for determining an appropriate training budget. Specifically, we monitored the validation F1-score for class 1 (`label=1`) across all training epochs.

The rationale for this was straightforward: since the goal was to identify summary-worthy sentences, we were primarily interested in the model's ability to predict class 1 accurately. In an imbalanced setting, global accuracy and even loss may be misleading. For instance, a model that predicts all inputs as class 0 could still achieve over 80% accuracy, but such a model would have zero F1-score on class 1. Hence, the F1-score for label 1 was chosen as the central metric for convergence tracking.

We trained the baseline 1D-CNN model for a total of 400 epochs. After each epoch, we evaluated the model on a held-out validation set and recorded the F1-score for class 1. Figure 7-1 illustrates the progression of the F1-score across training epochs. As observed, the F1-score steadily increases during the initial phases of training and begins to plateau around epoch 350. Beyond epoch 375, no consistent improvement was observed, and in some cases, slight overfitting causes minor fluctuations.

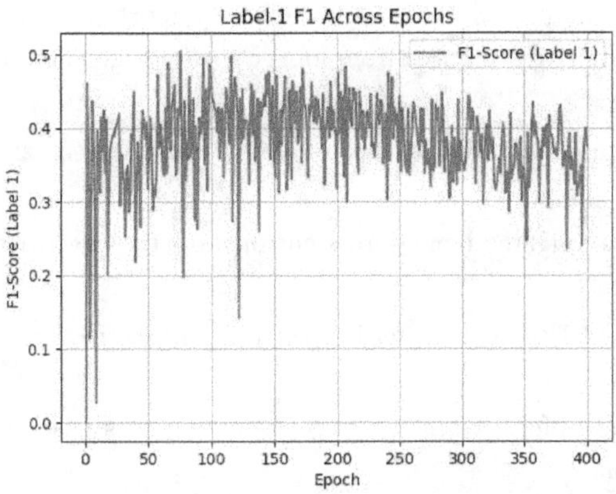

Figure 7-1: Training progression of F1-score across epochs for the neural models. *F1 was monitored every 50 epochs and smoothed to reduce noise. Based on convergence patterns, a uniform training budget of 400 epochs was selected for fair comparison across model variants.*

To reduce the effect of random noise, we monitored the F1-score at intervals of 50 epochs and plotted a smoothed trend. Based on these observations, we set the final training budget at 400 epochs for all model variants, ensuring consistent comparison across architectures.

These findings guided our decision to use a fixed training schedule, rather than adopting adaptive strategies like early stopping, as further discussed below.

7.2.5.4 Fixed Epoch Budget and Plateau Justification

Although it is common practice to apply early stopping based on validation loss, such a strategy was suboptimal in this case. As discussed, validation loss was not a reliable indicator of the model's ability to detect summary-worthy sentences in an imbalanced setup. Instead, we rely on direct monitoring of the F1-score for label 1. This score reflects the true task objective more faithfully.

The final decision to fix the epoch count at 400 was based on the empirical observation that model performance for label 1 saturates by this point. Furthermore, using a fixed training budget enables fairer comparisons across models, since all architectures were trained under identical conditions without model-specific stopping criteria.

7.2.5.5 Summary of Training Protocol

To summarize, the training process was carefully tailored to address the unique challenges of extractive summarization in speech. These challenges include severe class imbalance, limited labeled data, and the importance of detecting a small number of informative sentences from longer speech segments. The final training strategy includes:

- Treating summarization as an inherently imbalanced binary classification task.
- Using class-weighted binary cross-entropy loss to prioritize summary-worthy sentences.
- Monitoring F1-score for label 1 as the primary metric for convergence tracking.
- Selecting a uniform training budget of 400 epochs based on empirical validation trends.

This principled approach ensures that all neural architectures were trained in a way that directly supports the end goal of extractive summarization, while remaining robust to imbalance and task-specific constraints.

7.3 Experimental Setup

7.3.1 Corpus and Session Definition

The speech corpus used in this chapter was derived from the same manually segmented and annotated Assamese broadcast news dataset introduced in Chapter 3. Each audio file corresponds to a single spoken sentence, and collectively, these files were grouped into recording sessions corresponding to full news broadcasts.

For each session, gold-standard summaries were created by human annotators, marking sentence-level binary labels: `label = 1` if the sentence belongs in the summary, and `label = 0` otherwise. The total number of sessions and sentences was relatively modest due to the challenges of manual annotation in low-resource language contexts.

All features used in this chapter were derived solely from the speech signal. No textual or ASR-transcribed data was used at any stage, preserving the fully text-independent nature of this summarization task.

Key characteristics:

- Each input instance corresponds to one sentence-long audio segment.
- Sessions were treated as independent summarization units.
- Summary labels were binary and sentence-level.

7.3.2 Data Splits and Preprocessing

To evaluate the summarization models, we divide the corpus into fixed training, validation, and test splits based on sessions (not shuffled across sentence-level instances). This respects session integrity and avoids leakage of speaker-specific or content-specific prosodic patterns between train and test sets.

7.3.2.1 Split Strategy

From the dataset procured from the Assamese portion of Broadcast news sub-corpus (the same dataset used in Chapter 6), we reserve three sessions as the test set, which remain fixed across all experiments for fair model comparison. The remaining sessions were used for training and validation. From the dataset procured from the Assamese portion of Broadcast news sub-corpus, we reserve three sessions as the test set, which remain fixed across all experiments for fair model comparison. The training and validation sets were created by splitting the remaining sessions at the document (i.e., session) level, ensuring that each complete broadcast session used for testing remained entirely unseen during model training—thus better reflecting real-world summarization scenarios.[1].

- **Training set:** Majority of sessions used for model learning.
- **Validation set:** Held-out sessions used to monitor label-1 F1-score and guide training.
- **Test set:** Three fixed sessions used for final evaluation of classification and summary generation.

[1]Each session refers to a full spoken broadcast segment, approximately 15 minutes in duration, taken from Assamese All India Radio news bulletins (morning or evening editions). Each session was treated as a distinct document for summarization, with sentences segmented and labeled for summary inclusion.

7.3.2.2 Feature Preprocessing

Each sentence-level audio file was converted into a fixed 47-dimensional feature vector. These features were entirely acoustic-prosodic in nature, capturing pitch, energy, duration, and MFCC-based information. Specifically, the 47 features include:

- **Pitch-related (4):** Minimum, maximum, mean, range of pitch contour.
- **Energy-related (3):** Minimum, maximum, and root mean square energy.
- **Duration (1):** Total duration of the audio segment.
- **MFCCs (39):** 39 Mel-Frequency Cepstral Coefficients.

No raw waveform data was used. All features were computed from time-aligned sentence-level audio clips using standard signal processing tools. These features were normalized per-dimension to zero mean and unit variance using the training set statistics.

7.3.2.3 Input Formatting for Neural Models

The final input to each neural model was a tensor of shape `(47, 1)` per instance, reshaped for compatibility with `Conv1D` layers. All models operate on the same input features, without any additional embeddings, transcriptions, or context windows. Labels were converted to binary class targets and cast to `int` format.

- **Input:** 47 acoustic-prosodic features per sentence (reshaped to 47×1).
- **Output:** Binary label indicating summary inclusion.

This fixed input pipeline was used consistently across all architectures (1D-CNN, CNN+Dropout, CNN+BiGRU, etc.), ensuring that performance differences stem from model design and not data handling.

7.3.3 Evaluation Metrics

The performance of our proposed and comparative neural models was evaluated using both classification metrics and summary-level metrics. Given the extreme class imbalance in sentence-level extractive summarization, we prioritize metrics that highlight performance on the minority class (label=1), which corresponds to summary-worthy sentences. We also include complementary visualizations to provide a transparent view of model behavior across training epochs.

7.3.3.1 Why Standard Accuracy was Misleading

Extractive summarization was inherently imbalanced: only a small subset of sentences in any session was considered summary-worthy (label = 1), while the majority of the sentences were not (label = 0). A model predicting all inputs as class 0 can achieve deceptively high accuracy while failing entirely at the summarization objective. Therefore, accuracy alone cannot serve as a reliable metric in this task.

7.3.3.2 F1-Score for Label 1: Core Metric

Our primary evaluation signal was the F1-score for class 1. This score was tracked at every epoch during training, and it serves as the primary criterion for model selection and comparison across architectures.

7.3.3.3 Supporting Metrics and Visualizations

To supplement label-1 F1-score, we include the following metrics and visualizations across all architectures:

Table 7.1: Visualization and Reporting Strategy for Neural Summarization Models

Plot / Metric	**Purpose**	**Why It Matters for Summarization**
Training / Validation Loss	Track optimization and detect instability	Helps identify underfitting or overfitting, particularly when label-1 gradients were underrepresented
Training / Validation Accuracy	Baseline learning sanity check	Useful for diagnostics but secondary due to class imbalance
F1-Score for Label 1 (per epoch)	Core classification evaluation	Directly reflects the model's ability to identify summary-worthy content
Confusion Matrix	Show class-wise prediction performance	Highlights misclassification trends, especially false negatives on label 1
ROC Curve (optional)	Visualize threshold-agnostic discrimination	Reviewer-friendly but limited under class imbalance
Final ROUGE Scores	Evaluate summary-level output quality	Measures overlap between predicted and reference summaries; bridges classification and downstream summarization utility

These metrics were visualized and discussed in the Results section for each architecture. F1-score trajectories, confusion matrices, and ROUGE trends were key to interpreting model behavior, convergence, and summary quality.

7.4 Results and Analysis

This chapter presents the classification-based evaluation of the proposed 1D-CNN architecture and its comparative variants for sentence-level extractive summarization in a text-independent setting. Performance was evaluated using label-wise metrics, standard classification scores, and training visualizations. The primary focus remains on label 1, which corresponds to summary-worthy sentences.

7.4.1 Classification-Based Evaluation

This section presents the classification performance of all neural architectures explored in this thesis. Each model was evaluated on a held-out test set, using the same 47-dimensional prosodic feature inputs. All models were trained with identical hyperparameters: 400 brute-force epochs, identical train-validation splits, and class-weighting enabled to address imbalance. The goal was to isolate the impact of architectural variation under fair conditions.

7.4.1.1 Label-Wise Performance Metrics

Table 7.2 summarizes the label-wise precision, recall, and F1-score for each model. As extractive summarization prioritizes the correct detection of summary-worthy sentences (label 1), we highlight F1-scores for label 1 as the primary metric of interest.

Table 7.2: Label-wise Precision, Recall, and F1-Score for Each Model

Model	$\mathbf{P_0}$	$\mathbf{R_0}$	$\mathbf{F1_0}$	$\mathbf{P_1}$	$\mathbf{R_1}$	$\mathbf{F1_1}$
CNN-Basic	0.7442	0.7805	0.7619	0.4194	0.3714	0.3939
CNN-Dropout	0.7372	0.7012	0.7188	0.3718	0.4143	0.3919
CNN-BiGRU	0.6993	0.6098	0.6515	0.2967	0.3857	0.3354
CNN-Attention	0.7246	0.7378	0.7311	0.3582	0.3429	0.3504
MLP	0.7397	0.6585	0.6968	0.3636	0.4571	0.4051

Key Insight: Despite the class imbalance, all models retain reasonable recall for label 1, but precision suffers due to false positives. The MLP model surprisingly outperforms more complex variants in label 1 F1-score, while CNN_Basic remains the most balanced overall.

7.4.1.2 Secondary Evaluation Metrics: Accuracy, Loss, and AUC

To support the above analysis, Table 7.3 reports global metrics—classification accuracy, binary cross-entropy loss, and Area Under the ROC Curve (AUC). These give an overview of model generalization and probabilistic separability.

Analysis:

1. CNN_Basic offers the best accuracy and highest AUC overall, validating its use as the primary architecture.
2. CNN_BiGRU and MLP models have poorer generalization, likely due to overfitting (MLP) or optimization difficulty (BiGRU).

Table 7.3: Overall Accuracy, Loss, and AUC for All Models

Model	Accuracy	Loss	AUC
CNN-Basic	0.6581	0.9993	0.6203
CNN-Dropout	0.6154	0.7531	0.5915
CNN-BiGRU	0.5427	1.1731	0.5022
CNN-Attention	0.6197	0.7322	0.5763
MLP	0.5983	1.2088	0.6113

CNN_Dropout improves regularization but slightly hurts recall for the summary class.

Attention mechanisms did not offer benefit in this small-scale prosody-only setup, as temporal granularity was already coarse (sentence level).

7.4.1.3 Training Behavior and Visual Analysis

Each model's training behavior was further illustrated using visual assessment. These include: confusion matrices, training/validation accuracy, loss over epochs, and ROC curves.

- **Figure 7-2**: Accuracy, loss trend for CNN-Basic.
- **Figure 7-3**: Confusion matrix for CNN-Basic.
- **Figure 7-4**: ROC curve for CNN-Basic.
- **Figures 7-5–7-13**: Similar visualizations for other architectures.

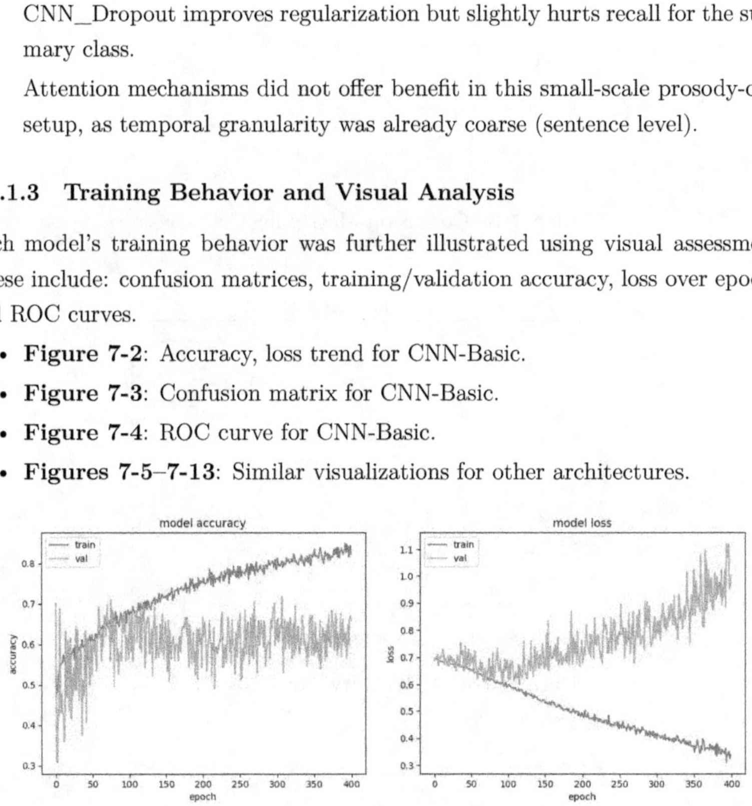

Figure 7-2: Training/Validation Accuracy and Loss for CNN-Basic

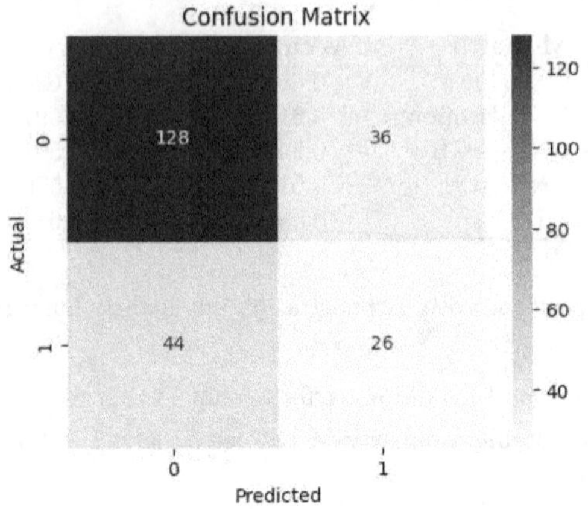

Figure 7-3: Confusion Matrix for CNN-Basic

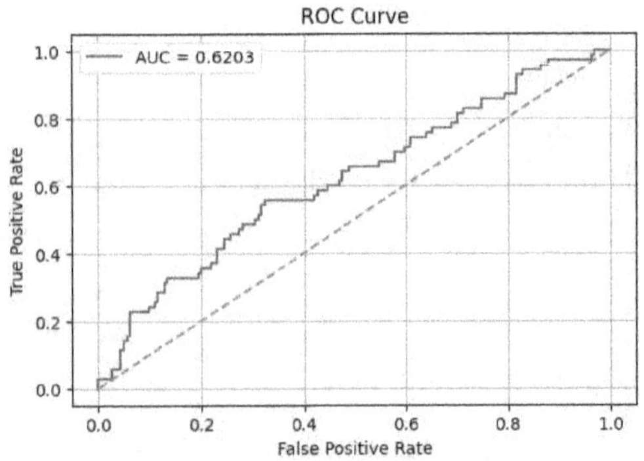

Figure 7-4: ROC Curve for CNN-Basic

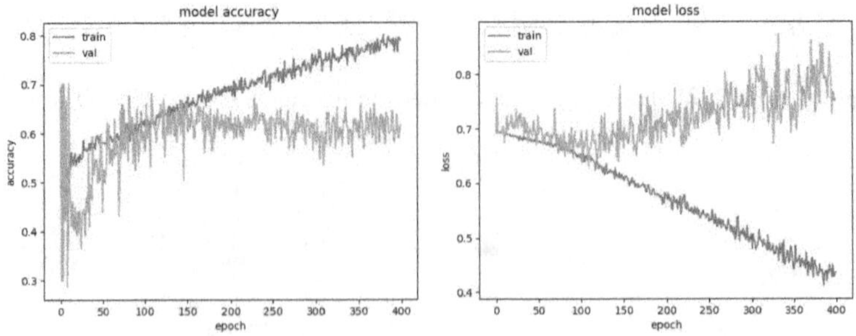

Figure 7-5: Training/Validation Accuracy and Loss for CNN-Dropout

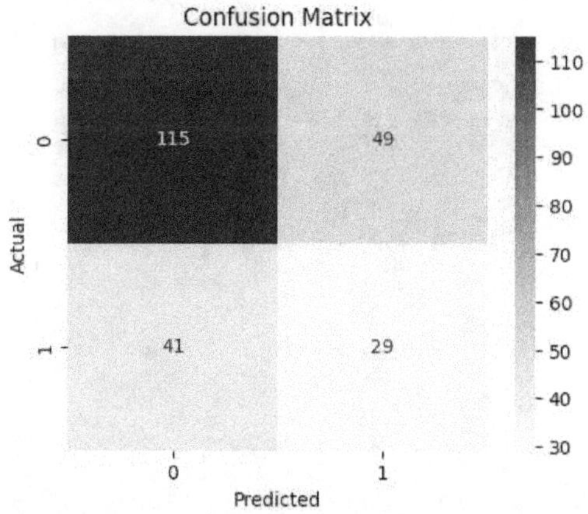

Figure 7-6: Confusion Matrix for CNN-Dropout

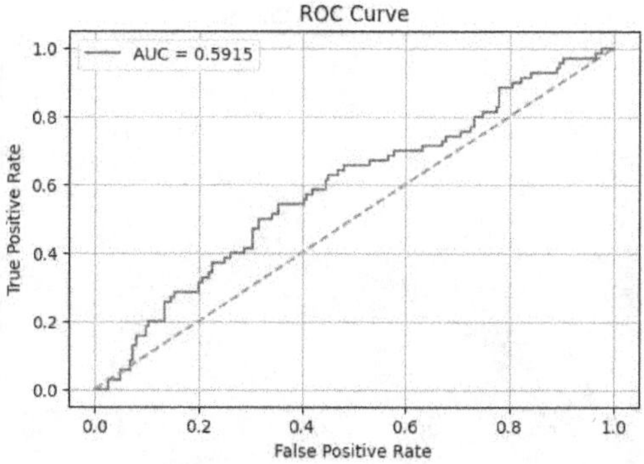

Figure 7-7: ROC Curve for CNN-Dropout

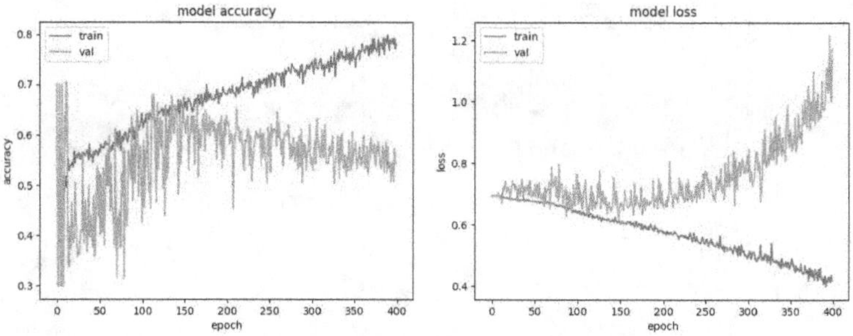

Figure 7-8: Training/Validation Accuracy and Loss for CNN-BiGRU

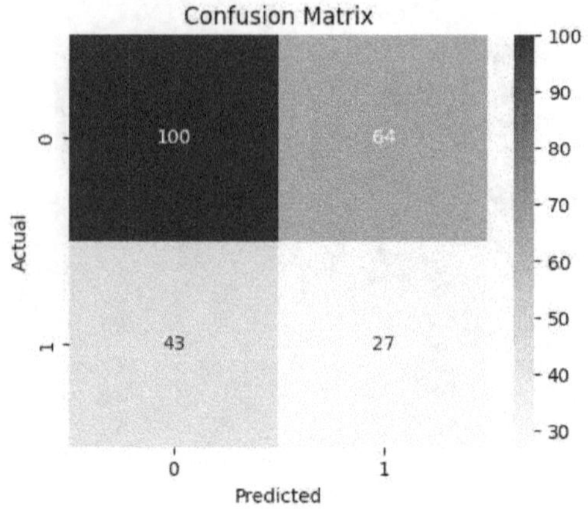

Figure 7-9: Confusion Matrix for CNN-BiGRU

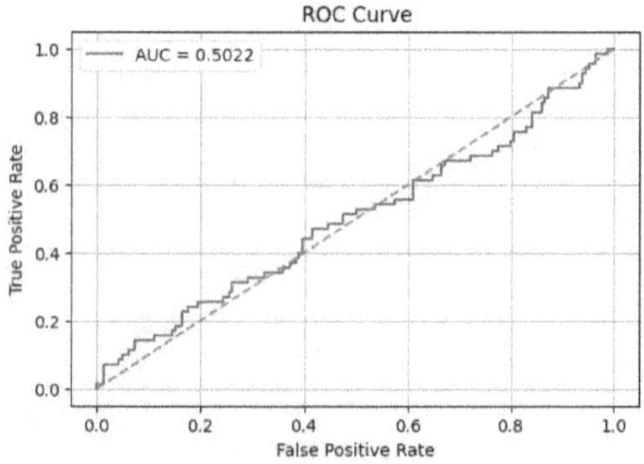

Figure 7-10: ROC Curve for CNN-biGRU

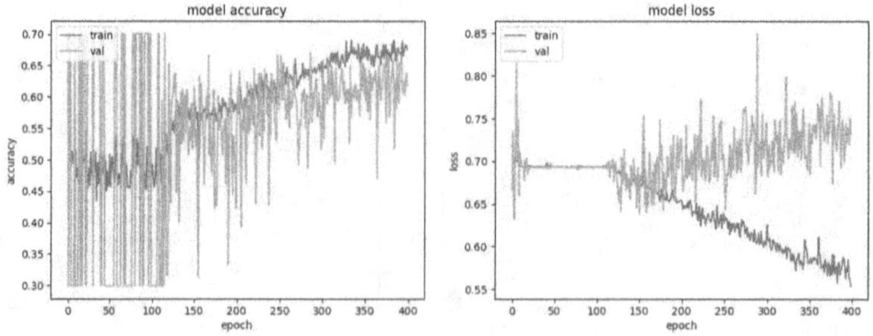

Figure 7-11: Training/Validation Accuracy and Loss for CNN-Attention

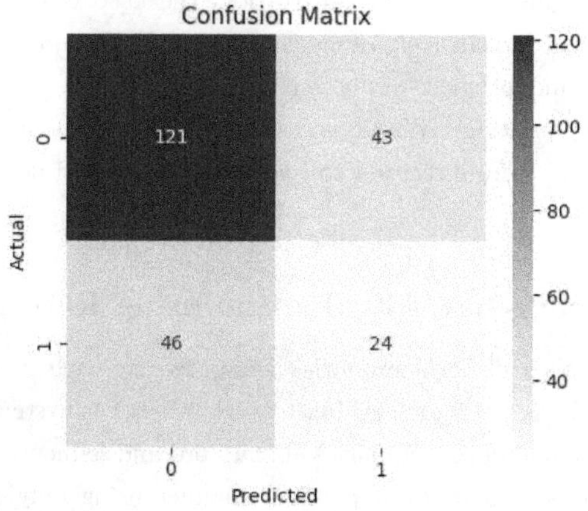

Figure 7-12: Confusion Matrix for CNN-Attention

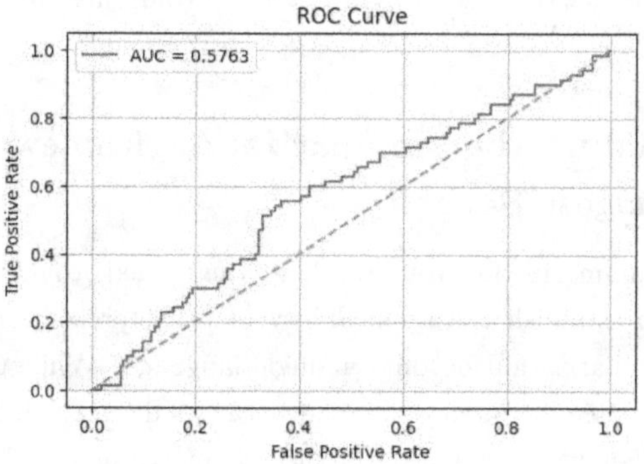

Figure 7-13: ROC Curve for CNN-biGRU

To provide a qualitative perspective on the predictions made by the proposed neural model, Table 7.4 presents a side-by-side comparison between system-selected utterances and the gold-standard human summary for a representative Assamese broadcast news segment. For this illustration, the base 1D-CNN model (Model CNN_Basic), trained exclusively on acoustic-prosodic features, was used. As the table shows, the model successfully recovers several core summary-worthy utterances despite operating without access to transcripts or lexical information. Matches and misses were indicated to help interpret model decisions at the sentence level.

7.4.2 Summary-Level Evaluation using ROUGE

To assess the quality of the summaries generated by each neural architecture, we report ROUGE scores, which evaluate overlap between system-generated summaries and human reference summaries at the word and sequence level. Given that the model operates in a text-independent manner using only acoustic-prosodic features, this evaluation bridges the gap between sentence-level classification and real-world summarization utility.

As shown in Table 7.5, the proposed CNN_Basic model achieved the highest ROUGE-1 and ROUGE-L F1-scores, indicating its superior ability to select summary-worthy sentences. CNN_BiGRU and CNN_Attention models followed closely, while CNN_Dropout and MLP showed relatively lower performance, reflecting their instability under small-data, imbalanced conditions. These results reinforce the feasibility of prosody-only summarization in low-resource settings and highlight the effectiveness of lightweight convolutional architectures for this task.

7.4.3 Extending the summarization framework to other languages: Bengali

The proposed summarization framework was extended from Assamese to Bengali, in order to establish the applicability of using prosodic features for text-independent summarization beyomd a single language. While the initial experiments were conducted on Assamese broadcast news data, the inclusion of Bengali enables a multi-language evaluation of the role of prosodic and spectral features in extractive speech summarization.

Table 7.6 presents a comparative performance analysis across Assamese and Bengali using three feature configurations: prosody-only, spectral-only, and combined prosodic–spectral features, all modeled using the same CNN architecture. The re-

Table 7.4: Extractive Summary Comparison: 1D-CNN vs. Human Summary

#	**System Summary (Classifier-selected)**	**Human Summary (Reference)**
	Original Assamese Sentences	
	(1) দেশৰ ১৬খন ৰাজ্য অচিৰেই কৰ'নামুক্ত হোৱাৰ দিশত ✓ (2) ২০ মে'ৰ ভিতৰত ভাৰতত নোহোৱা হ'ব সংক্ৰমণ শিৰোনামৰ এটা বাতৰি দৈনিক জনমভূমি কাকতে প্ৰধান বাতৰি হিচাপে প্ৰথম পৃষ্ঠাত প্ৰকাশ কৰিছে ✓ (3) ৮জন ৰোগীক কালি চিকিৎসালয়ৰ পৰা যাবলৈ দিয়া হয় ✓ (4) অৱশ্যে চৰকাৰী কৰ্মচাৰীসকলে যিহেতু সম্পূৰ্ণ দৰমহা লাভ কৰিছে ✗ (5) কেতিয়া খুলিব লকডাউন, উদ্বিগ্ন জনতা ✓	(1) দেশৰ ১৬খন ৰাজ্য অচিৰেই কৰ'নামুক্ত হোৱাৰ দিশত (2) স্বাস্থ্যমন্ত্ৰীগৰাকীৰ সৈতে স্বাস্থ্য ৰাজ্য মহৰী পিযুয হাজৰিকাও উপস্থিত থাকে । (3) ৮জন ৰোগীক কালি চিকিৎসালয়ৰ পৰা যাবলৈ দিয়া হয় (4) কোভিড-19ৰ আক্ৰমণত ক্ষত-বিক্ষত বিশ্ব (5) কৰণাত দুই লক্ষাধিকৰ মৃত্যু শীৰ্ষক এটা বাতৰি দৈনিক অগ্ৰদূত কাকতে প্ৰধান বাতৰি হিচাপে প্ৰথম পৃষ্ঠাত প্ৰকাশ কৰিছে
	English Translation of the corresponding Assamese summary-sentences	
1	16 states in the country were on the verge of becoming free of the virus soon ✓	*(Match)*
2	The Daily Janambhumi made a front page headline with the headline 'Infection will disappear from India by May' ✓	*(Match)*
3	Eight patients were discharged from the hospital yesterday ✓	*(Match)*
4	However, government employees have received their full salaries ✗	*(Miss)* The world was wounded by the onslaught of COVID-19
5	The Daily 'Agradut' headlined in its first page that more than 2 lakh died due to Corona ✓	*(Match)*

✓ *Match:* Semantically aligned utterance in both summaries (highlighted in green).
✗ *Miss:* System-selected utterance not found in reference summary (highlighted in red).
Extractive Summary Comparison (short excerpt): Comparison between the system-generated extractive summary using a 1D-CNN model trained on acoustic-prosodic features and the corresponding human-generated gold-standard summary.

Table 7.5: Summary-Level Evaluation: ROUGE-1 and ROUGE-L Scores for All Models

Model	ROUGE-1 F1	ROUGE-L F1
CNN_Basic (Proposed)	0.598	0.318
CNN_Dropout	0.391	0.229
CNN_BiGRU	0.436	0.25
CNN_Attention	0.49	0.245
MLP	0.398	0.198

sults indicate that prosodic features consistently contribute to summarization performance across both languages, demonstrating their language-agnostic relevance. Spectral features show competitive performance in certain metrics, particularly for Assamese, while the combined feature set reflects complementary behavior depending on the language and evaluation measure.

The observed variations between Assamese and Bengali highlight that, although the overall modeling framework remains unchanged, language-specific prosodic realization influences summarization outcomes. This evaluation establishes that the proposed prosody-driven summarization approach is not confined to a single language and can be extended to other low-resource languages, thereby partially addressing the lack of publicly available established datasets in this domain.

Table 7.6: Performance comparison of CNN model based on various feature-sets: Assamese and Bengali

Feature-set	Assamese			Bengali		
	R1	R2	R3	R1	R2	R3
Prosody	0.4613	0.2634	0.2225	0.4416	0.2345	0.3701
Spectral	0.4907	0.3291	0.1963	0.457	0.2528	0.2358
Prosody + Spectral	0.4622	0.2846	0.2407	0.4179	0.2347	0.1944

7.4.4 Comparison with State-of-the-Art Speech Summarization methods

Since most state-of-the-art speech summarization systems rely on an intermediate automatic speech recognition (ASR) stage, this comparison was conducted by converting the Bengali spoken documents into text using Google ASR (as detailed in Chapter 5). The proposed text-independent summarization framework were evaluated against established summarization approaches, namely TextRank and Maximal Marginal Relevance (MMR).

The ASR-generated transcripts were represented using GloVe word embeddings. TextRank and MMR were then applied to these textual representations to generate summaries. The performance of these text-based methods was compared against the proposed CNN-based models using prosodic features, spectral features, and their combination. Table 7.7 presents the ROUGE-1, ROUGE-2, and ROUGE-L scores obtained for the Bengali spoken documents.

Table 7.7: Performance comparison of the proposed text-independent CNN-based summarization models with text-based state-of-the-art methods (TextRank and MMR) on Bengali speech data using ROUGE metrics

Method	R1	R2	RL
PROSODY (CNN)	0.4416	0.2345	0.3701
SPECTRAL (CNN)	0.457	0.2528	0.2358
PROSODY+SPECTRAL (CNN)	0.4179	0.2347	0.1944
TEXTRANK (GLOVE)	0.4012	0.2091	0.1623
MMR (GLOVE)	0.3909	0.1859	0.2164

The results indicate that the proposed text-independent models achieve competitive and, in several cases, superior performance compared to the text-based state-of-the-art methods. In particular, prosody-driven and spectral-based CNN models outperform TextRank and MMR across most evaluation metrics, despite not relying on ASR-generated transcripts. This highlights the effectiveness of acoustic-prosodic cues for summarization in low-resource and ASR-error-prone scenarios. The comparison demonstrates that, while contemporary state-of-the-art speech summarization approaches are predominantly text-based, the proposed framework offers a viable and robust alternative that avoids error propagation from ASR systems.

7.5 Discussion

7.5.1 When and Why Brute-Force Training Works

One of the most important insights that emerged during the development of this neural summarization framework was that standard deep learning regularization strategies—such as dropout and early stopping—can underperform or even fail in low-resource, imbalanced speech summarization tasks. In contrast, a brute-force training strategy, where models were trained for a fixed number of epochs without interruption, consistently led to better outcomes for detecting summary-worthy sentences.

This counterintuitive result stems from the nature of the task. Summary-worthy sentences, which form the minority class in extractive summarization, were acoustically subtle and sparsely distributed in the training data. Their signals were weaker, both in frequency and representation. Dropout, while effective in high-resource settings for preventing overfitting, introduces stochastic noise by disabling neurons at random. In scenarios where critical patterns were already rare, this noise can suppress the emergence of discriminative features necessary for the minority class.

Furthermore, when dropout was combined with early stopping based on validation loss, the problem compounds. Since the validation signal was noisy—due to both data sparsity and imbalance—the model often halts training long before it has seen enough examples to begin reliably predicting class 1. In practice, such setups resulted in near-zero F1-scores for class 1, despite the presence of class-weighted loss functions.

In contrast, when the same models were trained for a fixed 400 epochs—without dropout and without callbacks—F1-scores for class 1 improved markedly. Even architectures that previously failed under early-stopping regimes began to learn meaningful representations for the minority class. This suggests that brute-force training allows the model enough time to gradually discover subtle acoustic-prosodic patterns associated with summary-worthy sentences, even in the absence of strong class signals or text-based context.

7.5.2 Limitations of Early Stopping in Low-Resource Settings

Early stopping was widely used to prevent overfitting in deep learning by terminating training once the validation loss stops improving. However, this technique assumes that validation loss was a stable and reliable indicator of model generalization. In low-resource, highly imbalanced tasks such as speech summarization, this assumption breaks down.

First, the validation loss itself was heavily dominated by the majority class, and may not reflect the model's ability to detect rare but important class-1 instances. Second, the instability introduced by dropout or class noise makes the validation curve highly volatile, especially in early epochs. This volatility can trigger premature termination even before the model begins meaningful learning for the minority class. As a result, early stopping becomes not a safeguard against overfitting but a barrier to underrepresented class learning.

In such settings, convergence for the minority class often occurs much later than for the majority class. Stopping early—based on aggregate metrics like total loss—risks freezing the model before it has had a chance to begin learning the most crucial distinctions. These observations led us to abandon early stopping in favor of a fixed-length training protocol.

7.5.3 Handling Summary Length Variability

Another subtle challenge in this work arises from the variability in reference summary lengths across speech documents. In extractive summarization, this translates into inconsistent numbers of positive (class 1) labels across different training instances. For some documents, only a handful of sentences were labeled as summary-worthy; in others, the number was slightly higher—but in all cases, they remain a small minority.

This variability introduces additional noise during training. A model may overfit to documents with longer summaries or underperform on shorter ones. More importantly, early learning may be biased by batches dominated by documents with few or no summary sentences, skewing the gradient updates in favor of class 0.

By adopting brute-force training over many epochs, the model was exposed repeatedly to all types of documents, allowing it to accumulate gradient signals for class 1 even if they were sparse or inconsistently distributed. Moreover, the use of class-weighted loss ensures that documents with fewer positive examples do not lose importance in training simply due to their lower count.

Although this approach does not fully resolve the issue of summary length variability, it mitigates its effects sufficiently to allow the model to generalize better across different types of documents. This highlights a generalizable insight: in speech-based summarization, robust training often requires time, repetition, and patience—not aggressive regularization or early termination.

7.6 Limitations

This work presents a principled, text-independent approach to extractive speech summarization using only acoustic-prosodic features. By removing dependence on automatic speech recognition (ASR) and framing the task as a classification problem over prosody-based sentence embeddings, the proposed framework offers a lightweight and interpretable alternative for low-resource languages where text transcriptions were unreliable or unavailable.

However, several limitations constrain the generalizability and extensibility of the current system.

Lack of End-to-End Feature Learning

The present approach relies exclusively on handcrafted acoustic-prosodic features—such as pitch, energy, duration, and MFCCs—which were known to correlate with information structure in speech. While these features were selected for their interpretability and computational efficiency, they do not capture the full complexity of prosodic variation across contexts. The absence of learned representations limits the model's ability to discover latent prosodic cues that may be predictive of sentence importance. Future work could explore hybrid architectures that combine manually engineered features with end-to-end neural encoders trained directly on raw audio.

No Multilingual or Cross-Domain Scaling Tested

Although the system was explicitly designed with low-resource generalizability in mind, all experiments in this thesis were limited to Assamese and Bengali. These languages share similar prosodic and grammatical structures, which may not hold in typologically distinct languages. The framework has not yet been tested across broader language families or domains (e.g., spontaneous conversations, oral narratives, interviews), which may exhibit different prosodic markers of salience. The extent to which the proposed method generalizes beyond the current language pair remains an open question.

Limited Handling of Prosodic Ambiguity

Even with speaker normalization, prosodic expression varies significantly based on speaker style, discourse context, and affect. In structured broadcast speech, prosodic features such as pitch range and emphasis tend to align well with informational prominence. However, in more spontaneous or emotionally charged speech, prosody may reflect interpersonal dynamics rather than informativeness. The model does not currently account for this ambiguity, which may affect its robustness in real-world usage.

No End-to-End Training Pipeline

The current approach involves multiple separate steps for preprocessing and feature extraction, outside the main model. While this makes the system easier to understand and control, it also means that the model cannot learn or fine-tune those steps during training. An end-to-end system—where everything is trained together—could allow the model to improve its features based on the task. However, such a setup has not been explored or tested in this work.

In summary, this thesis introduces a tractable and interpretable model for prosody-based summarization in low-resource settings, but further work was needed to extend its applicability across languages, domains, and speech styles. Addressing the above limitations would not only enhance robustness but also allow the model to approach the performance of more complex ASR-dependent systems—while retaining its language-agnostic strengths.

7.7 Chapter Summary

This chapter proposed a lightweight, transcript-free speech summarization model using a 1D Convolutional Neural Network trained entirely on acoustic-prosodic features. Evaluated on Assamese broadcast news, the model outperformed stronger neural variants despite its simplicity, demonstrating that prosody alone can reliably indicate summary-worthy content in low-resource settings. To the best of our knowledge, this is among the first attempts to apply 1D-CNNs for prosody-based summarization in a setting where textual transcriptions are either unavailable or unreliable. The model provides a practical and reproducible framework, supporting the broader aim of this thesis—to explore the feasibility of summarization driven primarily by acoustic cues.

www.ingramcontent.com/pod-product-compliance
Lightning Source LLC
LaVergne TN
LVHW010721061126
851857LV00014B/1293